Aspiring in Later Life

Global Perspectives on Aging

Series editor
Sarah Lamb

This series publishes books that will deepen and expand our understanding of age, aging, ageism, and late life in the United States and beyond. The series focuses on anthropology while being open to ethnographically vivid and theoretically rich scholarship in related fields, including sociology, religion, cultural studies, social medicine, medical humanities, gender and sexuality studies, human development, critical and cultural gerontology, and age studies. Books will be aimed at students, scholars, and occasionally the general public.

Jason Danely, *Aging and Loss: Mourning and Maturity in Contemporary Japan*
Parin Dossa and Cati Coe, eds., *Transnational Aging and Reconfigurations of Kin Work*
Sarah Lamb, ed., *Successful Aging as a Contemporary Obsession: Global Perspectives*
Margaret Morganroth Gullette, *Ending Ageism, or How Not to Shoot Old People*
Ellyn Lem, *Gray Matters: Finding Meaning in the Stories of Later Life*
Michele Ruth Gamburd, *Linked Lives: Elder Care, Migration, and Kinship in Sri Lanka*
Yohko Tsuji, *Through Japanese Eyes: Thirty Years of Studying Aging in America*
Jessica C. Robbins, *Aging Nationally in Contemporary Poland: Memory, Kinship, and Personhood*
Rose K. Keimig, *Growing Old in a New China: Transitions in Elder Care*
Anna I. Corwin, *Embracing Age: How Catholic Nuns Became Models of Aging Well*
Molly George, *Aging in a Changing World: Older New Zealanders and Contemporary Multiculturalism*
Cati Coe, *Changes in Care: Aging, Migration, and Social Class in West Africa*
Megha Amrith, Victoria K. Sakti, and Dora Sampaio, eds., *Aspiring in Later Life: Movements across Time, Space, and Generations*

Aspiring in Later Life

*Movements across Time,
Space, and Generations*

Edited by
Megha Amrith
Victoria K. Sakti
Dora Sampaio

Rutgers University Press
New Brunswick, Camden, and Newark, New Jersey
London and Oxford

Rutgers University Press is a department of Rutgers, The State University of New Jersey, one of the leading public research universities in the nation. By publishing worldwide, it furthers the University's mission of dedication to excellence in teaching, scholarship, research, and clinical care.

Library of Congress Cataloging-in-Publication Data

Names: Amrith, Megha, editor. | Sakti, Victoria K., editor. | Sampaio, Dora, 1987– editor.
Title: Aspiring in later life : movements across time, space, and generations / edited by Megha Amrith, Victoria K. Sakti, and Dora Sampaio.
Description: New Brunswick : Rutgers University Press, [2023] | Includes bibliographical references and index.
Identifiers: LCCN 2022049233 | ISBN 9781978830417 (hardback) | ISBN 9781978830400 (paperback) | ISBN 9781978830424 (epub) | ISBN 9781978830431 (pdf)
Subjects: LCSH: Older people—Cross-cultural studies. | Older immigrants—Cross-cultural studies. | Older people—Social life and customs. | Older people—Psychology | Hope. | Desire.
Classification: LCC GN485 .A83 2023 | DDC 305.26—dc23/eng/20230302
LC record available at https://lccn.loc.gov/2022049233

A British Cataloging-in-Publication record for this book is available from the British Library.

This book is also freely available online as an open-access digital edition.

This collection copyright © 2023 by Rutgers, The State University of New Jersey

Individual chapters copyright © 2023 in the names of their authors

All rights reserved

No part of this book may be reproduced or utilized in any form or by any means, electronic or mechanical, or by any information storage and retrieval system, without written permission from the publisher. Please contact Rutgers University Press, 106 Somerset Street, New Brunswick, NJ 08901. The only exception to this prohibition is "fair use" as defined by U.S. copyright law.

References to internet websites (URLs) were accurate at the time of writing. Neither the author nor Rutgers University Press is responsible for URLs that may have expired or changed since the manuscript was prepared.

⊚ The paper used in this publication meets the requirements of the American National Standard for Information Sciences—Permanence of Paper for Printed Library Materials, ANSI Z39.48-1992.

rutgersuniversitypress.org

It is not true that people stop pursuing dreams because they grow old, they grow old because they stop pursuing dreams.

—*Gabriel García Márquez, 2004*

Contents

Introduction   1
Megha Amrith, Victoria K. Sakti, and Dora Sampaio

PART I
Desire and Self-Realization

1. Growing Old Hand in Hand: Aspirations of Romantic Love in Later Life among Romanian Transmigrants in Rome   19
Dumitrița Luncă

2. Letting Go and Looking Ahead: The Aspirations of Middle-Aged Migrant Domestic Workers in Singapore and Hong Kong   39
Megha Amrith

3. Aspirational Movements: Later-Life Mobility as a Female Resource to Age Well   56
Lisa Johnson

PART II
Intergenerational Negotiations

4. Aspiring to Retire: Intergenerational Care in a Ghanaian Transnational Family   77
Cati Coe

5. Between Aging Parents There and Young Children Here: The Aspirations of Late-Middle-Aged Peruvian Migrants in Santiago as a Transnational Sandwich Generation   95
Alfonso Otaegui

6 Whose Aspirations? Intergenerational Expectations and Hopes in Eastern Uganda   112
Susan Reynolds Whyte

PART III
Living in the Present

7 Before It Ends: Aging, Gender, and Migration in a Transnational Mexican Community   129
Julia Pauli

8 Disrupted Futures: The Shifting Aspirations of Older Cameroonians Living in Displacement   145
Nele Wolter

9 "Setting Off from the Mountain Pass": Facing Death and Preparing for the Journey Ahead in Tibetan Exile   159
Harmandeep Kaur Gill

Afterword   177
Erdmute Alber

Acknowledgments   183
Contributors   185
Index   189

Aspiring in Later Life

Introduction

Megha Amrith, Victoria K. Sakti, and Dora Sampaio

If to aspire is to breathe, then aspirations can be thought of as being the force of life itself: "the breath of life that flows through families and crosses borders."[1] As we write this introductory essay two years into the COVID-19 pandemic, it is strikingly and painfully clear how this force of life, for many people around the world, has been put on hold, whether for a migrant whose aspirations for a better life have been interrupted by the public health situation, insecure employment, or the inability to cross borders or for someone struggling to be together with and in the care of loved ones at the end of life. In public discourse during the pandemic, "some ethicists and medical policy makers have defended prioritizing time left in the 'life cycle,' directing resources away from older people" so that younger people would be able to enjoy a wide range of opportunities available to them at different stages of their lives (Ciafone and McGeehan Muchmore 2021, 9). By looking at how people aspire in and for later life, we seek to challenge normative and static arguments that present later life as a time of decline and passivity and instead to illuminate it as a time and space in life that can open up new possibilities and horizons. Equally, we recognize the profound and debilitating impacts that the pandemic and its policies have had on the realization of such aspirations.

On Not Settling: Aspiring as Process

Studies of migration and mobility often center on aspirations for and constructions of alternative futures. There is an implicit presumption, however, that it is younger mobile generations who are most concerned with the pursuit and negotiation of these aspirations and that, over time, people eventually settle. Yet how and when do they imagine settling and achieving a "good life"? This book makes the case that people do not stop aspiring in later life. It challenges popular assumptions that aspirations are exclusively located and achieved in earlier life phases and that older age is a passive stage of life for receiving care, staying put, and accepting things as they are.

This volume argues that aspirations are produced and reconfigured across time, space, and generations. We understand aspirations as articulations of life goals that relate to the construction of specific identities, values, and life trajectories. While aspirations are intrinsically subjective, they are mediated by the broader structures of everyday life. They emerge from specific cultural and historical contexts; they are shaped and constrained by social categories of gender, class, race, sexuality, and (dis)ability; and they are framed by diverse moral imaginaries and principles on how to live a good life. Central to our inquiry is a recognition that the pursuit of aspirations is intricately tied to different forms of mobility and negotiated across the life course. In exploring these intersections between aspirations and mobilities in later life, two central questions underpin this volume: How are aspirations imagined and expressed in later life? How do mobilities shape individual and collective pursuits of these aspirations?

In this volume, we speak of *aspiring* as an ongoing process of imagining and constructing a good life (with its diverse and subjective meanings). We take aging as a lens to explore the extended and nonlinear character of aspirations, the pursuit and fulfillment of which may span decades. In particular, we consider the ethnographically diverse and specific ways through which aspirations are expressed in the times of life broadly known as later life. We understand later life to be a fluid life space that brings to light new and old commitments, ambivalent life projects, dialectic tensions between continuity and discontinuity, expressions of agency, and relationships with other generations. Contrary to widespread popular ideas about older people being sedentary or fixed to a single place, our volume demonstrates that people in later life hold a complex sense of place, with commitments and life projects that span different milieus. They are either highly mobile themselves or profoundly influenced by the movements of others. Such mobilities are both social and spatial. They refer not only to transnational migration but also to rural-urban mobilities, forms of displacement, travels back and forth across locales, and movements between households. Mobilities might also refer to the movement of ideas, images, media, lifestyles, technologies, expectations, and institutions across places, just as they might concern practices of social mobility to change one's class position or status, bodily (im)mobilities, and the mobile lives of the dead. These movements, however, are not seamless but are often shaped and constrained by deep-seated inequalities and by institutions, states, and borders. In this way, immobilities are equally important to our inquiry.

Aspiring in Later Life brings together ethnographic work in different regions of the world, from the Americas to Europe, Africa, and Asia. The contributors to this volume show how local, regional, transnational, and also social forms of mobility play an important role in supporting or hindering people's aspirations for a good life. The chapters take us on a journey to explore the reconciliation of future aspirations and present desires among older migrant women in Rome, Singapore, and Montreal at the end of long years of work abroad; the shifting of individuals' aspirations across time and space in accordance with those of kin in Cameroon and Uganda; Peruvian and Ghanaian migrants planning their futures to align with the next generations' priorities; multiple generations of women wanting the present to last *un poco más*, "a little more," in a Mexican town shaped by migration; and Tibetan exiles in India meditating on death and rebirth.

Our discussions on this theme first began at a panel on later-life negotiations at the German Anthropological Association conference in Constance in October 2019, with the participation of four of the authors. The lively discussions that ensued encouraged us to organize a second meeting to include an extended and in-depth discussion of draft papers in a virtual workshop, which was held in November 2020. In this workshop, we examined the different ways through which aspirations cut across our different regional cases as an important feature in later life and in intergenerational relationships. In these conversations, we talked about later life as a culturally heterogeneous space that is fundamentally shaped by mobilities at different scales of people, things, and ideas, all of which are themes that continue to underlie this volume's central concerns.

Aspiring in Later Life: Conceptual Notes

Our use of the term *aspiring* as an ongoing process of imagining and constructing a good life is informed by Arjun Appadurai's (2004, 60) writing on aspirations as having to do with "wants, preferences, choices, and calculations" that are shaped by and embedded in diverse cultural practices and imaginaries. While "aspirations about the good life, about health and happiness, exist in all societies" (67), they take on different cultural meanings, which, we further argue, shift in contexts of mobility. Appadurai further reminds us that "aspirations are never simply individual (as the language of wants and choices inclines us to think). They are always formed in interaction and in the thick of social life" (68). Aspirations "entail planning, hoping for, and imagining the future" (Bryant and Knight 2019, 19), but they also include moments of frustration, stillness, and remaining in an extended present (Sakti and Amrith 2022). Such ebbs and flows can widen and narrow temporal horizons. We base our discussions in this volume on this broad conceptualization of aspirations and analyze how they emerge and develop in different regions of the world and in translocal settings.

Aspirations have emerged in anthropological and social scientific debates in recent years as a topic of shared interest. They are discussed in relation to many spheres of life, from urban spaces (Van der Veer 2015) to migration contexts (Carling and Schewel 2018), age-related positionalities (Robertson, Cheng, and Yeoh 2018), and future life projects (Bunnell, Gillen, and Ho 2018). In migration studies, for instance, there has been keen interest in how younger people construct their migration aspirations, particularly in the face of increasingly restrictive border regimes. As younger people wait or become stuck at different points of their migration journeys, initially held aspirations—for education, work, love, or family—often have to be reevaluated in the circumstances (see, e.g., Honwana 2012; Robertson, Cheng, and Yeoh 2018). Aspirations in these studies are often tied to questions of the future, the underlying assumption being that youth have futures to aspire toward.

Aspirations, however, have featured less prominently or explicitly in studies of later life in migratory contexts. A growing body of literature on the relationship between aging and migration examines what it means to age in transnational lifeworlds. In a volume edited by Parin Dossa and Cati Coe (2017), for instance, contributors ethnographically explore how transnational aging shapes and reconfigures kinship relations, while Azra Hromadžić and Monika Palmberger (2018) bring together in their volume diverse ethnographic explorations of how people in different parts of the world care for loved ones across geographical distances and how migration might overturn normative assumptions about care. Other themes that scholars in the social sciences have explored in relation to aging and migration include the connections between aging, home, and belonging (Walsh and Näre 2016); aging in transnational contexts (Horn and Schweppe 2016; Karl and Torres 2016); aging and (im)mobilities (Ciobanu and Hunter 2017); and independence and subjective well-being in later life (King et al. 2017). In all of these cases, aspirations are often implicitly present but rarely explored as a motivating force in people's lives. Later-life aspirations thus warrant further research attention, in conjunction with examining how aspirations are shaped over the life course and intergenerationally. Notable exceptions are very recent studies that address novel questions relating to aging and futurity (Ho et al. 2022; Kavedžija 2020; Taylor 2020), Iza Kavedžija's (2019) ethnography on how older people in Japan construct meaningful lives in ways that have little to do with ageing itself, and Sarah Lamb's (2017) volume *Successful Aging as a Contemporary Obsession: Global Perspectives*, which explores the different aspirations or visions that people hold of what it means to age successfully and live meaningfully in older age across five continents.[2] Lamb's volume challenges the binary that often features in public debates about aging, with decline in older age on one end of the spectrum and the neoliberal move toward "active aging" on the other end.[3] Instead, it captures more nuanced and culturally situated experiences of "successful aging" that lie in between.

Our volume on aspiring in later life is distinctive in that it takes discussions of aging beyond the dominant focus on topics of health, illness, care, and (in)dependence, to understand how older people are actively shaping their worlds and relationships in contexts of mobility and social change through aspirations. In placing aspirations front and center, our work challenges widespread assumptions (especially in Western Europe and North America) "that everyone from their sixties to past one hundred is similar, identically dependent, and past useful life" (Katz, Sivaramakrishnan, and Thane 2021, 18). We argue that people do not stop living, aspiring, moving, and changing in the later phases of their lives and suggest that aging does not have to do only with problems of kin and care or the aging process itself (see also Kavedžija 2019). Instead, aspirations for a good life might revolve around the search for new lifestyles and forms of consumption, aspirations for class mobility and status, plans for the next generation's future, desires to be with intimate others, the rejection of dominant social expectations, and plans for an afterlife. Our focus is on how aspirations are intertwined with the practicalities of everyday life but also tied to broader social, political, economic, and cultural projects and imaginaries. We further show how mobility, at multiple scales and across different spaces, shapes aspirations over the life course in ways that connect people's pasts, presents, and futures.

Shifting Aspirations: Time, Space, and Scale

Later-life aspirations are not static. Aspiring, as we have argued, is a process that connects people to a range of spaces and places. Our book adopts a sustained focus on movement to explore how such life projects are enacted and reconfigured across different locales and scales in an increasingly mobile world. Our volume situates itself in a globalizing world where people's lives are profoundly shaped both by experiences of mobility and immobility and by movement and stasis over long periods. While some people engage in transnational migration projects, others move translocally, or their family members do. Sometimes it is not people who move but rather ideas, institutions, and imaginaries of the good life, which circulate and transform over time and space. At the same time, these kinds of mobilities are never neutral. Aspirations can be shaped, but also choked, by mobility. They might be affected by the restrictive migration regimes that constrain people's abilities to shape their livelihoods and aspirations transnationally; by the racialized, classed, and gendered structures that confront postcolonial migrants; by political conflict and violence that create experiences of displacement; or by the global inequalities that deny opportunities for (physical, social, or economic) mobility and reproduce structures of poverty and precarity across different regional contexts. These structures, and the different scales of mobility they enable or disable, deeply shape the circumstances in which one feels able to aspire. Scale is also inherent to how aging as a process is constituted if we consider bodily changes, intra- and intergenerational representations and negotiations, and historical shifts in how age and aging are perceived. This book attends to the messy, uneven, and asynchronous nature of pursuing aspirations on different scales.

The ability to pursue aspirations is thus contingent on one's resources and position within a given social field. Likewise, one's aspirational horizons depend on varying degrees of precarity and privilege and the position that the aging body occupies in diverse sociocultural and political structures. As Raymond Williams notes, the present is a process of emergence (Williams, cited in Berlant 2011). In the same way, it is through the fragilities, hopes, and unpredictability of everyday life, in friction with systemic changes and ordinary crises and failures, that aspirations are created and managed. At a more foundational level, one's "capacity to aspire" (Appadurai 2004) is tied up with local specificities and with the enduring inequalities produced by the historical legacies of colonialism, war, exploitation, and dispossession (Sivaramakrishnan 2018). Colonial pasts, their continuities in the present, and their ramifications for welfare and forms of state protection, demographic policies, and international development agendas have rendered some bodies deserving of dignified aging experiences, while "those who are racialized aging bodies from low-income backgrounds may entail multiple layers of exile and invisibility" (Rajan-Rankin 2018, 34). Protracted states of displacement and the multiple impossibilities in humanitarian care for the aging and the dying may further contribute to experiences in which the future appears foreclosed for certain groups of people (Feldman 2017). Those othered by their marginal positioning, be it due to their ethno-racial background, nonbinary identity, migrant status, or bodily and mental impairment, have remained overlooked under a hegemonic gaze on later life and what it ought to look like and for whom, which in turn has consequences for their aspirations. The contributions in the book ethnographically illustrate both the possibilities of and the limits to aspiring across different societies.

Many of the chapters in this volume deal with people living in relative scarcity or with insecure status in the Global South, or in the framework of South to North migrations.[4] Some might consider themselves "middle class," having secured this positioning through their migration journeys. New inequalities also emerge within communities and families when some are able to follow their aspirations through mobility and others not. In these different circumstances, aspirations are never absent, but they might vary in scale and scope, from grand visions to establish intergenerational legacies to the search for love or the small desires for sugar in tea. For others, notions of the good life are essentially about constructing and sustaining a "livable life," as Judith Butler (2004) puts it, which is shaped by prevailing socioeconomic conditions but also by normative sociopolitical understandings of what counts as a life worth living and which lives may or may not be given the conditions to flourish.

Across the contributions in the book, aspirations encapsulate how people manage the messiness and incoherence of life in the face of ongoing uncertainty and threats to the good life they wish for. The pursuit of aspirations can therefore be deeply fragile and precarious, and it might at times "fail." In the different cases presented by the authors, we see how people make sacrifices or endure hardships or humiliation as they pursue a good or livable life. There are echoes of Lauren Berlant's (2011, 2) notion of "cruel optimism," whereby "the object/scene that ignites a sense of possibility actually makes it impossible to attain the expansive transformation for which a person or a people risks striving." As people continue to pursue the ever-elusive "moral-intimate-economic thing called 'the good life'" (2), the desired objective keeps people living in the impasse with a sense of both possibility and anxiety. In this way, aspirations and hope are sometimes entangled with each other.[5] As Nauja Kleist and Stef Jansen (2016, 388) argue, "combinations of uncertainty, anticipation and aspirations . . . generate specific degrees, forms and intensities of hope," which express "visions of possible lives, and thus of possible futures." However, they rightly suggest that "it makes little sense to use 'hope' as a blanket feel-good word in the way that it often seems to appear in the contemporary moment" (388), making more sense to see how hope is generated as a part of different, often unequal, social and political configurations. As the authors in this volume suggest, individuals and communities still seek personal and social transformations in the face of inequality. Migration, for instance, can "fundamentally reshape . . . emotional worlds and aspirations" in spite of the impediments of a global capitalist economy, as Alexia Bloch (2017) convincingly puts it.

There are, furthermore, important temporal dimensions to aspiring. Rather than seeing aspiring as part of a linear path with a fixed outcome, we might imagine aspiring as part of a process through which aspirations are reconfigured and reevaluated at different points of the life course (Fischer 2014). The contributors further show throughout the volume that aspiring in later life is tied to past memories, present concerns, and future imaginaries, rather than being exclusively future-oriented, as much of the discussion on aspirations puts forward. Aspirations connect different temporal moments and encompass divergent temporal horizons (Amrith 2021). For example, people may choose to orient their aspirations to the present, a space that is familiar, when the future signifies dramatic change or fears of the unknown. Temporality is also important when thinking about how aspirations are mediated between and across generations, and how migration and familial aspirations are often enabled and sustained through intergenerational relationships and solidarities in a globalized world (Cole and Durham 2007; Yarris 2017). We concur with Dossa and Coe (2017, 5), in that "time, timing, the life course, cohorts, and generations [are] central to transnational migration." Aspirations straddle different times, spaces, and scales.

Overview of the Book

The ethnographic cases presented in this book take "later life" to be a broad and heterogeneous category that covers those in late middle age, those who have retired, or those aspiring to retire. The cases also include the stories of people anticipating death and awaiting the next journey, those confronting frailty and bodily immobility, and those aspiring for intimacy and self-actualization. All contributors adopt a relational perspective, highlighting that one's aspirations in later life are connected to one's past, present, and future. They are also tied to the aspirations of other generations and "age categories," for the relations between midlife and later life or relations between younger and older members of a family are central.

The book's sections focus on desire and self-realization (part 1), intergenerational negotiations (part 2), and living in the present (part 3). These sections are followed by an afterword by Erdmute Alber. Although the book is organized into different parts, many of the chapters address themes that cut across the sections, with a number of themes intertwined with one another. Crosscutting themes include the negotiation of aspirations and well-being across generations; desires to return to one's homeland; navigating intimate relationships with kin and lovers in later life; confronting end-of-life care, death, and imagining afterlives; grappling with the multiple emotions that accompany the fragile pursuit of aspirations; and the gendered nature of aspiring in later life. Together, these chapters argue that while aspirations in later life do sometimes center on how to arrange old-age care, they go far beyond medicalized framings of care to consider its social, intimate, relational, and culturally situated dimensions. Aspirations in later life, moreover, may not always revolve around aging itself, even as state policies and gerontological discourses focus on the question of "optimizing" one's aging experience (Lamb 2017).

Drawing on rich ethnographies situated across multiple regions, the chapters reveal diverse understandings, expressions, and scales of aspirations. Aspirations take on material expression—through the building of houses, new consumption practices, and strategies for social and class mobility—and ritual performance. They also relate to the less tangible processes of self-realization, finding comfort and fulfillment, and the quest for belonging. Some aspirations are voiced and planned, others are embodied and felt, or both. Sometimes it is the aspirations of others that impinge on one's later-life possibilities. Aspirations might follow certain normative scripts around ideas about (in)dependence, reciprocity, and success, or they may move in unexpected directions.

Part 1: Desire and Self-Realization

The chapters in part 1 explore the desires, yearnings, and processes of self-realization that emerge in later-life contexts of mobility. The three chapters in this section revolve around middle-aged and older migrant women, many of whom are or were employed in domestic and care work in Italy, Singapore and Hong Kong, and Canada, respectively, and are approaching retirement. In this section, retirement is narrated not as a taken-for-granted space that strictly follows formal or institutional definitions but as a time-space that is imbued with multiple meanings, imaginaries, and ideas and constructed afresh in contexts of mobility. Retirement aspirations become important to migrants approaching the end of their working lives abroad as they recalibrate their relationships and connections to a range of people and places. Retirement aspirations might involve returns to the homeland or plans to move back and forth between countries in search of security, care, a better climate, and affordable living. They may equally involve looking for or renewing relationships of love and romance or delving into new life projects, learning new skills, and striving for self-realization. The three chapters show that, more than a period of stagnation and acceptance, later life is experienced as a moment to discover new passions, to pursue lifelong dreams, and to build new life possibilities and social relationships. Such plans, however, can also be limited by precarious migration circumstances and border regimes that affect migrant women's abilities to achieve all that they desire.

In the first chapter in this section, Dumitrița Luncă (chapter 1) examines romantic aspirations of middle-aged Romanians living in Rome, Italy. Through a focus on migrants' aspirations, her chapter demonstrates how love, partnership, and sexuality can be driving forces in midlife and that these are constitutive of what makes a good later life. Her chapter underlines the ways that migration experience and retirement aspirations challenge normative ideas associated with "older womanhood" and are bound up with the desire for not giving up on love and intimacy.

Midlife aspirations that emerge at the end of migration journeys and transition to retirement are also the focus of this section's second chapter. Megha Amrith (chapter 2) conceptualizes midlife as a vantage point that enables us to see how diverse aspirations start to shift or take on renewed energies when women reach their forties, fifties, and sixties. Focusing on migrant women in Singapore and Hong Kong, she argues that this specific phase of their lives offers insights into how aspirations are variously shaped through letting go of past selves and decisions, anticipating an uncertain future and reconfiguring aspirations for self-realization in the present. The chapter's ethnographic cases emphasize the relevance of understanding migrants' aspirations as integral to their identities, which are always in a state of becoming rather than static.

In this section's third chapter, Lisa Johnson (chapter 3) investigates the affective practice of yearning among Jamaican older women aspiring to reconnect with and return to the homeland after prolonged and racialized periods of working in Canada. She follows their return migration journeys and argues that in their efforts of "aging well," Jamaican older women depend on continued transnational mobility in later life. Through an exploration of yearning, Johnson shows how aspiring is, on the one hand, deeply subjective and surrounded by idealized memory of the past and, on the other hand, an act on which women meticulously plan and pursue.

Part 2: Intergenerational Negotiations

Plans in later life concern not only older people themselves but also their family members. The chapters in the second section explore how later life for some people is a time to organize their aspirations alongside those of the next and previous generations and to continue to invest in ensuring the best possible conditions for the next generation's future. Those in late middle age will be relating to and caring for those both younger and older than themselves, and their plans and aspirations also consider the needs and desires of older relatives. Synchronizing aspirations across generations, however, often comes with some difficulty and conflict, requiring negotiation and accommodation. Similarly, the mobilities and plans of younger generations may affect the aspirations of older people, generating complex moral debates on intergenerational interdependence and reciprocity that are shaken over time and space.

In the first chapter of this section, Cati Coe (chapter 4) delves into the story of one Ghanaian transnational family and the complexities of their intergenerational relationships and aspirations over time. Specifically, she explores the competing aspirations of an aging Ghanaian home care worker in the United States, who wanted both to retire to Ghana and to launch her young-adult daughter into successful adulthood in the United States. Coe's chapter discusses how people use and flip between cultural scripts that guide them to synchronize kin-time across different life courses, toward a sense of a good life, and in situations of conflict. She argues that later-life aspirations are not only individual projects at a particular stage of the life course but also intergenerational ones, with effects across the generations.

The following chapter, by Alfonso Otaegui (chapter 5), focuses on the so-called sandwich generation of older Peruvian migrants living in Chile. His chapter investigates migrants' ambivalences toward constructions of older age while caring and providing support for their parents in the homeland and adult children in the destination country. Intergenerational aspirations in this context extend beyond those related to care, to include desires to continue work life and contemplations of cremation arrangements after death so as not to burden their children. This chapter raises an important discussion about the ambivalent, and at times conflicting, aspirations of late middle age, as it is a phase in migrants' lives "in between" the past, present, and future; vitality and frailty; and obligations and aspirations for different generations.

In the next chapter, Susan Reynolds Whyte (chapter 6) draws on ethnographic work with very elderly people living in conditions of poverty in eastern Uganda. She argues that the aspirations of older people must be understood within the shifting configurations of relatives, through whom, and with whom, they try to make a livable or comfortable, if not a good, life. Her chapter expands on Appadurai's (2004) work on imagination, anticipation, and aspiration. She raises a critical issue on whether Appadurai's conceptualization of "the capacity to aspire" applies to late older age because, in this case, people are frail and approaching death. Particularly in the context of poverty, she reflects on how, in this phase of life, horizons to aspire may be diminished. This offers a contrast from other chapters in this volume focusing on midlife.

Part 3: Living in the Present

Aspirations do not follow linear temporalities, nor are they exclusively future-oriented. They importantly connect the past, present, and future and can develop as comparative projects. Pasts impinge on how people make a good life in the present, just as people evaluate, reshape, and take actions in present lives to confront unknown futures. These unknown futures are sharpened in uncertain and precarious contexts of migration, mobility, and displacement, leading people to adopt a range of temporal strategies for seeking well-being, building livelihoods, and living purposefully. Hindsight and approaching significant life transitions (such as retirement or the end of life) offer critical points for introspection and reassessment. The chapters in this section bring in the perspectives of multiple generations of people situated at different points in the life course to illuminate the diverse temporalities of aspirations and "the time that is left" to aspire.

Julia Pauli's chapter (chapter 7) draws on long-term ethnographic research with several generations of women in a Mexican village shaped by transnational migration and examines what they perceive as a "good life." She identifies a layering of temporalities in which feelings that one has to get ahead, *adelantarse*, are mixed with nostalgic longings for an imagined, more idle, past. Between these past and future makings, Pauli focuses on a third sentiment, which is women's wish to prolong the present. In scrutinizing the "art of living" in the very present, she demonstrates how the desire that things stay as they are, just a little longer, is used to reconcile with a troubling and often insecure future.

The next chapter, by Nele Wolter (chapter 8), takes us to Bafoussam, Cameroon. She discusses the interplay between past, present, and future aspirations with a discussion on hope. Focusing on older internally displaced persons' narratives, she examines how people realign their future lives in forced displacement contexts. Wolter suggests that the protractedness of displacement and the everyday present shape the shifts in older people's aspirations and that familial ties affect their decisions to stay where they are, to move on to new places, or to return to their homeland.

In the final chapter of this section, Harmandeep Kaur Gill (chapter 9) explores life's end in a Tibetan exile context. Through a rich ethnographic description of the everyday life of a ninety-three-year-old monk, whom she calls Genla, she tunes in to his aspirations of achieving a peaceful death and a good rebirth through his commitment to performing everyday rituals and practices in the present. Gill situates Genla's aspirations and biography within the contexts of the Tibetan exile and the contemporary out-migration of the younger generation. In doing so, she shows us how Genla, like her other research companions, draws on the Buddhist notion of impermanence in steering his aspirations for older age and dying in the absence of family. This contribution invites us to think about the afterlives of aspirations and the role of religion in configuring aspirations.

Finally, Erdmute Alber, in her afterword to the volume, offers a powerful reflection on how older age is still a time when a *whole* life is waiting to be lived, even if one does not know how long a life will last. This perspective is a contrast from medicalized health policies that presume that life stops at a certain age. And while we often look to older generations for their wisdom based on past life experience, these experiences may offer insights into understanding the novel and unexpected possibilities that can emerge later in life.

The COVID-19 Pandemic

Our conversations on the topic of aspirations in later life took place in the midst of a global pandemic, requiring us to reflect on how this health crisis and its social, political, and economic ramifications have halted or reconfigured aspirations for older populations living in a world of movement.

The coronavirus pandemic has resulted in a disproportionately high number of fatalities among older populations, their vulnerability to the virus stemming from not only epidemiological but also social, political, and institutional factors. Old age came to be at the center of public health and political debates relating to the necessity (or not) of social protection measures, lockdowns, and triage decisions. News reports of multiple fatalities of older people in eldercare institutions have been devastatingly common (Cohen 2020).[6] In some parts of the world, there has been an intensified concern for and protection of older populations, with increasing forms of intergenerational support. In other cases, older people have felt intensely isolated.[7] One political response—that life must go on "as usual," without health-based restrictions on social life—has implicitly or explicitly suggested that older people's lives are disposable or less valuable (Cohen 2020). In all such cases, the category of "old age" or the "elderly" is often homogenized, overlooking the very diverse spectrum of experiences of later life that exist across the world, including how old age intersects with other social experiences such as mobility and migration. Older migrants and their families, for instance, have faced even stronger barriers to mobility than usual during the pandemic, affecting the provision of intergenerational care across locales and borders.

Crucially, as some of the chapters show, the sudden onset of COVID-19 disrupted and complicated later-life aspirations for many, altering future plans (which were already precarious in many cases) and creating a sense of unresolved existential anxiety. In this volume, we see how aging Jamaican women who counted on the ability to move across borders between Jamaica and Canada as a retirement strategy suddenly found themselves "stuck" and constrained by containment measures that particularly affected older groups. Middle-aged migrant domestic workers in Singapore found themselves isolated in their employers' homes with high workloads, unable to meet their peers or pursue projects of self-realization. An aging interlocutor in Mexico was in ill health after a COVID infection exacerbated her asthma, while a Tibetan monk living in exile in India found himself altering his daily routines after the onset of the pandemic. Some families were separated, others lost their livelihoods, while some, ironically, found augmented sources of income, as in the case of Ghanaian home-care workers in the United States, given that more people sought out live-in home care during the pandemic. In Cameroon, there was a sense that the internal displacement as a result of the civil conflict was more pressing an issue than the pandemic itself in people's everyday lives. The cross-cultural perspective that the contributors bring to this volume thus reveals a range of responses and experiences of the pandemic in different localities.

The pandemic also had significant impacts on the very modes of ethnographic inquiry that many researchers in the social sciences have taken for granted, until now. A number of the contributors to this volume reflect on how plans for ethnographic fieldwork were disrupted and on the possibilities and limits of keeping in touch with their research participants through phone calls and digital media channels. We must therefore acknowledge that working on this book project during the (still ongoing) global pandemic has made us rethink our methodologies as digital connections become ever-more salient. It has also pushed us to think deeper about what it means to aspire in the current conditions of containment, fragility, and (im)mobility, where questions about life and death are ever present. The volume as a whole and our discussions on aspirations in a world of movement must therefore be read with all of these open-ended and still unresolved questions as a backdrop. At the same time, we cannot but recognize that not everyone, everywhere, became stuck in the same or in equal ways.

Looking Ahead

With *Aspiring in Later Life*, we seek to make an original contribution to expand and nuance our understandings and imaginations of how aspirations shift across the life course and across generations. By bringing together ethnographically rich and conceptually innovative perspectives on the dynamic life projects that emerge in later life and how they take shape in a world of movement, the volume contributes to broader debates on how questions of aging are configured in relation to transnational care and globalization. People are not necessarily growing older "in place," as much policy work on aging would imply, but are aging in relation to families, homes, and memories that span multiple locales.[8]

The variety of lived experiences that the contributors present in this volume offer a window onto understanding how aspirational horizons are both shaped and limited in conjunction with broader societal structures and norms and to global inequalities in gender, class, and race. Aspirations in and for later life are influenced by migrant experiences of exclusion and discrimination over the life course; by the everyday poverty or long-term precarity that might characterize the lives of people displaced; by experiences of immobility (which might be chosen or forced); or by the failed promises and the sacrifices of migration for working bodies from the Global South. At the same time, the rich stories that are presented in this volume speak to the myriad ways through which people creatively and resourcefully confront and surpass these unequal structures in their own ways, finding joy, love, a sense of purpose, and meaningful relationships in the process. These opportunities, encounters, and constraints together contribute to animating and reconfiguring later-life aspirations, revealing different visions of what constitutes a "good life," or at least a "livable life," and what one is able to aspire toward.

Another important contribution of the volume is to show that aspiring is not a linear process. Aspirations are woven in through the textures of time. They are adjusted on the basis of hindsight and past experiences, they feature prominently in the present, and they also speak to projects of the future, including the afterlife. Aspiring is a process that shifts over the life course yet not always in predictable ways or through fixed life stages. Different generations within a family may share aspirations or aspire to different things, sometimes in contested ways.

Together, we make the case in this volume that later life is not a romanticized phase of life without challenges, nor is it a time of life characterized exclusively by dependency, passivity, pain, and despair. By examining aspirations in diverse cultural contexts—how they are given expression, but also the limits they come up against—the chapters in this book highlight the ambivalence and the indeterminacy that occupy the space in between these two ends of the spectrum. In other words, the focus on aspirations in a mobile world critiques static, normative, taken-for-granted assumptions about the life course and its stages and mirrors instead the more fluid, messy, and tentative entanglements of everyday life.

NOTES

1. These are the words of an anonymous reviewer of this volume, who has articulated so well the significance of aspirations in a time of COVID-19.
2. A few studies have also explored people's aspirations in old age in terms of where and how they would like to receive care and the medicalization of older age and death (see, e.g., Gunaratnam 2013; Hunter and Ammann 2016).
3. See Ciafone and McGeehan Muchmore (2021) for a valuable discussion on how critical gerontologists and historians of age also challenge these binaries.
4. See Sampaio and Amrith (2022) for a more extensive discussion on aging and migration in the Global South.
5. In our view, aspirations can encompass hope but might also exceed them. We see aspirations as more active, something that people work on with the capacities and possibilities they have and a way of living in pursuit of certain goals, projects, and desires that might carry across generations. Meanwhile, hope is an affective state, active or passive, linked to a desire for a better outcome or the possibility that something desired may happen, and often emerges in periods of crisis.
6. See, for example, Fiona Sun, "Old, Unvaccinated, a Disaster Waiting to Happen: How Hong Kong's Care Homes for Elderly Fell to Covid-19 When Omicron Arrived," *South China Morning Post*, 6 March 2022, https://www.scmp.com/news/hong-kong/health-environment/article/3169399/old-unvaccinated-disaster-waiting-happen-how-hong; and Robert Booth, "Why Did So Many People Die of Covid-19 in the UK's Care Homes?," *Guardian*, 28 May 2020, https://www.theguardian.com/society/2020/may/28/why-did-so-many-people-die-of-covid-19-in-the-uks-care-homes.
7. See, for example, Louise Aronson, "For Older People, Despair, as Well as Covid-19, Is Costing Lives," *New York Times*, 8 June 2020, https://www.nytimes.com/2020/06/08/opinion/coronavirus-elderly-suicide.html.
8. This example offers one definition of "aging in place": National Institute on Aging, "Aging in Place: Growing Older at Home," 1 May 2017, https://www.nia.nih.gov/health/aging-place-growing-older-home.

REFERENCES

Amrith, Megha. 2021. "The Linear Imagination, Stalled: Changing Temporal Horizons in Migrant Journeys." *Global Networks* 21 (1): 127–145. https://doi.org/10.1111/glob.12280.
Appadurai, Arjun. 2004. "The Capacity to Aspire: Culture and the Terms of Recognition." In *Culture and Public Action*, edited by Vijayendra Rao and Michael Walton, 59–84. Stanford, CA: Stanford University Press.
Berlant, Lauren. 2011. *Cruel Optimism*. Durham, NC: Duke University Press.
Bloch, Alexia. 2017. *Sex, Love, and Migration: Postsocialism, Modernity, and Intimacy from Istanbul to the Arctic*. Ithaca, NY: Cornell University Press.
Bryant, Rebecca, and Daniel M. Knight. 2019. *The Anthropology of the Future*. Cambridge: Cambridge University Press.
Bunnell, Timothy, Jamie Gillen, and Elaine Lynn-Ee Ho. 2018. "The Prospect of Elsewhere: Engaging the Future through Aspirations in Asia." *Annals of the American Association of Geographers* 108 (1): 35–51.
Butler, Judith. 2004. *Precarious Life: The Powers of Mourning and Violence*. London: Verso.
Carling, Jørgen, and Kerilyn Schewel. 2018. "Revisiting Aspiration and Ability in International Migration." *Journal of Ethnic and Migration Studies* 44 (6): 945–963.

Ciafone, Amanda, and Devin McGeehan Muchmore. 2021. "Old Age and Radical History: Editors' Introduction." *Radical History Review* 139: 1–12.
Ciobanu, Ruxandra Oana, and Alistair Hunter. 2017. "Older Migrants and (Im)mobilities of Ageing: An Introduction." *Population, Space and Place* 23 (5): e2075.
Cohen, Lawrence. 2020. "The Culling: Pandemic, Gerocide, Generational Affect." *Medical Anthropology Quarterly* 34 (4): 542–560.
Cole, Jennifer, and Deborah Durham, eds. 2007. *Generations and Globalization: Youth, Age, and Family in the New World Economy*. Bloomington: Indiana University Press.
Dossa, Parin, and Cati Coe, eds. 2017. *Transnational Aging and Reconfigurations of Kin Work*. New Brunswick, NJ: Rutgers University Press.
Feldman, Ilana. 2017. "Humanitarian Care and the Ends of Life: The Politics of Aging and Dying in a Palestinian Refugee Camp." *Cultural Anthropology* 32 (1): 42–67.
Fischer, Edward F. 2014. *The Good Life: Aspiration, Dignity, and the Anthropology of Wellbeing*. Stanford, CA: Stanford University Press.
Gunaratnam, Yasmin. 2013. *Death and the Migrant: Bodies, Borders and Care*. London: Bloomsbury.
Ho, Elaine Lynn-Ee, Leng Leng Thang, Shirlena Huang, and Brenda S. A. Yeoh. 2022. "(Re)constructing Ageing Futures: Insights from Migration in Asia and Beyond." *American Behavioral Scientist* 66 (14). https://doi:10.1177/00027642221075265.
Honwana, Alcinda. 2012. *The Time of Youth: Work, Social Change, and Politics in Africa*. Sterling, VA: Kumarian Press.
Horn, Vincent, and Cornelia Schweppe, eds. 2016. *Transnational Aging: Current Insights and Future Challenges*. New York: Routledge.
Hromadžić, Azra, and Monika Palmberger, eds. 2018. *Care across Distance: Ethnographic Explorations of Aging and Migration*. New York: Berghahn Books.
Hunter, Alistair, and Eva Soom Ammann. 2016. "End-of-Life Care and Rituals in Contexts of Post-Migration Diversity in Europe: An Introduction." *Journal of Intercultural Studies* 37 (2): 95–102.
Karl, Ute, and Sandra Torres, eds. 2016. *Ageing in Contexts of Migration*. London: Routledge.
Katz, Stephen, Kavita Sivaramakrishnan, and Pat Thane. 2021. "'To Understand All Life as Fragile, Valuable, and Interdependent': A Roundtable on Old Age and History." *Radical History Review* 139: 13–36.
Kavedžija, Iza. 2019. *Making Meaningful Lives: Tales from an Aging Japan*. Philadelphia, PA: University of Pennsylvania Press.
———. 2020. "Introduction. The Ends of Life: Time and Meaning in Later Years." *Anthropology and Aging* 41 (2): 1–8.
King, Russell, Aija Lulle, Dora Sampaio, and Julie Vullnetari. 2017. "Unpacking the Ageing-Migration Nexus and Challenging the Vulnerability Trope." *Journal of Ethnic and Migration Studies* 43 (2): 182–198. https://doi.org/10.1080/1369183X.2016.1238904.
Kleist, Nauja, and Stef Jansen. 2016. "Introduction: Hope over Time—Crisis, Immobility and Future-Making." *History and Anthropology* 27 (4): 373–392.
Lamb, Sarah, ed. 2017. *Successful Aging as a Contemporary Obsession: Global Perspectives*. New Brunswick, NJ: Rutgers University Press.
Rajan-Rankin, Sweta. 2018. "Race, Embodiment and Later Life: Re-animating Aging Bodies of Color." *Journal of Aging Studies* 45: 32–38.
Robertson, Shanthi, Yi'En Cheng, and Brenda S. A. Yeoh. 2018. "Introduction: Mobile Aspirations? Youth Im/mobilities in the Asia-Pacific." *Journal of Intercultural Studies* 39 (6): 613–625. https://doi.org/10.1080/07256868.2018.1536345.
Sakti, Victoria K., and Megha Amrith. 2022. "Introduction: Living in the 'Here and Now': Extended Temporalities of Forced Migration." *Journal of Intercultural Studies* 43 (4): 457–463.
Sampaio, Dora, and Megha Amrith. 2022. "Introduction: Southern Reconfigurations of the Ageing–Migration Nexus." *Journal of Ethnic and Migration Studies*. https://doi.org/10.1080/1369183X.2022.2115624.

Sivaramakrishnan, Kavita. 2018. *As the World Ages: Rethinking a Demographic Crisis.* Cambridge, MA: Harvard University Press.

Taylor, Janelle. 2020. "Afterword: Situating Time, Futurity, and Aging in the Pandemic." *Anthropology and Aging* 41 (2): 90–92.

Van der Veer, Peter, ed. 2015. *Handbook of Religion and the Asian City: Aspiration and Urbanization in the Twenty-First Century.* Berkeley: University of California Press.

Walsh, Katie, and Lena Näre, eds. 2016. *Transnational Migration and Home in Older Age.* New York: Routledge.

Yarris, Kristin. 2017. *Care across Generations: Solidarity and Sacrifice in Transnational Families.* Stanford, CA: Stanford University Press.

PART I

Desire and Self-Realization

CHAPTER 1

Growing Old Hand in Hand

ASPIRATIONS OF ROMANTIC LOVE IN LATER LIFE
AMONG ROMANIAN TRANSMIGRANTS IN ROME

Dumitrița Luncă

"I want a partner," Anastasia says with tears in her eyes during our first meeting. "But my sons say that I am too old for this, I am a grandmother already. And besides, haven't I had enough of men already?"[1] In 2002, at thirty-six, twice divorced, and taking care of her two sons, Anastasia was struggling to make ends meet as a nurse in a provincial hospital in Romania. Seeing more and more friends, neighbors, and colleagues emigrate to find care and domestic work in Italy, she decided to give it a try too. When I met her in the summer of 2017, she was fifty and had been in Rome, Italy, for fifteen years, working as a *badante* and sharing a rental flat with her two grown sons and their girlfriends.[2]

About six months after our first meeting, I visited Anastasia in a flat she was sharing with a man, Tudor. They met on Facebook soon after our encounter, realized they came from the same town, were the same age, and had friends in common, but did not know each other. They were also both divorced and looking for love, so things moved fast from thereon. Soon after they started their relationship, they visited Romania together and met each other's friends and families. Then they decided to move in together. "I have never felt this way for someone so fast," Anastasia told me, her eyes filling again with tears, but happy ones this time. Tudor too seemed to be head over heels, darting about the kitchen, excited to have guests, both looking at each other like adolescents in love. Later in the afternoon, when Anastasia and I retired to their bedroom, she recounted her life story, focusing on her two failed marriages and a string of unhappy relationships, all marked by lack of emotional closeness and sexual pleasure, by jealousy, unfaithfulness, unwanted pregnancies, and emotional and physical violence. At the end, she told me: "You know, my boys didn't want me to find someone, but they always left me alone during holidays while they went to party with their friends. Last year, I spent New Year's with a friend, also a *badante*. We went to a Romanian party at a restaurant, and when the clock struck midnight, we both made a wish. We wished to find love. And I did! And she did too."

Aging, Migration, and Aspirations

Aspirations have been discussed in relation to cultures of migration (Cohen 2004; Horváth 2008; Massey et al. 1994; Sirkeci, Cohen, and Yazgan 2014; Van Mol et al. 2018), oftentimes with an emphasis on the ways in which young people are envisioning their futures (Robertson, Cheng, and Yeoh 2018; Skrbiš, Woodward, and Bean 2014; Van Mol 2016). Some authors draw direct connections between aspirations to migrate and actually undertaking the trip (Creighton 2013), while others observe a gap between stated intention and action (Carling 2002), where migration aspirations are not concrete plans toward mobility, but rather a form of social critique, a "metaphor for disappointment and disengagement" among immobile youth (Bal 2014, 286). Jørgen Carling (2014) notes that aspirations are tightly intertwined with migration because, with the exception of extreme poverty and involuntary mobility due to famine or war, people migrate as a result of not absolute but relative poverty. In other words, migration is oftentimes not just a means of survival but a path toward an envisioned better life. Whether material or spiritual, on a grand or small scale, for oneself, for another, or for a community, all human wants are embedded into culturally established ideas about the good life (Appadurai 2004, 67; see also Amrith, Sakti, and Sampaio, this volume).

Aspirations also have a temporal quality. They are always oriented toward what is yet to come and hinge, like hopes, "on the capacity for imagination, on a sense of time and of temporal progress, on a desire to believe in a better future or in the possibility that something can change" (Pine 2014, S96).

In this chapter, I focus on aspirations of *migrants*, not of migration. Instead, I look at the aspirations of romantic love among middle-aged Romanians living in Rome. I aim to show that love, partnership, and sexuality can be driving forces for migrants of this age and significant components in their definition of good, meaningful, and successful later lives (Lamb 2017; Lulle and King 2016b). In focusing on migrants' intimate lives, I also follow Lena Näre, Katie Walsh, and Loretta Baldassar (2017, 517), who propose that analyzing the micro level of everyday and personal relationships of aging migrants offers insights not only into their emotions, experiences, and sense of identity but also into meso- and macro-level social structures.

In order to contextualize my analysis, I begin with a discussion of the literature on migration, love, and aging, followed by a brief historical account of the Romanian migration phenomenon and a description of my research field in Rome. I then proceed to introduce some of my interlocutors and the role of romantic love in their lives. Although past experiences, present romantic situations, and future aspirations vary greatly among the middle-aged people I met, I identify two large themes: nurturing love and looking for love. I illustrate each of these categories with my own observations and with my interlocutors' stories.

The data presented here were collected during thirteen months of fieldwork between 2017 and 2018, as part of my doctoral research project on the intersection of love, sex, and migration among Romanians living in Rome. I did participant observation and informal interviews with numerous people at various meetings, concerts, dinners, church masses, and other events that this very active community organizes weekly, as well as in parks, on buses, in stores, in cafés, on Facebook groups, and anywhere else I happened to meet a fellow Romanian. I also did expert interviews with community leaders and extensive life-history interviews with sixty interlocutors, whom I had selected by mixing convenience and snowball sampling. For my project, I spoke with adults of all ages about their intimate experiences and desires, past, present, and future. In this chapter, however, I concentrate on twenty-seven interviewees who were between forty-five and sixty years old at the time—twenty women and seven men.[3] They were all of post-reproductive age, and, except for one man who was childless and had a longtime partner with no intention to tie the knot officially, they had all married young, all had grown children, and many were already grandparents.[4] They had completed varying levels of formal education, from high school to master's programs. Before emigrating, some of them had been qualified workers in factories, while others had worked as teachers, army personnel, chemists, or small business owners. At the time of the interviews, some had low-paying jobs in care, cleaning, or construction, but others had managed to have their qualifications recognized and were decidedly middle class, working in the culture and education fields.

Aging, Migration, and Love

Romantic love has only recently emerged as a "serious" subject of scientific inquiry (Ahearn 2001; Campbell 2006; Cole 2009; Gell 2011; Illouz 2012; Jackson 1993; Jankowiak 2008, 2017; Jankowiak and Fischer 1992; Lindholm 2006; Luhmann 1986). Nevertheless, it is very rarely prominently featured in scholarly work on migration. Not only does this omission fail to fully understand the migrant experience, but, as Walsh points out, studying love in a transnational context may offer insights into "contemporary cultures of intimacy" more generally (2009, 443). In a similar vein, Nicola Mai and Russell King make an impassioned appeal for an "emotional and sexual turn in migration studies." They call for scholarship looking at a wide array of factors that all fit under the umbrella of intimacy to better understand the importance that "these dimensions play in determining life choices, their centrality in people's understanding of themselves and each other, their links to moralised notions of freedom, coercion and respectability" (Mai and King 2009, 300).[5] In a more recent volume, Christian Groes and Nadine T. Fernandez highlight the manifold incarnations of the intimacy-mobility articulation, thus underscoring its ubiquitous and essential quality in people's lives: "For us, 'intimate mobilities' involve all forms of mobility shaped, implied or facilitated by bodily, sexual, affective or reproductive intimacy, spanning what has been coined as marriage migration, family migration, sexual migration, romance travel, erotic adventure, sex work migration and sex tourism, as well as any kind of mobility motivated by emotions, desires or pleasures, or conditioned by kinship, family ties or reproductive ambitions" (2018, 1).

As Martina Cvajner and Giuseppe Sciortino point out, these intimate mobilities not only impact migrants' own lives but also lead to wider "socio-cultural changes in the sexual stratifications and categorical systems of the erotic spheres established in sending, transit and receiving spaces," which they call "lovescapes" (2021, 45). Ethnographers who have explicitly focused on romantic love and couplehood in the context of migration, such as Jennifer S. Hirsch (2003), Gloria González-López (2005), and Alexia Bloch (2017), have all noted that romantic love is an arena of (re)negotiating seemingly private issues, such as gender roles, reproductive practices, pleasure, power, agency, and money, as well as larger issues, such as generational social change, modernity, and the process of migration itself. The ways in which people "do" romantic love is oftentimes transformed by the migration process, but the former can also be a catalyst for the latter (Mai and King 2009, 296). Aspirations of migration, therefore, become entangled not only with hopes of material stability or professional success but also with romantic and sensual aspirations, all of which are different facets of collective and individual understandings of the good life.

In most of the studies on intimacy and migration mentioned so far, older people are not in focus and are usually not the ones to be mobile themselves, but rather are background characters, or those left behind by their mobile kin. Some notable works on aging and transnationalism have appeared in the past two decades (Alber 2018; Baldassar 2007; Baldassar, Baldock, and Wilding 2007; Ciobanu, Fokkema, and Nedelcu 2017; Dossa and Coe 2017; Gardner 2002; Horn and Schweppe 2016; Lamb 2009; Näre, Walsh, and Baldassar 2017; Nedelcu 2017; Zontini 2015), but the "default protagonist" (King et al. 2017) of migration studies continues to be a young or early middle-aged adult. Similarly, I would argue, the "default person in love" or "sexual person" is also usually perceived as young, which leads to a scarcity of research on the topic of intimate aspirations in later life. It follows, then, that the articulation between intimacy, aging, and migration is rarely addressed, with very few exceptions (Sampaio 2018; Lulle and King 2016a).

As Anastasia's account at the beginning of this chapter suggests and as other interlocutors have confirmed, according to the socially sanctioned ways of aging Romanian womanhood, those who have grown children or grandchildren and who have had several unsuccessful attempts at love should sexually and romantically "close up shop." They are encouraged to focus on an asexual, domestic retirement, on regularly attending church and nurturing the new generations. Elsewhere, I focus more narrowly on sexual (re)discoveries such as "sexual agency, sexual communication, and consent, giving and receiving oral sex, and even experiencing (multiple) orgasms and squirting" (Luncă 2020, 61) among middle-aged Romanian women in Rome. These findings echo those of Aija Lulle and Russell King (2016a) among middle-aged Latvian women in other European countries, some of whom were also discovering their "erotic agency" (Sheller 2012)—"a sexual reawakening and a triumphal rejection of their framing in Latvia as nonsexual older or middle-aged beings" (Lulle and King 2016a, 93).

These sexual explorations were not universal among the middle-aged women I encountered in Rome, but I considered them important specifically because they ran counter to what was expected. In this chapter, I apply a different logic and focus on aspirations of romantic love and partnership in later life, specifically because these *were* almost universal among the people I encountered during my fieldwork, regardless of gender.

My interlocutors' intimate aspirations, I propose, were partly shaped by the "culture of intimacy" (Walsh 2009, 443) during their youth in state socialism and by their migration experiences. In the following sections, I offer some background necessary to frame their present lives in Italy and their view of the future.

From Closed Borders to Mass Phenomenon

The life trajectories of working and middle-class people during the state socialist dictatorship of Nicolae Ceaușescu (1965–1989) followed a predictable pattern: get married young, have children early on, and find a lifelong stable job in the industrial, services, administrative, or cultural sectors (Massino 2019). Ceaușescu's austerity measures led to limited access to certain consumer goods (televisions, washing machines, and cars), foods (milk, bread, meat, and coffee), and services (gas, electricity, and heating) (Chelcea 2002). Migration and international travel were restricted, and political dissent was discouraged. Draconian pronatalist policies (Kligman 1998) led to the death of an estimated twenty-five thousand women as a result of illicit abortions and to countless abandoned children between 1966 and 1989 (Anton 2011–2012, 10). At the same time, most of the population benefited from education, guaranteed employment, and housing, a stability that the country has not enjoyed since its "move to democracy" in 1989 and which many, including some of my interlocutors, miss.

Women especially benefited from the official policy of gender equality during state socialism, which allowed them, despite continuing to do most care and domestic work, to participate in the labor market at almost the same level as men and at much higher rates than their Western counterparts (Massino 2009). This in turn led to women's increased financial independence and presence in the public sphere in an otherwise patriarchal society (Miroiu 2007). Men were still considered heads of the household and main providers. Despite glorifying motherhood as part of pronatalist policies, government propaganda was also promoting egalitarian family models (Massino 2010, 53) and an image of spouses as *tovarăși de viață* (comrades in life) (Biebuyck 2010, 61). Marriage was an important institution during state socialism, and it has remained so after 1989, despite a slight delay in establishing the first union and reproduction, along with an increase in reproduction outside of marriage, cohabitation, and divorce (Mureșan 2007).

In the 1990s, the country's industrial infrastructure collapsed, leaving most of its workers jobless. The transitional economic crisis pushed many Romanians to emigrate in search of work. At first, Germans and Hungarian ethnics were "returning" to their ancestral lands in Germany and Hungary, while Roma ethnics were applying for asylum in Western Europe. Then, temporary and circular labor migration slowly emerged, first toward Hungary, Israel, and Turkey and later to other European Union (EU) countries, especially Spain and Italy.

During the 1990s, Romanians were able to circulate within the Schengen Area only with tourist and short-term visas or they would cross borders illegally. They usually found irregular work and remained in their countries of destination after the expiration of the visas (Anghel 2008; Sandu 2005). In 2002, the EU introduced the right to free movement within the Schengen Area for Romanians, which allowed them to find work legally, to visit home, and to bring their families. In 2007, Romania joined the EU, which allowed more and more Romanians to establish permanent residence in other EU countries, to acquire long-term work, and to access temporary or seasonal formal employment (Marcu 2015). After three decades, an estimated four million Romanians are living outside the country's borders. More than 1.2 million of them are in Italy alone, where they are also the largest minority. More than two hundred thousand Romanians live in Rome, the capital of the country (ISTAT 2020).

A large portion of the migrants who were part of the first few waves of migration to Italy in their twenties and thirties are now in their fifties and sixties. Many had only planned a short stay to make some quick money for their families' immediate needs. Due to their strong material and affective ties in Romania—families, friends, homes, jobs, and responsibilities—their planned short stints in Italy were simply a means toward achieving their aspirations back home. However, as is the case with other labor migrant populations around the world, such as Mexicans in the United States (Pauli and Bedorf 2018) or Turks in Western Europe (Klok et al. 2017; Palmberger 2017), various factors—legal, economic, political, social, and emotional—have contributed to many of these first Romanians in Italy extending their stay from a few months to decades.

Migration and Intimacy

In the initial stages, Romanian migration was led by men, but it later became feminized. According to Ionela Vlase (2018, 204), one reason why men migrated first is the inherent danger and uncertainty associated with the initial trips abroad in the early 1990s, when migration networks were essentially nonexistent. This was more likely to attract young, adventurous men and to discourage most women. A second reason was the belief that women migrating alone might be attracted into the sex industry or sex trafficking, which not only might have deterred women but also threatened fathers' and husbands' masculinities. Finally, a third reason was that men were more likely to be able to access resources to cover the costs associated with migration, such as visas, transportation, bribes, or smugglers.

The nature of the initial stages of Romanians' migration, along with the border regimes in force at the time, has led to a popular belief that "străinătatea destramă familii" (going abroad breaks up families). Indeed, young Romanian families immigrating to Italy today might find it easy to emigrate together, making arrangements for jobs and housing in advance, making use of extended networks of kin and friends, and safely, legally, and quickly traveling by plane from one country to another. Twenty to thirty years earlier, all of these things were extremely different, and couples were usually separated in the migration process. In most cases, one spouse (usually the man) emigrated, found a job, and secured a place to live, with the other spouse and children joining later. But this might have taken years. All the while, the migrating spouse was living in crammed migrant accommodation, able to contact their loved ones only by letter or prohibitively expensive public telephones, and unable to return for long stretches of time due to their undocumented status. In many cases, one partner permanently stayed in Romania, while the other worked abroad and sent money. In other cases, men and women might have had access to different transnational networks and migrate to two different countries altogether.

The time and space that couples put between them likely had a strong impact on the relationship, but many other factors came into play in either strengthening or weakening marital bonds. Many of my interlocutors were in fact already divorced or widowed when they migrated, and only in a few cases did marriage dissolution occur afterward. In each of these situations, however, distance only served as the final nail in the coffin and never as the main reason for the separation.

During my fieldwork in Rome, I observed a very active and well-organized transnational community, with hundreds of shops, restaurants, churches, and cultural and political associations, which regularly organized events. While men and women working in low-paying jobs, such as cleaning, construction, care, and hospitality, were the most numerous and visible, I also met journalists, doctors, students, business managers, politicians, educators, priests, and poets, as well as unhoused or unemployed people. Before arriving, I could not have imagined the amount of interest the topic of intimacy would generate. Sometimes people would approach me at events, or they would write to me on Facebook proposing to meet. Whether single, newly in love, married for decades, widowed, or divorced, and no matter the age or social background, people would always be interested to hear about what I had observed in the field and to share their own stories. I was twice approached by a person who, with tears in their eyes, wanted to share the story of their successful and enduring marriage, which had lasted decades despite the difficulties of migration (or rather which made the difficulties of migration more bearable).

Once, I met a man who had become unhoused after his wife left him suddenly for another man, a situation that made him confused and depressed, disconnected him from old friends, and unable to work. It completely turned his whole life upside down. Another time I interviewed a young woman whose parents had managed to buy an apartment after years of hard work in Italy. Soon after, they separated

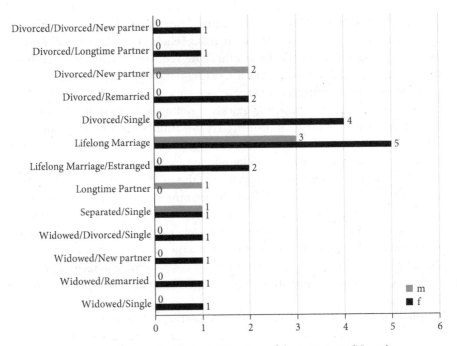

Figure 1.1. Romantic situation at the time of the interviews (N = 27).

but were forced to live together and even slept in the same bed without speaking to each other, because neither could afford to move out, as they were still paying the flat's mortgage. One middle-aged woman, who had been working low-paying jobs in Rome for twenty years, had an affair for about the same amount of time with a wealthy, married Italian man, who supported her and her family, both emotionally and materially. After his wife's death, he invited the woman to move into his home as his official partner, but they also had an arrangement through which she gave up her *badante* job and he paid a salary for her services as a full-time administrator, cook, and cleaner of their home.

Each of these instances illustrates how, for my interlocutors, love and partnership were not frivolous, superfluous things, but an integral part of life, tightly interwoven with daily activities, work, friends, family, finances, housing, religious and political beliefs, hobbies, investments, retirement plans, and the overarching transnational migration experience.

Although almost all of my informants started off similarly, by marrying and having children in their early twenties or even late teens, what immediately became obvious is that their intimate lives developed in dramatically different directions. To show the variety of their life (and intimate) trajectories, I compiled the romantic status of my interlocutors into precise categories (figure 1.1). Looking at their romantic aspirations at the time of the interviews, however, I identify two broader categories—those who had a partner and were looking forward to aging together and those who did not and were looking for love. Below I look more closely at individual stories.

Nurturing Love in Later Life

Out of the twenty-seven middle-aged interlocutors in my sample, nineteen were in romantic relationships at the time of the interviews and eight were single. Three who had migrated divorced or widowed were happily remarried with Italian citizens, while two were married but estranged from their spouses still in Romania. In this section, I focus on those who were married before migrating and who were still together. In my sample, eight people belonged in this category—five women and three men.

One couple, Corina and Marian, was especially striking because of their obvious, almost demonstrative closeness, despite having been together for almost three decades. I met them one evening at a vernissage, where the organizer invited me to present my project in front of the audience. Later in the evening, when the chairs for the audience were pulled back to make more room for dancing, Corina approached me by saying that she would really like to share her story. "When my husband emigrated, I stayed behind with our young son. I didn't see him for three years. You cannot imagine what this does to a couple! I want to tell you about it, so maybe others can learn from my experience." She also told me of the first time being intimate with her husband after his long absence. "It was like being with a stranger, like the first time all over again." She had tears in her eyes as she told me this. She then returned to her husband, and they continued to dance all evening, cheek to cheek, both smiling widely, spinning around with great energy.

They met very young, working together in a factory in the late 1980s. In 2001, after ten years of marriage, they were both thirty-three years old and had a young son. Marian went abroad, first to Germany, where Corina had a brother. He then went to Italy, where he had relatives from his side of the family, and soon found work transporting and assembling furniture. Because he purposely overstayed his tourist Schengen visa, Marian was only able to visit Romania after three years of absence, when his status was regularized as a result of a new immigration law (Ambrosini 2011). After two more years, Corina and their son joined Marian in Rome, where they have all been living ever since.

They both see the five years apart as one of the hardest moments in their lives, marked by loneliness and suffering. Corina, who continued to work in the factory, was struck not only by the pain of separation but also by the particularly insidious suspicion of immorality that oftentimes marks women in Romanian transnational families, whether they are the ones who migrate or the ones who stay behind (Potot 2005, 10). Because she was "husbandless," but not a virgin anymore, she was seen as a temptress by other married women, who forbade their husbands to socialize with her. At the same time, she experienced sexual advances from her boss and became increasingly isolated.

Corina and Marian are very similar in what they value in their relationship and what they wish for the future. Theirs is a classic "companionate marriage," which Hirsch describes as "a core ideology of modernity, related to the transformation of households from sites of production to consumption, to falling fertility and increased life spans, and to modern notions of personhood" (2003, 113). Respect, communication, but also sexual satisfaction and the sharing of household chores are at the core of their long-lasting and thriving marriage. "We do everything together," said Corina—laundry, shopping, cooking, socializing, taking all the decisions together—this is the most important. In fact, Marian oftentimes posts pictures of himself doing household chores, such as ironing clothes, on Facebook.

When looking at pictures of couples of different ages engaged in various activities, as part of photo elicitation, Corina chose one in which a man and a woman sit on the grass in front of a house, happily in each other's arms. Marian liked one where an elderly couple is holding a baby, saying he enjoyed imagining himself and his wife in the role of grandparents. Their aspirations are related to their return to Romania ("I live so I could go back," Corina says), to the personal and professional success of their son, and to their closeness with friends and family, both in Romania and in Rome. Their relationship, however, is the base for everything they see for themselves in the future and the only way they can imagine growing old. They oftentimes post on Facebook pictures of the two of them together on holiday, visiting Romania, attending events, eating, or dancing.

I have met many other middle-aged Romanian couples during my time in Rome, such as Victoria and Andrei, who had been friends since birth and romantic partners since adolescence. They had migrated together and, despite the initial difficulties of life in a new place, had made a good life for themselves in Italy. They recently marked their thirty-fifth anniversary by posting on Facebook a picture of themselves hand in hand and smiling. Another couple celebrated being married for thirty years in their Romanian Catholic church, where their priest organized a special mass dedicated to anniversaries of migrants.

In this community, a lasting marriage, which people oftentimes showed off at public events and on social media platforms, is a symbol of personal achievement and of successful migration, especially due to the belief that "going abroad breaks up families." It is also a coveted, essential ingredient in the way many people envision a peaceful, happy later life.

Looking for Love in Later Life

Among those who were single when I met them, some had fresh wounds, having recently lost their partner, while others had been alone for many years. In fact, one woman was celibate for two decades after her divorce, having decided to concentrate on the success of her daughter rather than on finding a partner for herself. Some of my interlocutors were divorced, while others were widowed, and yet others were both. Notwithstanding how and when they had lost love, most people who were not in a romantic relationship at the time of the interviews expressed their aspiration for finding love and companionship again in their later lives. This in turn reflected and was bound with individual ideas of the good (later) life (Lamb 2017), home, family, moral values, and belonging.

Figure 1.2. Women dancing at a Sunday Romanian event, summer 2017, Rome. Photograph by Dumitrița Luncă.

Single middle-aged people oftentimes attended events where traditional Romanian party music was played, and many danced for hours in pairs or in a *horă* (circle) (see figure 1.2). Another popular place to meet possible romantic partners among this age-group was church. While many younger people also attended services in one of the many Romanian churches in Rome, they were also more likely to have jobs that allowed for more socialization. For middle-aged people, many of whom worked more isolating jobs with strict schedules, Sunday mass was one of the few occasions to meet others with whom to have a coffee or a Romanian dish at a nearby canteen and exchange Facebook contacts with a romantic prospect. This observation echoes the findings of Ruxandra Oana Ciobanu and Tineke Fokkema (2016), who also concluded that among Romanian migrants in Switzerland, whether they migrated before 1989 or were new arrivals, going to church provided a sense of community and continuity, despite the fracture that migration had produced in their lives. For their aging interlocutors, practicing religion and attending services were preventing and reducing possible feeling of loneliness and isolation.

This was certainly the case for Gabriel, a fifty-six-year-old contractor, whom I first saw vividly talking to a woman and another man outside a small Romanian Orthodox church right after mass. Gabriel's first attempt to migrate was in the late 1970s, when he and two friends swam across the Danube, but they were caught and brought back to Romania. In the early 1990s, he was among the first to migrate for work, first to Yugoslavia, then to Turkey and Israel, and finally to Italy in 2000. His wife and three children remained in Romania. They finally joined him in 2005, but several years later, after thirty-four years of marriage, Gabriel's wife decided to get a divorce. The reason invoked was their religious conflict—Gabriel's wife is a Jehovah's Witness, while he is a Christian Orthodox. Living in Rome together, but socializing in separate religious communities, Gabriel and his wife started having issues. She began accusing him of being faithless as well as unfaithful and he had to leave their home.

When I met him, three years after his separation, he had recently met someone, a Romanian woman who had been once divorced and once widowed. They had met in church, and he liked that she was devout; she made the sign of the cross often. After watching her for some time, he approached her one day and asked for her phone number, and they started to go out. At the beginning of the relationship, she read prayers to him on the phone in the evenings. She was working as a *badante* and they were spending her days off together, at his place or going out for ice cream or pizza, to the seaside, and to Piazza Venezia. He was happy, she was diligent, often ironing his pants and shirts, cooking, and going to mass. They got engaged in church, a common practice among Romanian migrants who have been married before and who did not want to go through the hassle of civil marriage, but who wanted their union blessed in front of God. They exchanged rings. A week later she disappeared and never came back.

At the time of our interview, Gabriel no longer wore his engagement ring and told me he started talking to another woman from church. "I want to meet a nice Orthodox woman!" he told me, a good Romanian woman, not an Italian, because "they are cold and jealous." Instead, he wanted to meet someone who would care about him, someone he could respect, and someone to start over with and to provide for. After so many years of being away from Romania and after his marriage fell apart, he longed to go home and to start a construction business there so that people could see the skills he learned abroad. He gave himself one more year in Rome and wistfully said: "I would leave tomorrow if I could."

Another person who was planning to leave Rome soon is Vera. She was fifty-five when I met her, and, unlike most other Romanians her age, she had only been living in Italy for five years. Not part of the first waves of migrants who had to cross borders illegally, she saw her time in Italy as a learning experience and an adventure. She described having a perfect life before leaving Romania: a great relationship with her husband, a son, a job she loved, and colleagues she was best friends with. All this crumbled in 2012, when, after twenty-nine years of marriage, her husband died suddenly of a heart attack. Soon after, the chemical laboratory where she had worked her entire life closed and she was forced into unemployment. After she tried in vain to find work, her sister, who worked in Italy as a *badante*, found her a job, and Vera decided to take the leap.

After recounting her life story, Vera told me she was soon moving back to Romania. To live with her son? Her elderly mother? No, in fact, she was getting ready for a new beginning with a new partner. I was surprised. "I told you!" she said, with obvious satisfaction that the twist in her story had been so effective. "Life can be beautiful if you follow some rules," which I interpreted to mean that if you are patient, good things will come your way.

They met in a way that in the Romanian migrant community is very common: through a friend set-up. Matchmaking friends oftentimes connect migrants with possible romantic candidates at home or in other countries. Usually, the parties are shown pictures of each other and given some information, and, if they both agree, contact details are exchanged and courting commences. Social media and messaging platforms are extremely important in this process, and the middle-aged migrants I have met were very actively posting, commenting, and connecting virtually, whether with friends or romantic interests. This was especially the case for people working long hours and having few social interactions, such as *badanti*, for whom their phone is a window to the outside world and an important avenue toward establishing friendships, building romantic relationships, and finding jobs. With this man, Vera told me, things worked out very smoothly from the beginning.

> V: After we met, we started to talk every day on the phone, on WhatsApp on Messenger, on Facebook, on all the social networks.
> DL: And did you fall in love?
> V: Yes! Both of us!
> ...
> DL: Did you imagine finding someone? Is that what you wanted?
> V: Yes, yes, I wanted to.
> DL: But were you actively looking? Some people even search online on websites, they flirt on Facebook...
> V: My girlfriend first introduced me to someone else. And I didn't like it, there wasn't that *feeling* [in English in original].
> DL: Here, in Italy? Or at home?
> V: No, I wanted a Romanian man.
> DL: But a Romanian in Italy or a Romanian at home, so you know you have something to return to?
> V: I always wanted a Romanian, I always planned to go home. I sometimes joke with my girlfriends, I tell them, "I'm on standby."

They met for the first time face-to-face after a few months, on New Year's Eve, when Vera went home for the holidays. When I met her, eight months later, she was preparing to move back to Romania within weeks, and she seemed glowing with excitement.

Like Gabriel, Vera had a lasting relationship, which ended suddenly. Both of them longed to re-create that stability and imagined their later lives in Romania together with a new life partner. They both saw migration as an experience that had enriched their lives, but still only a phase before going back and starting to live their later years.

Finally, I introduce Maia, who was sixty when I met her at the monthly poetry club attended by many Romanians in Rome. Most attendants were middle-aged, and some read poems they wrote, while others came just for socializing. Maia worked as a *badante*, taking care of an elderly woman whose health was deteriorating fast, but she had been a qualified chemist in Romania. Whenever her job contract would be "over," that is, when her employer would inevitably pass away, Maia would go back to Romania and start anew.

Unlike most of the other people I had met, she was very reserved and mingled very little with the others in the community, except for attending the poetry club once a month. She even preferred to work on the usual days off for *badanti*, Thursday and Sunday, and during holidays. She spoke minimal Italian after eighteen years in Rome, which was unheard of among Romanians, who rather reveled in their quick proficiency, and which suggested her unwillingness to adapt to her condition as a migrant laborer. Like Vera saying she was "on standby," Maia too seemed to keep herself above the reality of her work as a *badante* in Rome and concentrate her energy on her rich inner life and her aspirations of a new start at home. Many of her writings, which she sometimes read at the club and which she often posted on Facebook, were very sensual and spoke of an intense romantic longing. "I am a passionate woman, romantic, my poetry is born out of love," she told me.

In Maia's case, her husband emigrated first, in 1995, and she followed five years later. She had to come and start working herself to make extra money, especially since her husband seemed to not do a good job in her absence. "I was always the administrator, he always counted on my strength." After five more years of living together in Rome, she found out that he was unfaithful. The relationship started to deteriorate, and, despite efforts to work through the problems, it soon dissolved. She had only had one attempt at a romantic relationship since the divorce, some ten years before our interview, but it did not work out. She nevertheless persisted in her hope to meet someone: "I've said it all along and I will say it again: I don't hide the fact that I want someone." For Maia, as for Gabriel and Vera, desire for a partner was, in turn, tightly related to her return to Romania and to a social status that she wanted to regain after the years of working a low-paying and low-prestige job. She imagined a happy retirement, full of intellectual stimulation, a life close to her children and grandchildren, but not as a full-time grandmother. When I asked her where she saw herself in five years, she replied: "I hope that in two years, maximum, I will be in Bucharest for good. And there I hope to find someone for me, someone to travel with. It is very difficult because single men [this age], there is a reason why they are single. . . . I'm not saying that there are no bad women, but less so. Percentagewise, men hold the record. It's very hard, but I hope, I dream, I hope to find someone!" Despite her desire for love, she had not yet found anyone because she was very "picky." Besides, where could she meet someone in Rome?

> M: I am an independent, pretentious, elegant, luxurious woman. This is not just because of Italy; I've always been like that. I want to find someone so that I am not alone, but he must be a smart man.

DL: And your plan is to return to Bucharest and start attending cultural events, exhibitions...?

M: Yes, exhibitions, yes, and something has got to give, someone must appear, I say!

Like many of my other single interlocutors in this age-group, Maia had had unhappy romantic experiences, and looking for love and a partner to her liking at her age was not an easy task. Nevertheless, like the others, she too persisted in her optimism and aspiration, as if growing old without a partner was not even an option.

Conclusions

When I last saw Anastasia, she said about her relationship with Tudor: "Every day I hope that it will be forever, until death do us part." This was especially important for her because of all the unhappy relationships she had had before; she wanted to have true love at least in later life. Several years later, in early 2022, I found out she was back in Romania taking care of her ill mother. Her relationship with Tudor did not last, but she later married again, as she had aspired. Her New Year's wish finally came true. Vera's relationship also did not work out as planned, and she was back in Rome. "My dream of forming a family was not realized," she wrote to me in a message a few years after our last meeting. "But I remain a person who sees the positive in everything." Maia, who had moved to Bucharest after her employer eventually died, was also still single, but judging by her Facebook page, she seemed to be very active, traveling and attending many cultural events.

Vera's and Gabriel's first marriages were happy, so they wanted to replicate that, while Maia's and Anastasia's were not, so they both wanted to compensate by finding better partners at least later in life. Despite their different past experiences, all of them maintained their romantic aspirations, even when faced with failed attempts.

Like Dora Sampaio's (2018) lifestyle migrants in Azores and Lulle and King's (2016a, 2016b) Latvian labor migrants, many of my interlocutors saw retirement as a new and exciting stage in their lives, full of plans, desires, and aspirations, of which romantic ones were a crucial aspect. For many of them, their greatest wish was to return to Romania upon retirement, where they had heavily invested in buying, renovating, and furnishing homes, preparing their homecoming for decades.[6] Some, like Gabriel, wanted to start businesses, while others, like Maia, wanted to travel or enjoy some well-deserved rest. Being close to family, especially parents and grandchildren, was also important, as it was for Corina and Marian, who had extensive kin networks at home and abroad.

Aside from these more common later-life aspirations, my interlocutors, regardless of whether they had a partner or not and notwithstanding the bitter past experiences they might have had, often mentioned love and partnership as essential ingredients for a good life. Having a strong, lasting relationship, such as the ones between Corina and Marian, Victoria and Andrei, and others who have managed to stay together despite migration, becomes a symbol of a successful (later) life and of successful migration, just as much as building a house and putting children through school.

These findings echo those of Lulle and King, who write: "A 'good life' for a labour migrant means not only accessing a decent income and acceptable working conditions but also more 'personal' practices, such as developing new interests and activities, renewing lapsed hobbies, and pursuing healthy pastimes such as walking, dancing, travelling, and reclaiming a more sensual, 'alive' body" (2016a, 80–81).

In my interlocutors' parents' generation, divorce was unheard of, remarriage later in life was rare, and widowhood followed by singlehood was rather the norm. In many ways, it was fantastic to see their strength, energy, and capacity to dream and plan, their readiness to start anew, in contrast with the previous generations' rather fatalistic acceptance of body ailments and loneliness as part of the aging process. At the same time, it is easy to see their aspirations as culturally bound (Appadurai 2004) to neoliberal Western discourses about love and partnership as essential to happiness (Illouz 1997) and about healthy, active, and successful aging (Lamb, Robbins-Ruszkowski, and Corwin 2017). These ideas were also likely heavily influenced by the Romanian traditional view of marriage as an essential and universal institution, especially during their youth in state socialism.

At the same time, seeing couples who had been together for decades through thick and thin and who still held hands, danced together, and seemed to be so supportive of one another, it was also easy to understand why those less lucky in love might want the same for themselves. For better or for worse, despite experience having made them wearier and more selective in their searches, middle-aged Romanian transmigrants could only imagine growing old hand in hand as they looked toward retirement. All of those interviewed, including those who were happily, although not always effortlessly, nurturing a decades-old marriage, saw partnership as essential for their later lives, and none could imagine growing old alone as a viable or desirable option.

Acknowledgments

This chapter includes results in the doctoral thesis entitled "Intimate Luggage: Love, Sex and Gender among Romanian Transmigrants in Rome" submitted by Dumitrița Luncă to the Institute for Social and Cultural Anthropology at Hamburg University in 2023. This work would not have been possible without three equally important parties: all my interlocutors in Rome who have opened their hearts to me; Julia Pauli, my doctoral supervisor at the University of Hamburg, my mentor and inspiration; and the editors of this volume, who provided immensely helpful feedback and encouragements throughout this process. To all, I am extremely grateful, thank you.

Notes

1. All interviews were conducted in Romanian and translated by me. All names are anonymized.

2. *Badante* (s.)/*badanti* (pl.)—in Italian: a live-in care worker of any gender, oftentimes a migrant woman.

3. There is a gender imbalance in the sample, due to the fact that the combination of my own gender and the research topic made it difficult, awkward, and sometimes unsafe for me to approach men with the same forwardness I approached women. Women also showed more eagerness to discuss the topic, and they were usually present at higher rates at the public events I attended.

4. Depending on their sex and other factors, people can reproduce until later in life. However, none of the interlocutors were planning to have any (more) children. To my knowledge, all my interlocutors were heterosexual and cisgender. Due to the strict binary and heteronormativity of Romanian society and not wanting to antagonize anyone, I usually avoided discussing LGBTQI* issues. Throughout the chapter I refer to cis men and women exclusively.

5. *Intimacy* has many definitions, from closeness between kin or friends to a euphemism for the sexual act, but throughout this chapter I use it as an umbrella term for all matters regarding romantic love and sexuality.

6. See also chapters by Lisa Johnson and Cati Coe, respectively, for a discussion of return migration aspirations.

REFERENCES

Ahearn, Laura M. 2001. *Invitations to Love: Literacy, Love Letters, and Social Change in Nepal*. Ann Arbor: University of Michigan Press.

Alber, Erdmute. 2018. "Préparer la Retraite: New Age-Inscriptions in West African Middle Classes." *Anthropology and Aging* 39 (1): 66–81. https://doi.org/10.5195/aa.2018.171.

Ambrosini, Maurizio. 2011. "Immigration in Italy: Between Economic Acceptance and Political Rejection." *Journal of International Migration and Integration* 14 (1): 175–194.

Anghel, Remus Gabriel. 2008. "Changing Statuses: Freedom of Movement, Locality and Transnationality of Irregular Romanian Migrants in Milan." *Journal of Ethnic and Migration Studies* 34 (5): 787–802. https://doi.org/10.1080/13691830802106069.

Anton, Lorena. 2011–2012. "Socialist Mothers and Their Legacies: Migration, Reproductive Health and 'Body-Memory' in Post-Communist Romania." Work-in-Progress Seminar. Institute for Advanced Studies in the Humanities, University of Edinburgh.

Appadurai, Arjun. 2004. "The Capacity to Aspire: Culture and the Terms of Recognition." In *Culture and Public Action*, edited by Vijayendra Rao and Michael Walton, 59–84. Stanford, CA: Stanford University Press.

Bal, Ellen. 2014. "Yearning for Faraway Places: The Construction of Migration Desires among Young and Educated Bangladeshis in Dhaka." *Identities* 21 (3): 275–289. https://doi.org/10.1080/1070289X.2013.833512.

Baldassar, Loretta. 2007. "Transnational Families and Aged Care: The Mobility of Care and the Migrancy of Ageing." *Journal of Ethnic and Migration Studies* 33 (2): 275–297. https://doi.org/10.1080/13691830601154252.

Baldassar, Loretta, Cora V. Baldock, and Raelene Wilding. 2007. *Families Caring across Borders: Migration, Ageing and Transnational Caregiving*. Basingstoke: Palgrave Macmillan.

Biebuyck, Erin K. 2010. "The Collectivisation of Pleasure: Normative Sexuality in Post-1966 Romania." *Aspasia* 4 (1): 49–70. https://doi.org/10.3167/asp.2010.040104.

Bloch, Alexia. 2017. *Sex, Love, and Migration: Postsocialism, Modernity, and Intimacy from Istanbul to the Arctic*. Ithaca, NY: Cornell University Press.

Campbell, Colin. 2006. "'All You Need Is Love': From Romance to Romanticism: The Beatles, Romantic Love and Cultural Change." *Etnofoor* 19 (1): 111–123.

Carling, Jørgen. 2002. "Migration in the Age of Involuntary Immobility: Theoretical Reflections and Cape Verdean Experiences." *Journal of Ethnic and Migration Studies* 28 (1): 5–42.

———. 2014. "The Role of Aspirations in Migration." Paper presented at Determinants of International Migration, International Migration Institute, University of Oxford, 23–25 September 2014.

Chelcea, Liviu. 2002. "The Culture of Shortage during State-Socialism: Consumption Practices in a Romanian Village in the 1980s." *Cultural Studies* 16 (1): 16–43. https://doi.org/10.1080/09502380110075243.
Ciobanu, Ruxandra Oana, and Tineke Fokkema. 2016. "The Role of Religion in Protecting Older Romanian Migrants from Loneliness." *Journal of Ethnic and Migration Studies* 43 (2): 199–217. https://doi.org/10.1080/1369183X.2016.1238905.
Ciobanu, Ruxandra Oana, Tineke Fokkema, and Mihaela Nedelcu. 2017. "Ageing as a Migrant: Vulnerabilities, Agency and Policy Implications." *Journal of Ethnic and Migration Studies* 43 (2): 1–18. https://doi.org/10.1080/1369183X.2016.1238903.
Cohen, Jeffrey H. 2004. *The Culture of Migration in Southern Mexico*. Austin: University of Texas Press.
Cole, Jennifer. 2009. "Love, Money, and Economies of Intimacy in Tamatave, Madagascar." In *Love in Africa*, edited by Jennifer Cole and Lynn M. Thomas, 109–134. Chicago: University of Chicago Press.
Creighton, Mathew J. 2013. "The Role of Aspirations in Domestic and International Migration." *Social Science Journal* 50 (1): 79–88. https://doi.org/10.1016/j.soscij.2012.07.006.
Cvajner, Martina, and Giuseppe Sciortino. 2021. "The Sexual Dimension of Migration: From Sexual Migration to Changing Lovescapes." In *Handbook of Culture and Migration*, edited by Jeffrey H. Cohen and Ibrahim Sirkeci, 40–53. Cheltenham, UK: Edward Elgar Publishing.
Dossa, Parin, and Cati Coe, eds. 2017. *Transnational Aging and Reconfigurations of Kin Work*. New Brunswick, NJ: Rutgers University Press.
Gardner, Katy. 2002. *Age, Narrative and Migration: The Life Course and Life Histories of Bengali Elders in London*. Oxford, UK: Berg.
Gell, Alfred. 2011. "On Love." *Anthropology of This Century* 2: 1–10.
González-López, Gloria. 2005. *Erotic Journeys: Mexican Immigrants and Their Sex Lives*. Berkeley: University of California Press.
Groes, Christian, and Nadine T. Fernandez, eds. 2018. *Intimate Mobilities: Sexual Economies, Marriage and Migration in a Disparate World*. New York: Berghahn Books.
Hirsch, Jennifer S. 2003. *A Courtship after Marriage: Sexuality and Love in Mexican Transnational Families*. Berkeley: University of California Press.
Horn, Vincent, and Cornelia Schweppe, eds. 2016. *Transnational Aging: Current Insights and Future Challenges*. New York: Routledge.
Horváth, István. 2008. "The Culture of Migration of Rural Romanian Youth." *Journal of Ethnic and Migration Studies* 34 (5): 771–786. https://doi.org/10.1080/13691830802106036.
Illouz, Eva. 1997. *Consuming the Romantic Utopia: Love and the Cultural Contradictions of Capitalism*. Berkeley: University of California Press.
———. 2012. *Why Love Hurts: A Sociological Explanation*. Cambridge, UK: Polity Press.
ISTAT (Instituto Nazionale de Statistica). 2020. "Stranieri residenti al 1° gennaio—Cittadinanza." Rome: ISTAT. Accessed 12 October 2020, http://dati.istat.it/Index.aspx?DataSetCode=DCIS_POPSTRCIT1#
Jackson, Stevi. 1993. "Even Sociologists Fall in Love: An Exploration in the Sociology of Emotions." *Sociology* 27 (2): 201–220.
Jankowiak, William R., ed. 2008. *Intimacies: Love and Sex across Cultures*. New York: Columbia University Press.
———, ed. 2017. *Romantic Passion: A Universal Experience?* New York: Columbia University Press.
Jankowiak, William R., and Edward F. Fischer. 1992. "A Cross-Cultural Perspective on Romantic Love." *Ethnology* 31 (2): 149–155.
King, Russell, and Aija Lulle. 2016. "Grandmothers Migrating, Working and Caring: Latvian Women between Survival and Self-Realisation." *Population Horizons* 13 (2): 43–53. https://doi.org/10.1515/pophzn-2016-0003.
King, Russell, Aija Lulle, Dora Sampaio, and Julie Vullnetari. 2017. "Unpacking the Ageing-Migration Nexus and Challenging the Vulnerability Trope." *Journal of Ethnic and Migration Studies* 43 (2): 182–198. https://doi.org/10.1080/1369183X.2016.1238904.

Kligman, Gail. 1998. *The Politics of Duplicity: Controlling Reproduction in Ceausescu's Romania*. Berkeley: University of California Press.

Klok, Jolien, Theo G. van Tilburg, Bianca Suanet, and Tineke Fokkema. 2017. "Transnational Aging among Older Turkish and Moroccan Migrants in the Netherlands: Determinants of Transnational Behavior and Transnational Belonging." *Transnational Social Review* 7 (1): 25–40. https://doi.org/10.1080/21931674.2016.1277656.

Lamb, Sarah. 2009. *Aging and the Indian Diaspora: Cosmopolitan Families in India and Abroad*. Bloomington: Indiana University Press.

———, ed. 2017. *Successful Aging as a Contemporary Obsession: Global Perspectives*. New Brunswick, NJ: Rutgers University Press.

Lamb, Sarah, Jessica Robbins-Ruszkowski, and Anna I. Corwin. 2017. "Introduction: Successful Aging as a Twenty-First-Century Obsession." In *Successful Aging as a Contemporary Obsession: Global Perspectives*, edited by Sarah Lamb, 1–24. New Brunswick, NJ: Rutgers University Press.

Lindholm, Charles. 2006. "Romantic Love and Anthropology." *Etnofoor* 19 (1): 5–21.

Luhmann, Niklas. 1986. *Love as Passion: The Codification of Intimacy*. Cambridge, MA: Harvard University Press.

Lulle, Aija, and Russell King. 2016a. *Ageing, Gender, and Labour Migration*. New York: Palgrave Macmillan.

———. 2016b. "Ageing Well: The Time-Spaces of Possibility for Older Female Latvian Migrants in the UK." *Social and Cultural Geography* 17 (3): 444–462.

Luncă, Dumitrița. 2020. "Migrant Women of a Certain Age: Midlife Searches for Self, Love, and Sex among Romanian Women in Rome." *Etnofoor* 32 (2): 49–66. https://www.jstor.org/stable/26964287.

Mai, Nicola, and Russell King. 2009. "Love, Sexuality and Migration: Mapping the Issue(s)." *Mobilities* 4 (3): 295–307. https://doi.org/10.1080/17450100903195318.

Marcu, Silvia. 2015. "From the Marginal Immigrant to the Mobile Citizen: Reconstruction of Identity of Romanian Migrants in Spain." *Population, Space and Place* 21 (6): 506–517. https://doi.org/10.1002/psp.1845.

Massey, Douglas S., Joaquin Arango, Graeme Hugo, Ali Kouaouci, Adela Pellegrino, and J. Edward Taylor. 1994. "An Evaluation of International Migration Theory: The North American Case." *Population and Development Review* 20 (4): 699–751.

Massino, Jill. 2009. "Workers under Construction: Gender, Identity, and Women's Experiences of Work in State Socialist Romania." In *Gender Politics and Everyday Life in State Socialist Eastern and Central Europe*, edited by Shana Penn and Jill Massino, 13–32. New York: Palgrave Macmillan.

———. 2010. "Something Old, Something New: Marital Roles and Relations in State Socialist Romania." *Journal of Women's History* 22 (1): 34–60.

———. 2019. *Ambiguous Transitions: Gender, the State, and Everyday Life in Socialist and Postsocialist Romania*. New York: Berghahn Books.

Miroiu, Mihaela. 2007. "Communism Was a State Patriarchy, Not State Feminism." *Aspasia* 1 (1): 197–201. https://doi.org/10.3167/asp.2007.010110.

Mureșan, Cornelia. 2007. "Family Dynamics in Pre- and Post-Transition Romania: A Life-Table Description." MPIDR Working Paper 2007-018, Max Planck Institute for Demographic Research, Rostock, Germany.

Näre, Lena, Katie Walsh, and Loretta Baldassar. 2017. "Ageing in Transnational Contexts: Transforming Everyday Practices and Identities in Later Life." *Identities* 24 (5): 515–523. https://doi.org/10.1080/1070289X.2017.1346986.

Nedelcu, Mihaela. 2017. "Transnational Grandparenting in the Digital Age: Mediated Co-presence and Childcare in the Case of Romanian Migrants in Switzerland and Canada." *European Journal of Ageing* 14 (4): 375–383.

Palmberger, Monika. 2017. "Social Ties and Embeddedness in Old Age: Older Turkish Labour Migrants in Vienna." *Journal of Ethnic and Migration Studies* 43 (2): 235–249.

Pauli, Julia, and Franziska Bedorf. 2018. "Retiring Home? House Construction, Age Inscriptions, and the Building of Belonging among Mexican Migrants and Their Families in

Chicago and Rural Mexico." *Anthropology and Aging* 39 (1): 48–65. https://doi.org/10.5195/aa.2018.173.

Pine, Frances. 2014. "Migration as Hope: Space, Time, and Imagining the Future." *Current Anthropology* 55 (S9): S95–S104. https://doi.org/10.1086/676526.

Potot, Swanie. 2005. "La place des femmes dans les réseaux migrants roumains." *Revue européenne des migrations internationales* 21 (1): 1–15.

Robertson, Shanthi, Yi'En Cheng, and Brenda S. A. Yeoh. 2018. "Introduction: Mobile Aspirations? Youth Im/mobilities in the Asia-Pacific." *Journal of Intercultural Studies* 39 (6): 613–625. https://doi.org/10.1080/07256868.2018.1536345.

Sampaio, Dora. 2018. "A Place to Grow Older ... Alone? Living and Ageing as a Single Older Lifestyle Migrant in the Azores." *Area* 50 (4): 459–466.

Sandu, Dumitru. 2005. "Emerging Transnational Migration from Romanian Villages." *Current Sociology* 53 (4): 555–582. https://doi.org/10.1177/0011392105052715.

Sheller, Mimi. 2012. *Citizenship from Below: Erotic Agency and Caribbean Freedom*. Durham, NC: Duke University Press.

Sirkeci, Ibrahim, Jeffrey H. Cohen, and Pinar Yazgan. 2014. "Turkish Culture of Migration: Flows between Turkey and Germany, Socio-economic Development and Conflict." *Migration Letters* 9 (1): 33–46.

Skrbiš, Zlatko, Ian Woodward, and Clive Bean. 2014. "Seeds of Cosmopolitan Future? Young People and Their Aspirations for Future Mobility." *Journal of Youth Studies* 17 (5): 614–625. https://doi.org/10.1080/13676261.2013.834314.

Van Mol, Christof. 2016. "Migration Aspirations of European Youth in Times of Crisis." *Journal of Youth Studies* 19 (10): 1303–1320. https://doi.org/10.1080/13676261.2016.1166192.

Van Mol, Christof, Erik Snel, Kenneth Hemmerechts, and Christiane Timmerman. 2018. "Migration Aspirations and Migration Cultures: A Case Study of Ukrainian Migration towards the European Union." *Population, Space and Place* 24 (5): e2131. https://doi.org/10.1002/psp.2131.

Vlase, Ionela. 2018. "Men's Migration, Adulthood, and the Performance of Masculinities." In *Gender, Family, and Adaptation of Migrants in Europe: A Life Course Perspective*, edited by Ionela Vlase and Bogdan Voicu, 195–225. Cham: Springer International Publishing.

Walsh, Katie. 2009. "Geographies of the Heart in Transnational Spaces: Love and the Intimate Lives of British Migrants in Dubai." *Mobilities* 4 (3): 427–445. https://doi.org/10.1080/17450100903195656.

Zontini, Elisabetta. 2015. "Growing Old in a Transnational Social Field: Belonging, Mobility and Identity among Italian Migrants." *Ethnic and Racial Studies* 38 (2): 326–341. https://doi.org/10.1080/01419870.2014.885543.

CHAPTER 2

Letting Go and Looking Ahead

THE ASPIRATIONS OF MIDDLE-AGED MIGRANT DOMESTIC WORKERS IN SINGAPORE AND HONG KONG

Megha Amrith

"I'm a late bloomer," said Lisa, laughing as we sat in the Hollywood Road park one weekend in central Hong Kong.[1] She continued: "I've been here for twenty-two years. When somebody asks me, 'Why do you stay so long in Hong Kong?' I don't have the answer! But then I realized, all the time I spent here, I didn't have a vision. You earn some money, give some money, spend some money. You always think you are far away and it's your responsibility to give. Most of us think we are responsible for everything. The kind of mind-set we have is that when you leave the Philippines, you become the breadwinner. That's why a lot of people are not happy—they couldn't enjoy life. I started very late."

Lisa, who comes from the northern Philippines, is fifty-one years old, and has worked in Hong Kong for over two decades, continued to talk about the "breadwinner mentality." By this, she is referring to the idea that migrant domestic workers like herself who work abroad in cities such as Singapore and Hong Kong blindly follow a well-known narrative: one of giving and sacrificing for the family who stayed in the country of origin. This narrative is consistent with the many normative, gendered expectations (constructed by states, kin, and wider public perceptions) that permeate domestic workers' lives and that dictate what their aspirations ought to be and whose interests they ought to serve. Similarly, there are linear assumptions about "age-appropriate" aspirations that migrant women ought to hold at different stages of their journey. Lisa's words, however, suggest that migrant aspirations and life projects are more complex and diverse than the dominant narratives might suggest and that they change and evolve, rather than settle, over time.

Lisa is one of the hundreds of thousands of migrant domestic workers who have worked to sustain households in Singapore and Hong Kong. Since the 1970s, both places instituted restrictive contract labor policies for domestic workers coming

39

from other countries in the region—the largest numbers come from the Philippines and Indonesia, and smaller numbers from other Asian countries such as India and Sri Lanka. Under these policies, domestic workers arrive on two-year (renewable) temporary contracts and are required to live in their employers' homes. They are barred from bringing their families with them, are excluded from national labor laws, and face restrictions on their mobilities and their social and intimate lives (Bélanger and Silvey 2020; Yeoh, Goh, and Wee 2020). In my fieldwork with domestic workers in both cities, I encountered a number of women who spent decades abroad on temporary contracts. While many women initially plan to work abroad for just a few years to earn money, it is not uncommon for migrants to continually renew their two-year contracts on a regular basis, prolonging their stays abroad for as long as possible. In Singapore, domestic workers can renew their contracts until the age of sixty, and in Hong Kong, it is until the domestic worker can no longer work due to old age or illness, which might be defined differently by domestic workers and their employers. Oftentimes, the age limit is de facto sixty-five, given the difficulties in finding insurance. At this point, migrant domestic workers have to return to their countries of origin since there are no pathways to long-term residence or citizenship for domestic workers in Singapore and Hong Kong on temporary contracts (regardless of the number of years they have spent abroad).

This chapter focuses on the broad-ranging aspirations of migrant women in middle to late-middle age as they start reflecting on their past lives and imagining their futures at the ends of their migration journeys. I argue that the vantage point of midlife thus enables us to see how aspirations start to shift or take on renewed energies when migrant women reach their forties, fifties, and sixties. This specific phase of migrant women's lives offers insights into how aspirations are shaped in relation to multiple temporal horizons: through letting go of past selves or undesirable past relationships, anticipating uncertain and insecure futures, and then reconfiguring projects of self and collective transformation in the present. Temporary border regimes also generate a certain impetus for migrant women to live in the present and to make the most of their remaining time abroad, which will inevitably end. Reconfiguring aspirations in the present is therefore one way for migrant women to better confront the uncertainties of the future, the present offering a safe, known space in which to develop projects of self-realization and to plan for the future.

For some women, it is migration itself that gives them the tools to pursue these projects of transformation in ways that they did not think possible at an earlier point in their lives. For others, aspirations shift within the migrant journey itself. Many of the migrant women I spoke with in my research felt themselves constrained by multiple normative expectations they faced in their younger days: for instance, to get married, to espouse a heteronormative gender identity, or to support their familial needs through migration before fulfilling their own personal aspirations. Given that these norms are gendered, so too are aspirations shaped and motivated by these gendered constraints. As migrant women grow older and learn to navigate these norms and structures, while anticipating new challenges ahead, new aspirations emerge and are put into practice while old ones are renewed and consolidated in what can be thought of as an ongoing process of "becoming" (Hall 1996). Aspirations thus take on novel characteristics in midlife that are often temporally at odds with the restrictive migration regimes and normative expectations that shape their transnational trajectories. Contrary to such normative expectations, migrant women reaching a certain age does not mean that they have exhausted their possibilities to aspire. The stories of migrants that feature in this chapter further reflect broader imaginaries of what it means to live a "good life" in mid-late life. These imaginaries of the good life, however, are not always in sync with how others script and define a good life (see also Coe, this volume; Pauli, this volume; Amrith, Sakti, and Sampaio, this volume). For the migrant women I spoke with, the "good life" is defined in multiple ways, whether this relates to projects of self-realization, financial and emotional independence, cultivating meaningful relationships, or living with dignity.

In this chapter, I first examine the gender and age-related norms that shape and constrain migrant women's lives and how domestic workers construct their aspirations in light of these dominant normative framings. I then outline the context and methodology behind the research and subsequently focus on the narratives of three women who came into their own in middle or late-middle age, pursuing aspirations that are financial, intimate, creative, and collective. Their aspirations revolve around cultivating the "right" friendships, expressing one's sexuality, finding ways to put aside regrets and to live with purpose, pursuing questions of social justice, and imagining entrepreneurial futures upon retirement from domestic work. These three stories in particular demonstrate the diversity of aspirations that emerge in midlife, a critical phase in which past decisions are reevaluated and unknown futures loom, pushing migrant women to live in the known present (see Pauli, this volume), to reconsider their values and priorities, and to use present activities to shape a more knowable "good life" in the future upon retirement. The chapter closes with a reflection on how aspirations emerge in the interstices between the constraints that limit older migrant women's mobilities and the possibilities for imagining and living life against the grain of normative expectations.

Becomings: Norms and Aspirations over the Life Course

There are two sets of norms that migrant domestic workers contend with: one set relating to gender and another relating to age. These norms in many ways attempt to define what domestic workers' aspirations ought to be. These norms also contribute to shaping migrants' motivations to go abroad in the first place, and they are intertwined with the migration policies that affect domestic workers' everyday lives.

The first set of norms relates to gender in the context of "global care chains," which refers to the movements of poorer women from "Third World" to "First World" countries, often resulting in their children or kin being left at home in the care of others. These movements, however, are never neutrally construed but often come with a series of moral expectations and assumptions. According to Martin F. Manalansan IV (2008), global care chains "[privilege] heteronormative subjects, such as married women with children and families" and "normative conceptions of care, love, and emotions." The discourses surrounding their movements abroad often focus on how "Third World women are torn away from their biological families" (Manalansan 2008), thereby creating deficits of care. This is echoed in public discourses on migrant women's journeys. Migrant women are, on the one hand, heroes who are celebrated for making the sacrifice of migration to give their families a better life and victims who have to endure exploitative conditions of work in making this sacrifice. On the other hand, domestic workers are shamed for their "immoral" behavior abroad, with public and political commentators remarking on their dress styles and intimate relationships (Chan 2018; Constable 2007). The implicit assumption underlying these narratives is that women migrate exclusively to support their families and that their aspirations should fully center around working and remitting money to their kin for their children's education and for buying a family house. This is also in line with how states see migrants' financial contributions as part of national development strategies (see, e.g., Guevarra 2009). A number of scholars, however, have echoed Manalansan's point by examining the ways in which migrant women's aspirations often far exceed the limits of these gender normative framings in practice. These studies have examined migrant domestic workers' activism, their intimate lives, their religious imaginations, and other diverse forms of self-expression (Constable 2007; Liebelt 2011; Johnson and Werbner 2010). In line with these rich ethnographic insights, I consider how migrant women themselves negotiate and challenge the aspirations that others (kin, states, public narratives) expect them to hold with their own aspirational horizons. It is also worth noting that these gendered, often heteronormative, patriarchal norms, shape women's lives before they decide to migrate, often serving as an impetus to go abroad in the first place in order to pursue an alternative path (Parreñas 2015).

The second set of norms shaping migrant women's experiences and aspirations relates to age (and its intersections with gendered norms). Referring to popular stereotypes about the life course, Jen Slater, Embla Ágústsdóttir, and Freyja Haraldsdóttir (2018) point out that while "adulthood is presented as a time of relative stability," youth is seen to be a turbulent life-stage marked by instability and insecurity. Older age, meanwhile, has widely been presented as a time of decline, passivity, and dependence on others. In ethnographic examinations of culturally situated understandings of the life course, however, a more complex picture emerges (Lamb 2017) that challenges the idea of fixed norms associated with particular life stages. In the field of migration studies, much of the scholarship on migrant aspirations has implicitly or explicitly focused on youth aspirations, considering how (im)mobilities shape the futures and the time ahead of younger people (see, e.g., Mains 2011; Robertson, Cheng, and Yeoh 2018). Unlike this common pairing of youth and aspirations, there is much less sustained attention on how aspirations are constructed in the mid-late stages of the migrant journey and how questions of the future are just as pertinent in these times of the life course. A notable exception relevant to this study is Paolo Boccagni's (2017) work on the shifting aspirations of migrant domestic workers in Italy, which looks at how the aspirations of migrant women when they leave home may differ significantly from what they aspire to now. Beyond the academic literature on this theme, policy prescriptions on age also shape migrant women's lives. The mandatory retirement age of sixty, which requires migrant domestic workers to leave the country upon retirement, reflects a policy that values only "able-bodied," "fit," and "agile" workers, deeming workers disposable when they are seen as "too old." These constructions of the aging migrant body, and the impending ruptures they bring into migrant women's lives, play an important role in configuring migrant women's aspirations in midlife as they look toward their later-life years.

The aspirations in migrant women's lives emerge at the intersection between "being" and "becoming," to draw on the postcolonial theorist Stuart Hall's (1996) conceptualization of identity. Many of the dominant normative narratives on gender and age that concern (older) migrant women construct their identities as fixed, as "being" as they are. Instead, migrant women construct forms of personhood that both dialogue with and move beyond these normativities through diverse aspirations that reflect a continuous process of "becoming" over the course of life. This idea also echoes work in feminist, queer, and disability studies scholarship, which illuminates how people with nondominant identities transgress societal structures that emphasize ablebodiness and heteronormativity in creative ways (Slater, Ágústsdóttir, and Haraldsdóttir 2018; Kafer 2013; Manalansan 2008). It also echoes Sarah Lamb's (2018) argument, in her study of single women in India, how an ethnographic focus on those who are seen to be living "outside the norm" offers unique insights into these very norms and institutions and how they operate to include or exclude certain bodies in everyday social life. Similarly, by exploring the narratives of middle-aged domestic workers, we see how their own aspirations emerge alongside and in tension with the aspirations that others construct for them, past, present, and future (see Whyte, this volume).

This chapter draws on ongoing ethnographic research since 2018 with an older generation of migrant domestic workers of different nationalities, primarily from the Philippines, but also Indonesia, India, and Sri Lanka. It primarily focuses on women who are between forty-five and sixty years old and who have been living in Singapore over multiple temporary contracts and are approaching the mandatory age of retirement. In-depth interviews were complemented with regular encounters and ethnographic observations in spaces where domestic workers meet and socialize, such as shopping malls, religious spaces, a domestic workers' clubhouse, parks, Sunday classes, and online spaces. The focus on an older generation of domestic workers, in particular those in "middle" and "late-middle" age, offers a distinctive vantage point for understanding aspirations from a life course perspective (Boccagni 2017; Lulle 2018). Aija Lulle (2018) rightly argues that research with middle-aged migrant women can offer insights into how they restructure their lives and seek out new experiences as they age, while also illuminating the effects of gender and age-related power relations. It also offers a lens onto how people begin to plan for and imagine their later-life years and how their aspirations shift in relation to structures and institutions that shape their futures. While most of the women I spoke with explicitly stated "conventional" aspirations to start with, such as building a house or seeing their children settled in life, I found consistently that their aspirations are rarely this limited. In what follows, I go in depth into the stories of three women as a way to demonstrate the multilayered nature of migrant women's aspirations, how these aspirations shift over the life course and take on new energies in midlife, in anticipation of retirement and later life. Moreover, their aspirations do not always follow a linear path to being fulfilled, but are constantly being renewed in light of past reflections, present desires, and future possibilities. The women also come up against the structural constraints and everyday insecurities that affect them as temporary migrants.

Rhea: Self-Expression and Financial Independence in Later Life

"I think I would say I'm a dreamer. Yes, I'm a dreamer!" Rhea said as she introduced herself to me when we sat down to talk one Saturday afternoon in a Singapore shopping mall. Rhea, now in her late fifties, is a domestic worker who has been working in Singapore for the past ten years. Rhea migrated to Singapore when she was in her forties, later than many of her peers. It was not her plan to come to Singapore, and she did not imagine herself employed as a domestic worker. Rhea studied business administration in the Philippines and, in her premigration life, worked as a sales agent. Rhea said that it was "easy money and then easy spending," as she got into a vicious cycle of taking out loans and then being swallowed by interest payments. After this episode in her life when she went broke, she then took care of her aging father. Rhea said, "At that time, I was thinking, Lord, my dad is old. Give me something so that I can support him and support myself. And then I think God heard my prayer and brought me to Singapore." Rhea first arrived in Singapore on a tourist visa, as she migrated to look after her cousin's children. Since Rhea was family, she did not get a specific day to herself (contrary to the legislation that specifies a mandatory day off) and found herself working far more than she ought to have been. When her cousin's family relocated away from Singapore a few years later, Rhea decided to stay on in Singapore as a domestic worker with a "work permit" for another family. She explained, "I told myself and I told them, this job is my retirement job.... If I stay home [in the Philippines], I will still do all these things. Here I get paid." Rhea saw her work in Singapore as a part of her retirement plan, a means to pursue other aspirations during her time abroad while still getting paid. With her current employer, she has more freedom to go out when she has finished her work (which is not always the case for domestic workers in Singapore). Rhea makes use of this situation, saying, "I'm not this 'yes ma'am' type of helper, that's not who I am, as if we don't have any brains."

Rhea spends a lot of her free time attending seminars on various themes and calls herself a "seminarista." When I met her, she had just attended a seminar on crowdfunding. Rhea is particularly active in a financial literacy group that meets on Sundays. The initiative, led by a Philippine-based nongovernmental organization (NGO), has a partnership with the Philippine state and works with grassroots groups of Filipina domestic workers in Singapore. The students in the course are a mix of ages, but many of the leaders are older women who have spent decades working abroad and whose own retirement and returns to the Philippines are looming. It was only later in their migration journeys that these women found themselves with little savings, thinking about their insecure futures, and trying to find ways to reach financial security. They are now keen to share their knowledge with both older and younger generations of domestic workers. Every few weeks, the group organizes afternoon workshops on different themes, including how to prepare for reintegration and return; investing in real estate, mutual funds, and stocks; and learning from other women in business. Rhea joined the group in 2014 and then later became a mentor in the group. The tone of such programs is decidedly neoliberal, in that they are clear that one has to take responsibility for one's own future. Nevertheless, those who join orient their aspirations toward finding this sense of financial freedom. One of Rhea's mentees was Ella, a single mother of two young children, who regularly sent money home to her family for her children's education, daily expenses, and emergencies, not keeping any for herself (modeling what Lisa, quoted at the beginning of this chapter, called the "breadwinner mentality"). However, a key lesson that this group teaches to its participants is not to be obligated to send money home to their families all the time, despite sometimes pressing needs, but rather to send small amounts for maintenance, freeing up money for their own savings and future planning. This strategy breaks with the expectations (from the state and migrants' families) that migrants should selflessly send as much money back as possible. That Rhea, Ella, and others in the group have dedicated themselves in midlife to seeking a good life that is defined by financial literacy and security, despite their precarious conditions of work as temporary migrant workers, reiterates how aspirations shift over time.

Beyond the financial education group, Rhea has also come into her own in Singapore. Being away from her judgmental kin and having a strong and supportive group of close friends have also been important to Rhea in expressing her sexuality more freely. Rhea reflected: "I'm old already, I am open about who I am now. Now I'm fifty-something, why should I hide? My mom, she used to say to me, 'Who are you? Do you love boys, or do you love girls? You are always so boyish, why are you like this?'"

Going abroad in her midlife years on her own and starting on a blank slate made Rhea feel more assured: "Even though I always knew, even if my family knows, now I don't hide anything. I was in denial for a long time. I just want to enjoy my retirement. Actually, being here is already a part of my retirement plan. I'm older and I met so many different people here, so now I'm much more open. This is who I am, what you see is what you get. Before I would never say, 'I am a lesbian.' Only now, recently, am I saying, 'I am a lesbian.'"

Rhea now wants to enjoy her life and is no longer afraid of what people think of her. Rhea confessed that she is in love with one of her friends and that even if it does not lead anywhere, it makes Rhea happy to spend her time around her. She and her friends also do makeovers on each other: "We all look young. You know why? We all love to sing and dance in our fifties. It keeps us young." Rhea plans to stay in Singapore for two more contracts (or four years) at least, adding, "But if I'm still healthy and able, why not stay until the Singapore government tells me I can't stay. Here I can still get some earnings and then save, save, save! The Lord is giving me another chance, and I want to make use of it. If you are aged fifty already, just stay here as long as you can, you won't find another job there [in the Philippines]." Rhea is anxious about returning to the Philippines, not only in terms of the lack of opportunities for financial security in later life, but also because she is tired, in her fifties, of having to justify to kin who she is and whom she desires. Her aspirations are thus centered around both financial security and expressing her sexuality. Both aspirations signal Rhea's desire to retain independence and control over her life decisions rather than be dependent on others financially in her older age or constrained by others diminishing her now secure sense of being.

Che: Strengthening the Fight for Social Justice

Che has been working in Hong Kong for the past twenty-five years. She arrived in the city in 1995 to support her family. Despite having a degree, she lamented that it was hard to find a job with decent pay in the Philippines and that she came from a poor family. As Che put it, "We had to survive, and I had to work. I did not have an option but to go abroad." Che reflected that she was not used to doing domestic work, and when she first arrived in Hong Kong, she found it very hard. She was demoralized, felt a sense of self-pity, and wanted to return to the Philippines. At her first employer's place, she slept on the sofa in the living room, not having any personal space for herself (a common experience for migrant domestic workers in Hong Kong). She also faced a language barrier since she did not speak Cantonese, and she had very limited time off. Over the years, Che changed employers a few times, until she found one who was a social worker in a church and who gave her more time to go out. Che then joined grassroots activist groups led by migrant workers in Hong Kong, and she has spent many of her years in the city campaigning for the rights of migrant domestic workers. Che was a student activist when she was in the Philippines, so she was already familiar with advocacy work.

Her own migration story, and those of many other migrant domestic workers in Hong Kong, motivates her activism. Che explains that she wants to go back to her son, who is seven years old, but as she herself is fifty, her chance of finding work back in the Philippines is very low, and she would rather stay on to provide for his education and future. She also provides an allowance for her mother's daily expenses, her diabetic mother-in-law's medical costs, and a niece who is going to school. Che explains, "I'm addressing the concerns of my family, and I'm concerned with the situation of my fellow domestic workers. We call it forced migration. This is not what we want." Che is referring here to the fact that many of her peers are driven to migrate because there are few options to improve their precarious familial livelihoods by staying in the Philippines. Once abroad, there are pressures (as we have seen in the previous examples) to send money back to their families to support their livelihoods and the next generation's future prospects. Her concerns as an activist are thus to break this cycle of migration and dependency by advocating for changes both to working conditions in Hong Kong and to the Philippines' labor export policy, a state-led project since the 1970s to promote out-migration as a strategy of economic development. She explains, "We are discussing the very reason why Filipinos go abroad, which is due to policies in our home country. If we have work, social services, good compensation, we won't leave. We would have a choice to stay and be with our families."

Given that Che had an activist background, her current preoccupations in this sense are not new but rather continuations of her past convictions. Nevertheless, they have only strengthened during her time abroad, and now as she begins her fifties, she is the chairperson of a major migrant organization in Hong Kong. Che has consolidated her position as a key community figure, building alliances between migrants of different nationalities and representing the interests of migrant workers in the city.

Che has been involved in numerous campaigns to speak out against discriminatory policies affecting migrant domestic workers in Hong Kong and the extractive policies of migrant-sending states. But there are now two issues she is particularly concerned with that directly relate to her midlife positionality as she ages abroad and looks ahead to her retirement in the near future. The first is the campaign for the right to permanent residence in Hong Kong. Given that all other migrants are eligible for permanent residence after seven years of living in Hong Kong, Che and her peers (some of whom have also lived and worked in the city for over twenty-five years) made the case that domestic workers should be entitled to the same rights. The case went before the Hong Kong Court of Appeals, but the ruling was that live-in domestic workers are not entitled to the right of abode. Those like Che, who envisioned futures with their families in Hong Kong, a city they now call home, once again have to grapple with familial separation for the duration of their working lives abroad and must confront both emotional and financial insecurity as they return home upon retirement.

The second campaign she is currently involved in is against excessive fees imposed by the Philippine government on social security and insurance, including the now mandatory social security payments. I asked Che why her group opposed social security contributions, thinking that the Philippines is one of the few sending countries that include their transnational migrants in their social security systems. For Che, the answer was simple: "The [Philippine] government says if you work for thirty years, [you] will receive fifteen hundred pesos—for thirty years![2] Never mind. It's useless, it's really a show. We are paying and paying every year, and you get this very insulting amount. We are calling for social pensions for retiring OFWs [overseas Filipino workers]. It should be a government responsibility, without us contributing to a scheme, because we have contributed so much money through our remittances, taxes, the goods we pay for in the Philippines."

Figure 2.1. Che and her peers on a Sunday march through central Hong Kong. Photograph by Megha Amrith.

Che's aspirations for social justice for migrant workers, and for dignified livelihoods and futures in later life, continue and remain at the center of her commitments. At this point in her journey, she is also keen to leave a legacy behind to improve conditions for the next generations of domestic workers and to ensure that her advocacy work is continued in the future. A few days after I first met Che, she invited me to a rally she was organizing in central Hong Kong, on Chater Road (figure 2.1). Che had a loudspeaker in hand as she gathered people around on the issue of the excessive fees imposed by the Philippine government, her phone ringing constantly and journalists approaching her for sound bites. As Che put it: "We need to do more to reach the average, everyday worker, we need to organize and maximize our social media presence." In short, "there is more work to do" and Che is nowhere close to stopping.

Madhu: A New Start in Middle Age

"I escaped from Tamil Nadu because I thought life would be better in Singapore. I thought the people here would be better. Money was not my prime motivation, I just wanted a change in my situation . . . that was my main motivation, to run away from there." Madhu studied for a bachelor's degree in economics in a government college in Tamil Nadu. She enjoyed studying, and her plan was to work and support her parents in their old age, but everyone around her kept "torturing" her, "Get married, get married!" Madhu said that she was fearful of being a single woman and that people treated her as if she were committing a crime. After her parents passed away, Madhu felt that everyone was out to exploit and cheat her, thinking she would be rich as a college-educated single woman. It was suffocating and she wanted to leave. Madhu did not know much about Singapore, only that her friends told her she could live well there. A relative of hers working in Singapore found her a job as a domestic worker and liaised with an agent to bring her over. Madhu said, "My main thought was, I need to go out and find some happiness." She did not say a word to her family and simply left.

Her arrival in Singapore, however, did not start off well. Like many migrant domestic workers, Madhu lost a lot of money through agency fees (for the agent who organized her travel and work). For the first three months, the agency deducted her entire salary in fees, which put her in debt. Her relative was working as a middlewoman for the agent, and, as Madhu put it, "Even she cheated me!" Her first employer did not allow her to go out on a regular basis. Madhu also kept her distance from other Tamil migrant women in Singapore and did not seek out friendships in her early days. She found that other women would judge how she "ran away" from home or the fact that she was single, even as Madhu remarked that many of the women she met were married yet having affairs with boyfriends in Singapore. She regrets that she encountered these people, whom she found toxic in their gossip and judgment, and did her best to avoid them.

After spending the first years of her contract with an employer who did not give her much freedom, she found a new employer, an Indian Singaporean Tamil-speaking retired sociologist who lives on her own with a dog. Madhu, now in her mid-forties, is starting anew, having developed a friendship with her employer, whom she sees as a sister (*akka* in Tamil), an ally, and a companion, who helped her see the way people took advantage of her in her youth and in the early stages of her migration journey and who supported her in finding her own identity. Madhu spoke of their close bond and shared experience as single women in mid-late life, despite the fact that they are employer and employee: "She did not marry, her life is also like mine. There is no one to support her, she is also alone. I am concerned that [someone might] cheat her. I want to be with her, so she doesn't get the feeling she is alone. Just like I tell her everything, she also tells me everything. I can't even imagine going away from her."

On Sundays, Madhu joined English classes organized by an NGO set up to empower Tamil migrant women. As part of this group, she put her story down on paper for a mobile library project and became inspired to write poetry. She also spoke at a Tamil feminist conference and recalled how it was the first time she held a microphone: "I won't ever forget this in my life." She felt in that moment that people did not look upon her as a "maid," but instead she was granted a lot of respect. Madhu explains, "Many people have a preconception that all the maids hang around Tekka [a lively marketplace in Singapore's Little India], just going with boyfriends, aimless. Not all of us are just lounging around."

For the first time, Madhu feels a sense of belonging and wants to put her past behind her. She does not even want to travel to India, as it would remind her of her life in Tamil Nadu when she was younger and constrained by the expectations of her kin around her, nor does she have other destinations on her horizon, since she has found a secure and safe space in Singapore.

Madhu feels that she has gained a lot of confidence through her experiences and wants to stay in Singapore as long as possible, especially to be with her *akka*. However, she knows the immigration regime requires her to leave when she reaches the age of sixty. She thinks ahead, often idealistically and wistfully, about what her life in India might look like in the future when she retires from domestic work in Singapore. "I want to build a house, a beautiful one, have a small business, not a big one. It will be a quiet place, with not much crowd and near the mountain. So, a nice house, restaurant, and I'll be the owner, sitting there . . . I'll be the head, not a slave," Madhu says with a giggle, and then explains that she would help the people working for her so that they do not struggle as she did. The image of the mountain, and the trope of solitude, features prominently in the poetry she writes.

Madhu is using her time in middle age to find her own independent voice, to transform her relationships into meaningful ones, and to imagine a fulfilling later life when she returns to Tamil Nadu. She thinks that women like herself have an opportunity to advance themselves and not to "fall into the pit" again. Madhu fervently believes that once you are abroad, you can break the social norms; otherwise, she says, "Being a woman, you are left with no identity."

Structures of Inequality and Reconfigured Personhood over Time

The narratives of Rhea, Che, and Madhu demonstrate the diversity of aspirations and processes of becoming that take shape through migration as well as the constraints that migrant domestic workers might face in shaping and realizing such aspirations. While each story is unique, there are common themes that emerge from looking at these three narratives together.

The first theme relates to the structures that shape or constrain aspirations. All three women highlight how they felt more vulnerable and isolated in their early days in Singapore or Hong Kong, which affected the extent to which they could put their own aspirations front and center. Madhu, for instance, pointed out the high agency fees that she was subjected to, which speaks to a common experience among migrant domestic workers, who are frequently in debt in the first months, and often years, of their migration journeys (Platt et al. 2017). The financial and emotional weight of debt can often be stifling, reducing the possibilities for the pursuit of aspirations. Meanwhile, Rhea and Che spoke about how their first employers (including Rhea's own cousin) did not give them the time and space to go out on a weekly basis. The ability for domestic workers to pursue their aspirations in these restrictive migration contexts is thus highly contingent on having a "good employer," and, in fact, finding such an employer is an aspiration in itself. Older domestic workers have often worked their way through different kinds of employment situations, some very exploitative, to find one that offers a balance in their lives. These different experiences reflect how aspirations are unequally distributed and dependent on the structural conditions that migrants face (Amrith, Sakti, and Sampaio, this volume).

Rhea and Che further recognize the ageism that confronts them in the labor market. They both point out that finding a new job (either in Singapore or in the Philippines) is very difficult once one reaches a certain age (fifty) and suggest that they might as well stay put in the jobs they already hold to ensure they have a steady income. For Che, this is the only way she envisages being able to continue supporting her young son and aging relatives in the Philippines, while Rhea's logic is that she wants to use this time as a domestic worker as her "retirement plan," a way for her to be paid to do the care work that she would in any case do (unpaid) in the Philippines, to save for the future, and to enjoy life. Their comments illuminate the precarity and undervaluation of care work: their skills are not recognized for other jobs, and this is work that they, as women, are expected to do anyway, paid or unpaid. Their comments also significantly demonstrate how ageism in the labor market operates to deny older migrant bodies possibilities. The aging body is perceived to be less able-bodied and thus not valued in a neoliberal economy.

The second theme that emerges out of the three narratives is on contesting norms, which are at the heart of all three women's midlife aspirational projects. A number of migrant women talk about how they were shortsighted in their younger days: either sending money back all the time, not putting themselves in the picture, trusting the wrong people, or not using their time well. All of these experiences can stifle aspirations, with migrant women's own desires diminished by overarching expectations or pressures from others. The norms that shape these women's lives are multiple and relate to sexuality, womanhood, marriage, age, and discipline, and all three women's stories reveal how they are often expected to live according to the dictates of others. Rhea, for example, has her whole life been confronting heteronormative expectations of how a woman should behave or dress or whom a woman should love. She grew up in a context where she did not feel able to express her sexuality and identity as a lesbian, and only when she went abroad and found a group of people with whom she felt comfortable did she begin to express herself and her desires.[3] For Rhea, a temporal or age-related dimension to her coming out story is that she is "old already." She believes that, at this stage in life, it is time to shed pretenses and start living and desiring. She has found a new sense of acceptance for herself and who she is, no longer worrying about how she will be judged by others. Meanwhile, Madhu, a single woman, has been taunted for years in a patriarchal context where marriage as an institution shapes one's social status and worth. She found that she was judged and taken advantage of not only by her kin back in India but also by other migrant women in Singapore. Over time, she began to realize that her marital status did not make her any less of a woman and that if she did not find ways to express herself and pursue her own aspirations for an independent life, she would be losing a key opportunity. Finally, Che's activism challenges the state-constructed normative discourses about the youthful, docile, and disciplined migrant woman, who is expected to diligently remit her money home to her family and to passively accept her conditions of work. Che's engagements illuminate the contradictions in these policies that govern migrant women's lives and the ways in which they stifle migrant women's wide-ranging aspirations. All three women also seek to challenge public perceptions of domestic workers: Rhea through her mentoring activities, Madhu through her poetry and public speaking, and Che through her relentless advocacy work for domestic workers' rights.

The third theme relates to ideas of the good life. On the one hand, all three women imagine the good life as a space of self-expression, self-realization, and communities of trust, which diverge from the norms and constrictions that define the lives of many migrant domestic workers. They also share the view that the good life is something that requires work, commitment, and using one's time well (rather than "wasting it" away), something that became clearer to them over time and with age. On the other hand, more specific ideas on how to live a good life vary widely among the three women and others in similar situations. For Rhea (as well as Lisa, and Ella), neoliberal ideas that construct the future and the good life in terms of financial security are seen as the way forward. Yet those who do not share in these financial aspirations are seen as victims of their own passivity or somehow "backward" in their thinking. In this sense, within communities of domestic workers, new inequalities and divisions can arise from these different aspirational logics. Che's perception of what makes a good life—social justice, state accountability, a critique of neoliberal policies—offers a sharp contrast. Finally, there are the more modest yet nonetheless pathbreaking aspirations that Madhu holds to write poetry and run a small restaurant at the mountainside. Aspirations for a good life among domestic workers in mid- to late life are thus variably collective, individualized, and even spiritual.

Conclusion

As the narratives in this chapter have demonstrated, migrant women do not stop aspiring once they reach middle or late-middle age, but rather their aspirations take on a novel and strengthened character, particularly in anticipation of retirement and return migration as migrant women begin to imagine their futures in later life. The aspirations that feature in these narratives are concrete projects of both self and collective transformation that reflect how ideas of the "good life" are reconfigured in diverse ways involving both grander aspirations and more modest ones. Moreover, the aspirations are not only occupational or family-related but are more broadly related to intimacy, creative self-expression, social justice, self-realization, and financial independence. In the stories of Rhea, Che, and Madhu (as well as Lisa and Ella), we see how aspirations are constantly renewed in relation to the multiple normative expectations that they face relating to their gender, age, and sexuality in both their "premigration" and migrant lives. The pursuit and expression of these aspirations can thus be thought of as an ongoing process of becoming over the life course, illuminating the importance of a temporal perspective on aspirations (Boccagni 2017; Amrith 2021). They also echo Tannistha Samanta's (2021) suggestion that in examining the social aspirations of women in midlife, we see how "middle aged selfhood is lived in all its fragility, ambivalence and emergent possibilities."

There are also some caveats that caution against seeing these stories through a romanticized lens. It is important to state here, for instance, that migrating abroad is not simply a straightforward route to "empowerment" or "success" (Amrith 2021). During the migrant journey, there is often a struggle back and forth between the pursuit of aspirations and starker realities that domestic workers face under restrictive temporary regimes, including the ageism that confronts them at a certain point in time. Moreover, that futures remain precarious and uncertain and that not all aspirations are realized demonstrate that these processes of becoming are not linear. The precarity of aspirations was laid bare during the COVID-19 pandemic, with new restrictions on domestic workers' movements and a heightened sense of existential anxiety in their lives. Domestic workers in both Singapore and Hong Kong were prevented from leaving their employers' homes for several months, experienced increased workloads, and could not return to visit their homes (which are still important to domestic workers despite the expectations and pressures they encounter) while facing anxieties about how their loved ones were faring. This meant that domestic workers could not use their days off—Sundays—to pursue their many aspirational projects. Some, of course, moved their engagements online—Rhea's financial education group, for instance, went online, organizing regular talks on how to spend one's time productively and producing YouTube videos and blog posts on why it is important to save and invest for the future. Online poetry readings and writing groups also offered alternative channels to share aspirations with diverse others. At the same time, not all domestic workers have internet access in their employers' homes, nor do they have the time and energy to pursue these activities in light of the new circumstances. A few of my interlocutors also prefer simpler modes of communication such as telephone calls and text messages, which do not offer the same possibilities. In short, it remains to be seen the extent to which the current pandemic has affected migrants' abilities to breathe life into their aspirations, to actively pursue and to sustain them, and how their engagements have suffered and changed as a result of these events.

What is clear, however, is that the aspirations of migrant women rarely settle and only become more diverse over time. Migrant women's aspirations come into tension at different points in their lives with the normative expectations of family and state, with many having sacrificed their well-being in their younger days or at an earlier stage of their migration journeys. Yet in midlife they begin to further question and contest established norms of what migrancy, gender roles, retirement, and older age might look like, often turning to prioritize their own well-being and pursuing collective goals for a good life with a clearer sense of purpose.

Acknowledgments

I am grateful to the migrant women who shared their time and trusted me with their stories. My thanks also to Victoria K. Sakti and Dora Sampaio for their insightful feedback on earlier drafts of this chapter and to the participants of the "Aspiring in Later Life" workshop, held online in November 2020, for the inspiring discussions.

Notes

1. Pseudonyms are used throughout this chapter to protect the identities of my interlocutors. When interviews were not conducted in English, all translations are mine.
2. Fifteen hundred Philippine pesos is equivalent to approximately thirty US dollars. Che is referring to a monthly sum.
3. See also Luncă (this volume) for a discussion on love and intimacy in later life among migrant women.

References

Amrith, Megha. 2021. "The Linear Imagination, Stalled: Changing Temporal Horizons in Migrant Journeys." *Global Networks* 21 (1): 127–145. https://doi.org/10.1111/glob.12280.

Bélanger, Danièle, and Rachel Silvey. 2020. "An Im/mobility Turn: Power Geometries of Care and Migration." *Journal of Ethnic and Migration Studies* 46 (16): 3423–3440. https://doi.org/10.1080/1369183X.2019.1592396.

Boccagni, Paolo. 2017. "Aspirations and the Subjective Future of Migration: Comparing Views and Desires of the 'Time Ahead' through the Narratives of Immigrant Domestic Workers." *Comparative Migration Studies* 5 (1). https://doi.org/10.1186/s40878-016-0047-6.

Chan, Carol. 2018. *In Sickness and in Wealth: Migration, Gendered Morality, and Central Java*. Bloomington: Indiana University Press.

Constable, Nicole. 2007. *Maid to Order in Hong Kong: Stories of Migrant Women*. Ithaca, NY: Cornell University Press.

Guevarra, Anna R. 2009. *Marketing Dreams, Manufacturing Heroes: The Transnational Labor Brokering of Filipino Workers*. New Brunswick, NJ: Rutgers University Press.

Hall, Stuart. 1996. "Introduction: Who Needs 'Identity'?" In *Questions of Cultural Identity*, edited by Stuart Hall and Paul du Gay, 1–17. London: Sage.

Johnson, Mark, and Pnina Werbner. 2010. "Diasporic Encounters, Sacred Journeys: Ritual, Normativity and the Religious Imagination among International Asian Migrant Women." *Asia Pacific Journal of Anthropology* 11 (3–4): 205–218. https://doi.org/10.1080/14442213.2010.517510.

Kafer, Alison. 2013. *Feminist, Queer, Crip*. Bloomington: Indiana University Press.

Lamb, Sarah, ed. 2017. *Successful Aging as a Contemporary Obsession: Global Perspectives*. New Brunswick, NJ: Rutgers University Press.

———. 2018. "Being Single in India: Gendered Identities, Class Mobilities, and Personhoods in Flux." *Ethos* 46 (1): 49–69. https://doi.org/10.1111/etho.12193.

Liebelt, Claudia. 2011. *Caring for the "Holy Land": Filipina Domestic Workers in Israel*. New York: Berghahn Books.

Lulle, Aija. 2018. "Mobilities and Waiting: Experiences of Middle-Aged Latvian Women Who Emigrated and Those Who Stayed Put." *Gender, Place and Culture* 25 (8): 1193–1208. https://doi.org/10.1080/0966369X.2018.1435512.

Mains, Daniel. 2011. *Hope Is Cut: Youth, Unemployment, and the Future in Urban Ethiopia*. Philadelphia: Temple University Press.

Manalansan, Martin F., IV. 2008. "Queering the Chain of Care Paradigm." *Scholar and Feminist Online* 6 (3). http://sfonline.barnard.edu/immigration/print_manalansan.htm.

Parreñas, Rhacel. 2015. *Servants of Globalization: Migration and Domestic Work*. Stanford, CA: Stanford University Press.

Platt, Maria, Grace Baey, Brenda S. A. Yeoh, Choon Yen Khoo, and Theodora Lam. 2017. "Debt, Precarity and Gender: Male and Female Temporary Labour Migrants in Singapore." *Journal of Ethnic and Migration Studies* 43 (1): 119–136. https://doi.org/10.1080/1369183X.2016.1218756.

Robertson, Shanthi, Yi'En Cheng, and Brenda S. A. Yeoh. 2018. "Introduction: Mobile Aspirations? Youth Im/mobilities in the Asia-Pacific." *Journal of Intercultural Studies* 39 (6): 613–625. https://doi.org/10.1080/07256868.2018.1536345.

Samanta, Tannistha. 2021. "Living Solo at Midlife: Can the Pandemic De-stigmatize Living Alone in India?" *Journal of Aging Studies* 56 (March). https://doi.org/10.1016/j.jaging.2020.100907.

Slater, Jen, Embla Ágústsdóttir, and Freyja Haraldsdóttir. 2018. "Becoming Intelligible Woman: Gender, Disability and Resistance at the Border Zone of Youth." *Feminism and Psychology* 28 (3): 409–426. https://doi.org/10.1177/0959353518769947.

Yeoh, Brenda S. A., Charmian Goh, and Kellynn Wee. 2020. "Social Protection for Migrant Domestic Workers in Singapore: International Conventions, the Law, and Civil Society Action." *American Behavioral Scientist* 64 (6): 841–858. https://doi.org/10.1177/0002764220910208.

CHAPTER 3

Aspirational Movements

LATER-LIFE MOBILITY AS A FEMALE RESOURCE TO AGE WELL

Lisa Johnson

Early one December morning in 2016, my interlocutor Rosalie, a sixty-three-year-old Jamaican-born geriatric nurse from Montreal, and I are standing in the departure hall of Toronto's Pearson International Airport, waiting for our flight to Jamaica. She has not been home to Jamaica in twenty-three years. As boarding starts, sixteen elders in sixteen wheelchairs, accompanied by several flight attendants, are queued up in the priority lane. Rosalie grunts, and she whispers toward me in Jamaican patois, "Dem fly home fi dead!," meaning they are returning home to die and be buried in Jamaica. It is an experience Rosalie is eagerly trying to avoid, so she will use this visit to plan and prepare for her own retirement return to the island. While a burial in her inherited family lot is certainly a deep-held wish, as soon as Rosalie starts receiving her pension she plans to return to Jamaica in order to live an active, mobile, and engaged retirement life there, as long as, she says, "Jesus provides me with good health and time."

This chapter elaborates on the return-migration aspirations of aging Jamaican women who emigrated through familial reunification programs in the 1970s, as children or teenagers from rural Jamaica, to the city of Montreal in Quebec, Canada. The analysis of these second-generation migrants' narratives and practices of mobility illustrates spatial, temporal, and familial contexts and trajectories of aspirations for later life. Narratives about where and how to age well give a more nuanced understanding of agency in migration processes. Aging well thus means to live an active, mobile, and engaged retirement life. Returning home as a mental and physical practice not only sheds light on female aspirations and capabilities to be mobile within a given set of socioeconomic opportunities and familial care structures but also contests common migration paradigms such as notions of linearity or permanent settlement. The chapter highlights how women's movement strategies can result in alternative forms of belonging, well-being, and human existence beyond national borders. At the same time, it considers the immense effects of the COVID-19 pandemic on the lives of people who were formerly highly mobile.

Jamaica is the third-largest, and largest English-speaking, island in the Caribbean, with a population of about 2.9 million, of whom 9 percent are aged sixty-five years or older (Statista 2021). Traditionally, older persons in lower- and middle-income countries live in multigenerational households. In Jamaica, the impact of urban and overseas migration, coupled with the absence of a public long-term care system since the island's independence in 1962, has resulted in the emergence of a private care sector. Having a good retirement in Jamaica, or generally aging well, is directly connected to reliable local and overseas familial contacts, for example, for monetary support or hands-on care arrangements, as official in-house or institutional elder care is in high demand but sparsely available and very expensive. Thus returning, as a migratory practice, entails thorough organization in preparing and getting ready (cf. Cassarino 2014), which in turn often results in a life-long, multi-layered process of yearning for reconnection (cf. Johnson 2021), filled with memories of loss, nostalgia, traditions, geographies, and temporal imaginaries (cf. Schmidt Camacho 2008) of the homeland. A closer examination of issues of time and place is thus relevant in unpacking returnees' aspirations for later life and retirement, and this chapter sheds light on how women "move" to their homeland long before they actually retire. The process of returning starts with a mental grappling with the meaning of the homeland and other localities as a retirement option, followed by in-depth planning ahead of actual relocation. This also includes ongoing communication with diverse social networks in the diaspora and homeland, the accumulation of wealth and material goods, and several physical returns, for example, to oversee the construction of a house. Familial care arrangements, such as for grandchildren or older or ill relatives, across different diasporic places are of special importance, because these responsibilities and agreements do not necessarily end with actual retirement.

Yearning is the fuel that maintains the flame of aspiration to reconnect with the homeland. This yearning is heavily influenced by the agency of the interlocutors, who actively shape and maintain social connections across cultural, geographical, and political borders. Aspiring to reconnect is a deep emotional yearning to retrieve one's homeland after emigration and is hence a lifelong process, constituted by dynamic socio-familial, cultural, and economic decisions and by mobile strategies in Jamaica and overseas. Already in 1999, the Jamaican-born cultural theorist Stuart Hall stated, "Migration has been a constant motif of the Caribbean story" (1999: 1). Recent census data underlines this ongoing pattern of Jamaican migratory mobility. There are 1,171,915 Jamaican-born people in the United States (United States Census Bureau 2019) and 309,485 Jamaican-born residents in Canada (Statistics Canada 2016), and the diaspora has grown over the past sixty years to nearly 1.3 million, or almost half the number of Jamaicans actually living on the island itself. Hence, many Jamaican households have either family members abroad or returnee family members in their familial networks.

For Jamaican women, aging well, actively, and in a self-empowered way depends on balancing multiple homes, connections, and possibilities to move between places. Even after returning, aspirations to later-life mobility and familial, as well as social, responsibilities continue to keep the lives and trajectories of Jamaican retirees active and fluid instead of sedentary. Many of Jamaica's aging citizens are return migrants who left Jamaica for Canada, the United States, or the United Kingdom in the 1960s and 1970s.[1] My research suggests that returned (senior) citizens have very different needs from those who have lived in Jamaica all their lives, including their expectations of market involvement, health care, security, and maneuvering the infrastructural, bureaucratic, and financial landscape (Johnson 2020b). Therefore, aging cohorts of Jamaican return migrants appear to move back and forth between their country of settlement and places in the United Kingdom or North America, benefiting from the social capital and economic resources they have accumulated over the course of their lives, such as entitlements, pensions, and multi-local family and friends networks.

Later-life mobility and return enable single, divorced, or widowed women in particular (cf. Gambold 2013) to age actively, well, and in a self-empowered way. Mobility is thus intertwined with Jamaican women's aspirations for a "good life" as they use mobility strategies to balance multiple connections, cross-border homes, and options. Typically, this later-life mobility involves traveling between family, kin, and nonbiological bonds within the diaspora. For many of these active women, the visits they make are socioculturally important caregiving arrangements and acts of communication within diasporic families. For example, as grandmothers, all of my retired interlocutors provide temporary caregiving or childcare services to their families, which means leaving their place of residence for short periods (one to six months) and moving to their families in the United States or Canada. These "seasonal grandmothers" are part of a coping strategy to raise children, especially during school summer breaks. The importance of grandmothers to childcare in matrifocal households in the Anglo-Caribbean has been shown by numerous studies over the years (cf. Foner 1975; Bauer and Thompson 2004; Horst 2011; Chamberlain 2017).

As my ethnographic research demonstrates, many aging women gain agency from the mobility of goods and personal travel between North America and Jamaica, or within North America, depending on where they choose to retire, and especially through seasonal travel between places of former residence, the homes of family members, and their retirement homes on and off the island (Johnson 2021). This chapter pays special attention to diasporic social networks among female relatives (grandmothers, mothers, daughters, and others), as they commonly bear the responsibility for care work and household expenditures. Finally, it also considers the immense effects of the COVID-19 pandemic on the cross-border lives of formerly highly mobile women, including the containment measurements by the Jamaican government that especially affected aging individuals.

Methodology

This chapter is based on an ethnographic study conducted during several periods in the field from spring 2016 to winter 2019 in North America (Canada and the United States) and Jamaica (see Johnson 2021). Throughout the field research, I accompanied returnees at different stages of migratory mobility, in different places, and at important intersections, in the sense of a "multi-sited ethnography" (Marcus 1995). However, it was not the comparative investigation of different places but the active travel with female migrants that enabled a "thick description" (Geertz 2003) of their manifold relationships, experiences, and interactions. The research focus on women, especially aging women, resulted from my inductive field approach in Montreal, where a community church was one of my initial key spaces and where I met Rosalie, one of my main interlocutors and gatekeepers to the local community.[2] In my research with aging Black women, who mainly work in lower- or middle-income professions such as nursing, I followed an intersectional approach that allowed age disparities to be analyzed in close relation to class, race, and gender (cf. Crenshaw 2017). The lens on women's migratory experiences became even more important when I found out that work programs to Quebec specifically hired Caribbean females from the 1960s onward.

Retirement and residential selection are important aspects in understanding women's later-life choices, agency, and social geographies. Active traveling between Canada, the United States, and Jamaica was possible due to the women's dual citizenships and the availability of regular and inexpensive air travel. Additionally, following up on real-time electronic communication via instant messaging, video calls, and social media during and beyond the fieldwork allowed for moments of time and space compression, in the sense of a virtual ethnography. This chapter utilizes ethnographic data from participant observation and narrative interviews, informal conversations, and the active accompaniment of interlocutors to explore intersections and practices among Jamaican retirees. Throughout the field research, my own positionality as a woman, mother, and German researcher, who nevertheless has family in Jamaica, helped me to sustain trusting research relationships with my interlocutors.

Historical Context

The influx of Caribbean immigrants to Canada reached its peak in the mid-1950s. Many Jamaicans left their homeland to escape increasing socioeconomic marginalization, political unrest, and crime. After the passage of the Immigration Act in 1962, Canada accepted one hundred Jamaican nurses and care workers annually, who were able to apply for permanent residency after one year of service (Labelle, Larose, and Piché 2019). Jamaican nursing staff were highly qualified at the time, and therefore emigration to Quebec was historically easier for women than for men, who mainly worked in seasonal horticulture programs. The demand for guest workers from the English-speaking Caribbean rose sharply until the mid-1960s, due to Canada's postwar economic boom and Jamaica's independence from Britain in 1962 (Labelle, Larose, and Piché 2019). Many Jamaican women belonging to that first immigrant generation remained in Quebec and later sent for their children, spouses, and close family members through governmental family reunification programs once they had established themselves legally and economically. Many of these labor or familial chain migrants returned successfully to Jamaica after several years overseas, either with their pensions or with accumulated assets to make their lives on the island comfortable.

Nowadays, returning Jamaicans mainly come from North American metropoles. Like emigration, voluntary return to Jamaica is a socioculturally accepted venture and is held in high regard.[3] The Jamaican government often welcomes returnees as honorary citizens, who have contributed through lifelong remittances and also through building local properties and who, in their last quarter of life on the island, contribute to local economic development through their spending capacities. This social structure is reflected in remittances amounting to USD 2.2 billion annually (Planning Institute of Jamaica 2016) that maintain the livelihoods of many islanders. This also makes individuals wish to emigrate themselves in search of a better life: for economic opportunities, study, seasonal work, or family reunification.

Many Jamaicans are cross-nationally and continually on the move, commuting for work, between family members, or due to lifestyle choices. Unfortunately, there is no quantitative data about these frequent movers, which makes it hard to estimate their exact number. However, given the geographical closeness between North America and Jamaica, and the availability of quick, low-cost air travel, cross-border exchanges seem readily attainable. In particular, privileged movers, such as dual citizens, green card holders, or those on long-term family and study visas, benefit from free movement to North America. Restrictive migration policies—in the United States after the 9/11 attacks in 2001 and the United Kingdom since 2003—have led Canada, with its numerous work programs, to become a preferred migration destination for many Jamaicans.

The majority of the research participants in this chapter left middle- to lower-income families in rural Jamaica and arrived in Montreal as children or teenagers in the 1970s–1980s to rejoin their mothers after having been in the foster care of their grandparents. These second-generation migrants are rapidly aging today, and with the prospect of receiving their pensions in sight, as well as the changing demographic environment in Montreal, many are seeking new ways of accommodating themselves by returning to Jamaica or finding new retirement locations elsewhere. Here, returning "home" not only promises upward social mobility but also counteracts the years of hard work, homesickness, and deprivation overseas.

Decisions to Return, Decisions to Be Mobile

One in five Canadians will be aged sixty-five years and over by 2024 (Statistics Canada 2019). For Jamaican women, a secure retirement in Canada or the United

States in terms of infrastructure and health-care access is carefully weighed against social marginalization and experiences of racialization in their considerations of where and how to age well. Carol, a retired Jamaican-born teacher from Montreal, gives several examples of these experiences in daily life: discriminatory acts in and outside the classroom, difficulty in finding well-paid employment, language issues for one who is not fluent in French (or rather Quebecois French), not being able to rent an apartment without a white friend acting as guarantor, racial profiling by the police, and so on. Such experiences led her to select Toronto instead of Montreal as her place of retirement, because in Toronto, she says, "it's more normal to be Black" and "life happens in English."

Montreal has changed tremendously since the 1990s, especially for Anglophones and Black individuals. The 1995 Quebec referendum (Gall 2013), called by the nationalist Parti Québécois, resulted in a radical French language policy, while remaining only one of many failed attempts to gain independence from Canada. Over the past thirty years, the nationalist party has increasingly pushed governmental agendas that negatively affect the lives of immigrants, Anglophones, Black people, people of color, and religious minorities. For example, in 2019 Bill 9 reformed the immigration system, setting out a strict framework for value tests of skilled workers, and canceled eighteen thousand immigration applications in the blink of an eye. Dwaine Plaza (2001) states that racialized older immigrant adults in Canada are mainly worried about their access to entitlements and health care and their social and financial security. Recent policy changes in Canada support this claim, as these have had negative effects on income support programs and made a (financially) secure retirement increasingly difficult to achieve (Matsuoka, Beaulieu, and Kitchen 2013).

For Carol, a secure retirement means living in Toronto and having good infrastructure and access to health care, while being able to fly to her homeland, Jamaica, frequently. The decision not to return to Jamaica permanently was one in which she put a lot of thought. She finally decided that seasonal returns to the island would quench her desire to reconnect, and she would not need to deal with the downsides of life in Jamaica, such as bad infrastructure or crime. The decision to visit Jamaica regularly from a place of choice in North America is not unique to Carol, but is highly dependent on individual and familial life courses, especially around the rearing of children or the responsibilities of caring for aging or sick family members. Carol, for example, has children and grandchildren in Canada and the United States, so the consideration to move "not too far away" was important. In that sense, aging Jamaican women who aspire to be mobile across various diasporic places must calculate the benefits of this mobility based on their sense of well-being, belonging, and future expectations. Especially since their Canadian pensions, at times, go further in their country of origin, some interlocutors choose to return to Jamaica, such as Rosalie, who also inherited land. Previous studies on Jamaican migrants often focused on their settlement in metropoles (e.g., in Canada, the United States, or the United Kingdom) or on a permanent return to Jamaica (Goulbourne and Chamberlain 2001; Thomas-Hope 2006).

However, return migration can be seen not as the final stage or outcome of their migration journeys but as ongoing aspirations of mobility—physical, virtual, or mental—between various diasporic lifeworlds, transcending binary experiences of settlement and return. Their considerations of socioeconomic stability and well-being extend beyond the realms of health or finances (see also Amrith, this volume; Otaegui, this volume). As they receive their pensions, retirement signals for many women the end of their purpose for being in Montreal. Their lifelong encounters with racism, discrimination, the harsh climate, demographic changes, and language issues are all relevant factors in saying good-bye to the city. Thus many people, including Jamaicans, choose to turn their backs on Montreal and migrate to other Canadian cities, such as Toronto, Vancouver, or Hamilton, or to the United States or to Jamaica, while staying mobile between various diasporic locales. In that sense, historical events, political decision-making, and globalization, as well as individual and familial choices of the "right" timing of return, are important in the anticipation and planning of retirement.

Yearning for the Homeland

As Rosalie, a geriatric nurse in her early sixties, explains:

> Leaving my grandmother's farm was one of the hardest challenges in my life.... Up until today, I have some days where I still feel robbed of staying with her and liv[ing] close to where I was born.... I had to go to live with my mother, who I hadn't seen for six years. She was a stranger, and I was just fifteen by that time, it was hard, so hard ... coming to this cold country, full of white people who side-eyed me and my sister every step of the way. Then we had to learn French right away.... Thinking of it now, though, I am also glad for my mother's choices, because she allowed us to get a stable life, she looked at the larger picture.

Biographical narratives of Jamaican migrants illustrate that many second-generation women face pronounced homesickness. This yearning for home is an expression of an affective affiliation with Jamaica, its land, and its people and plays a major role in their processes of return. By examining events and processes that are no longer, or not yet, perceivable, migratory narratives shed light on the cultural practices through which the actors either explicitly or implicitly aim to come to terms with the future. Remembering, as a practice, is thus both grievous and soothing; on the one hand, it arouses melancholy and romanticized sentimentality, and, on the other, it negotiates and mediates the past. This has a transformative power on the present and future. As Hall writes, "Poverty, underdevelopment, the lack of opportunities—the legacies of Empire everywhere—may force people to migrate, bringing about the scattering—the dispersal. But each dissemination carries with it the promise of the redemptive return" (1999, 3). Specifically, second-generation migrants uphold a strong attachment to the Jamaican homeland, people, traditions, and places, resulting from their often involuntary familial chain migration experiences. These displacement experiences often result in nostalgic stories about a childhood paradise left behind and explain current desires to return.

> It is because this New World is constituted for us as place, a narrative of displacement, that it gives rise so profoundly to a certain imaginary plenitude, recreating the endless desire to return to "lost origins," to be one again with the mother, to go back to the beginning. Who can ever forget, when once seen rising up out of that blue-green Caribbean, those islands of enchantment. Who has not known, at this moment, the surge of an overwhelming nostalgia for lost origins, for times past? And yet, this "return to the beginning" is like the imaginary in Lacan—it can neither be fulfilled nor requited, and hence is the beginning of the symbolic, of representation, the infinitely renewable source of desire, memory, myth, search, discovery. (Hall 1990, 236)

This mental time travel, through actively visiting memories of a life prior to emigration, results in a longing for an idealized past. The aspiration to reconnect often relates to carefree childhood days and a sense of fixed spatial and historical locations, which for many second-generation women are the homes of grandmothers or aunts where they were fostered as children. Women thus bring their situated pasts into a narrative order in which a mediated representation of the past also involves the (intended or unintended) exclusion of its less rosy aspects. In that sense, aspirations to returning and aging well in Jamaica are often accompanied by positive expectations, which are hardly attainable in the actual event of return. As the Hall quotation further shows, migration to Canada is also perceived by the women as a way of "getting ahead" in time, of altering the linear time of their families and their societal progress in life. For example, remittances are important in changing societal temporalities and lifeworlds, where "money from foreign" translates into building or buying houses, paying school fees for relatives' children, or supporting family or business ventures in Jamaica. Migration to North America is thus a process of upward social mobility for many Jamaicans and their families, fulfilling the sociocultural and moral obligations of individuals to take care of those who provided care or resources at an earlier period in life. Hence, before Jamaican women retire, they contemplate where they are able to age well to fulfill their longing for the homeland, while still being able to fulfill new responsibilities, such as caring for grandchildren. Their aspirations thus shift over the course of their lives, from gaining economic welfare to gaining more personal freedom, by deciding to age in their place of choice, while at the same time the aspiration to be able to move between various familial households and take care of grandchildren or other relatives remains an important motive.

These considerations result in spatial and temporal mobility between the country of origin, the country of settlement, and other diasporic localities. Returning to the island for retirement purposes is a lifelong process of yearning for "a home once lost," a positively connoted life stage of "having made it" and "being settled" in lavishly constructed houses thanks to the economic benefits of migrating abroad

(Johnson 2021). Women who return-migrate to Jamaica have a strong urge to "be at home" and come back to the place of their heart, one that is in line with their self-understanding, cultural identity, and familial history.

Josephine, a Jamaican returnee in her late sixties, explains why her life in Canada always had an end date: "When you come here as a young adult it's already too late for you to integrate in a classical sense . . . you have to be much, much younger. . . . Jamaican is who I am, you know, it can never get lost. . . . I see it with my grandchildren the best, you know, they have no problem, they are used to this life here. They don't ask questions, you know, it's a different generation, a different time."

Considerations on the selection of a final residence in Jamaica are thus highly influenced by a yearning for reconnection with land and people, the climate, childhood memories, and the wish to be buried in the land of one's ancestors. Stephen Katz and Debbie Laliberte-Rudman (2005) describe how retirement is a set of practices rather than a fixed institution, is provisional in nature, and creates identities and self-understandings that shape individual lifestyle choices and their boundaries over time. Within this context, after Jamaican women receive their pensions, they renegotiate residential choices to achieve livelihoods in old age that are in line with their aspirations to reconnect with the homeland. Due to the temporal limitations of aging and their mobility possibilities, women choose a final residence for their retirement, one that does not necessarily have to be on the island, as in Carol's case. However, no matter which location they choose, as long as they are healthy, able-bodied, and well, retirement does not necessarily signal the end of their travel endeavors.

Timing Returns, Returning Takes Time

Rosalie says in one of our interviews: "When I inherited my grandmother's house, I knew that's it, that's where I am going to spend my last couple of days. . . . I invested a lot in that house, in the renovation, the maintenance. . . . My sister takes care of everything. I send her the money and we discuss what needs to be done next. . . . Everything is so easy nowadays . . . I remember when there was only letters and long-distance phone calls, now I can see her right in front of my face [*laughs*]."

Aside from the material preparations for return, such as building or refurbishing houses and arranging land ownership (see Pauli 2008), interlocutors also speak of the importance of co-arranging female life courses in later life. As previous anthropological studies on care and migration (e.g., Coe 2013, 2015; Alber 2013; Drotbohm 2013) have also shown, time plays a crucial role in organizing and synchronizing life courses, especially when organizing child-rearing responsibilities and caring for elderly family members. Therefore, it is important to acknowledge the entanglement of different temporalities with women's aspirations to mobility. The biographical narratives of Jamaican women show the obligation to synchronize life courses by taking care of their own children, left-behind family in Jamaica, and ailing parents and co-organizing responsibilities for rearing their children's children, exemplified by the seasonal mobility of Jamaican grandmothers during the summer months. Especially the births of grandchildren, or the deaths of close relatives or a spouse, were seen to have a catalyzing effect on decision-making regarding return.

As Herminie, a Jamaican returnee in her mid-sixties, explains: "Grandmothers like me are vital in the development of the younger ones in American society. We are part of the coping strategy that helps out the family.... Grandmothers are needed for the nurturing and for instilling better morals in the children. They lack morals there a lot."

Regarding child-rearing responsibilities, many women of the second generation find great value in creating time to raise their children in Jamaican traditions—following Christian values, speaking patois (Jamaican English), or immersion in Jamaican food culture—which also entails making enough money to ensure that holiday trips to the island are feasible to socialize their children. In particular, transmitted knowledge from former generations such as mothers and grandmothers, their sociocultural practices, modes of living, and values, and their memories thereof, plays an important role in child-rearing practices. The symbolic meaning of ongoing connections with the homeland can therefore go beyond direct, personal relationships and be understood in terms of a community-based Jamaican reference system (Faist 2006). The learning of cultural customs, language, religiosity, and food culture through socialization and intergenerational narratives is fertile ground for glorified and romanticized views of life in Jamaica for the following generations. These form the basis of ongoing preoccupation with the homeland and of fluid and shifting reconstructions of a Jamaican cultural identity across generations (cf. Hall 2001).

Hence, I conceptualize yearning as the longing for past time memories and a "lost wholeness" of second-generation migrant women, which can be understood as discursive attempts and complex psychological strategies of cultural identification with Jamaica that emphasize the temporal dimensions that are of special symbolic and affective importance. Homeland, as a meaningful identification category, is marked by "multiple, woven together temporalities through feelings of belonging" (Easthope 2004, 135). The identification of the time in Montreal as being "completed," in the sense of a moral obligation to financially provide for their families, marks a new chapter in their life courses, one that is concentrated on the anticipation of returning home. We can thus observe how women's aspirations to spend their later lives in the homeland shift over time amid nostalgic and romanticized ideas of Jamaica.

On the question of how her return to Jamaica proceeded, Rosalie says: "I'm still returning, even after three years, I'm returning, because every other day you learn something new [*laughs*]. Sometimes I feel like I never left, and at other times I feel that I was gone for a very long time.... Change is good though, it keeps you fresh ... and I'm used to it from where I lived before, you always have to adapt."

Most female migrants return with secure pensions and live somewhat distinct and segregated from the local population in Jamaica. Rosalie indicates that she sold her apartment in Montreal and moved back permanently to Jamaica in order to maximize the value of her pension and the long-term payments she made for her dream house in Jamaica, as well as for the warm weather. As part of her later-life mobility practice, frequent travel to Canada and the United States in order to maintain her pension entitlement and to visit children and grandchildren is the norm for her, as it is for other returnees. Only rarely are aging and retirement in Jamaica, especially for women, defined as times of discovery in scholarly debates (see, e.g., James et al. 2012). However, interviews conducted with Jamaican returnees suggest that, far from being passive or settled, many are driven by aspirations to age well, resulting in the agency, desire, and capability to keep improving and reinventing themselves upon return to the island. In the event of returning and coming to terms with "real life" there, many returnees question their previous rosy imaginaries of the Jamaica they left behind years ago (Johnson 2021). While some returnees can become vulnerable when exposed to local infrastructural and bureaucratic realities and to financial expectations, jealousy, or even violence from locals (cf. Lemard 2004), many research respondents use their "flexible citizenship" (Ong 1999) and routine mobility to enjoy lifestyles that counteract local boredom, friction, and isolation. In order to come to terms with this new place of residence, and changing local sociocultural life, many use their mobility privileges to offset the challenges of reintegration. Their flexibility and social connections to North America enable them to address their misjudgments about Jamaica through ongoing mobile practices that increase their well-being. As Dimitris Papadopoulos and Vasilis S. Tsianos put it: "People on the move create a world of knowledge, of information, of tricks for survival, of mutual care, of social relations, of services exchange, of solidarity and sociability that can be shared, used and where people contribute to sustain and expand it.... The mobile commons is neither private nor public, neither state owned nor part of civil society; rather it exists to the extent that people share it and generate it as they are mobile and when they arrive somewhere" (2013, 190).

Globalizing factors, particularly digital communications and the new possibilities for networking that these offer, must also be taken into account in individual returns. These virtual connections demonstrate the importance of simultaneity and time-space compression across geographical borders. Continuous social interactions through "technoscapes" (Appadurai 1996) are important processes of transnational mediation and translation that structure the interactions between diverse spaces (Lehmkuhl, Lüsebrink, and McFalls 2015, 15). Thus, virtual communication networking is an important key to understanding residential selection. The quality of the networking, in the sense of being informed about happenings and contexts in Jamaica, is of central importance. As research on transnational Jamaican families suggests (Goulbourne and Chamberlain 2001, 41), telephones and new communication technologies are key instruments for maintaining connections with family and social networks in Jamaica across time and space. Many second-generation women report how important it is to stay connected with friends and family locally and across the diaspora. As Heather A. Horst and Daniel Miller's

(2005) study on cell phone use in Jamaica shows, family members but also, and especially, friends are of paramount importance for mutual help, recommendations, and support, both locally and globally. Virtual connection and keeping in touch through digital spaces is a cultural practice that can be understood as a preliminary stage in successful return and reintegration. It creates visibility of migrants in their places of origin and is useful for future needs. Many of the informants in Montreal stress the importance of social networking via their smartphones. Maintaining contacts over the years serves as an important tool for coordinating migration and mobility. Here, phone and video calls, texts, and voice messages are used to distribute friendly words, notes, or pictures to as many connections as feasible, helping to maintain the possibility of reactivating necessary connections whenever needed. Regular virtual conversations with family members, friends, housing providers, acquaintances, and even building contractors and relocation assistants are prerequisites for a successful return. It is relevant not only to stay in touch but also to gain knowledge about sociocultural changes. While living in the diaspora, members of the second generation exchange information and images of local events through their social networks (Appadurai 1996, 34). These exchanges can be ambivalent and may range, depending on whom they are talking to, from helping them to reconstruct their images of Jamaican reality to propagating an idealized imaginary of life on the island. While these images might vary, they are essential components of migrants' identity formation. Practical mobility is often preceded by mental mobility to maintain affective and effective social networks in different places. Therefore, "translocal figurations" (Etzold et al. 2019, 23) describe the simultaneous integration of mobile actors across various places and borders, which thereby cross and expand "social fields." Migratory people cannot be fixed in time or place but are embedded in their affective network relations.

Not all women in this study return to Jamaica as their final place of residence. When analyzing the strategic mobility movements of Jamaican women, it is necessary to move away from binary approaches in thinking about migratory returns. Migration is an ongoing process of mobility and belonging beyond national borders. Women's movements are not linear, but relational ways of entanglement and translation between transnational places, nations, and people, resulting from historical encounters (Clifford 1997, 7). Some remain in Canada and choose to stay closely connected to their local family and friends, but leave Quebec and reside in anglophone parts of the country, where they find life easier to navigate and where they have more social connections. Others choose to migrate to Jamaican diasporic enclaves in Florida, where the climate is better, the infrastructure is good, and they are close to family in the United States, and where they also retain geographical closeness to Jamaica while staying in North America. In both cases, many research participants explain that North America is considered a better location in which to age well in terms of medical care, access to entitlements, family connections, and infrastructure. However, this does not put their sense of belonging to Jamaica into question; rather, their selected residential locations are incorporated into a practical understanding of a "home away from home," which is often in response to ongoing familial and care responsibilities in North America. Choosing to remain in Canada or the United States indicates a high fluidity of belonging based on sentiment, familial obligation, life experience, and convenience.

Many women note the increased possibilities that retirement havens like Miami provide, with structured recreational programs for older adults, combined with the amenities of a warmer climate. Women such as Carol describe a desire to experience a more cosmopolitan or "modern" context of aging than they perceive to be available in Jamaica. Additionally, many retired women have the financial means to travel to Jamaica frequently, and often do so in the winter months. Others remain in North America due to health concerns or diminished social connections in Jamaica. Though Jamaica remains a figurative and ideational home for many, it is not the final destination for all research participants. However, cheap and easy flights, and modern communication, enable many to maintain their few social connections to friends and family on the island. The latter, especially, proved to be of great importance in maintaining connections across diasporic places when the COVID-19 pandemic began in early 2020. The coronavirus had immense effects on the aspirations and lifestyles of frequent movers, resulting in a cessation in the cross-border lives of my interlocutors.

COVID-19 AND THE COMING TO A HALT OF FREQUENT MOVERS

Herminie, a sixty-seven-year-old returnee, recalls her experience of the COVID-19 pandemic:

> My daughter, she cried on the phone, because I can't come this year. Ever since this pandemic started she got lost. . . . You know, when the school closed it was over. The money situation got really bad for them, too. . . . I feel like I'm in jail, you know. I mean, I give thanks for all that I have here, and that I'm safe and healthy and everything, but I don't like how they [the government] treat older people in this whole thing—it seems like we can't go nowhere again. I don't feel old, how they make "old" sound like? Sixty-seven years I walk this earth and been through all kinds of struggles and tribulations to get where I'm at. And now, after I just got to enjoy myself, they tell me I'm a risk group.

Herminie's words exemplify how the COVID-19 pandemic, and the drastic restrictions imposed for infection prevention, threatened aging individuals' lifeworlds and ruptured their strategies of resilience. Border closures and state regulatory practices had far-reaching consequences for Jamaican Canadian women's cross-border, familial, and local social networks, their health, well-being, and economic status, as well as their day-to-day practices in Jamaica. These women's aspirations to mobility came up against the context of hindered agency, immobility, and confinement, through the strict "stay-at-home orders" imposed on older people. The age limit for the stay-at-home orders was lowered during 2020, from seventy-five years in June to sixty-five in October (Jamaica Information Service 2020). While this change was based on the recommendations of medical experts, many of those categorized as "senior citizens" are far from being inactive or perceiving themselves as old. Moreover, as of March 2021, Jamaica has not received sufficient COVID-19 vaccines, which has meant that aging individuals have been forced to shelter in place, with allowances to leave home to purchase food or medicine, but these have changed over the course of the pandemic (at first, every twenty-four hours and, later, specific weekdays or hours of the day).

These measures affected their lifestyles and disrupted their social networks and gendered caring commitments. Because of COVID-19, familial care arrangements in transnationally organized households could not be met. Many women in the diaspora could not rely on their mothers for support and felt helpless, frustrated, and overburdened with simultaneous child-rearing and work responsibilities. An important socioeconomic transformation also came from the changing work opportunities for returnees' diasporic families in North America. The closure of businesses, borders, and entire cities changed the possibility of receiving regular remittances or goods from overseas. Nor were returnees able to engage in their former mobility and commuting practices. Many research participants described feelings of isolation, loneliness, and depression because they could no longer visit their grandchildren. Thus, COVID-19 infection control measures disrupted migratory reciprocal structures, the mobility aspirations of retired Jamaican women, and the cross-border familial networks of retirees. The vulnerability of many aging women, especially those who are single, divorced, or widowed, stems from the negative impacts of the pandemic on their agency, social behavior, and health.

Many returned retirees engage in local recreational activities, have part-time jobs, hold honorary positions, or are caregivers of ailing or older relatives in Jamaica. Unpaid caregivers or domestic workers were not exempt from the island-wide curfews (which changed from day to night curfews numerous times over the course of the pandemic), also raising questions about the reorganization of local households and reasons for possibly bypassing infection control measures. After an outcry from the Caribbean Community of Retired Persons, caregivers aged under sixty-five years were allowed to travel during curfew hours once they presented the required documents (Amour, Robinson, and Govia 2020). However, there was an ongoing lack of formal inclusion and consideration of older, unpaid, in-house caretakers as essential workers, especially aging women in caregiving positions, who are at higher risk of suffering severe COVID-19. Not only is health and care work still gendered labor in Jamaica, but it is rarely remunerated, particularly private, in-house care, which is generally provided by family, fellow congregants, or friends. The further loss of routines, such as attending church, and confinement at home, with its resulting inactivity, immobility, and lack of social exchange with peers and family, raise questions about women's physical and emotional well-being. A loss of informal income, caring, and social activities due to containment measures affects families and aging individuals, especially their health, and may lead to new arrangements, behavioral adaptations, and sociocultural practices of private, hidden care. Local acceptance of prescribed behavior changes (such as distancing and stay-at-home rules), and infection control measures (such as mask wearing) fell significantly over the course of the pandemic as many Jamaicans started to trivialize governmental measures (Johnson 2020a). In particular, many individuals seemed to minimize differences between COVID-19 and other diseases that already existed on the island, such as the Zika virus, dengue, or chikungunya, to bypass the measures because of their high social and economic costs.

Furthermore, the crisis cast a light on the fact that many retirees aged sixty-five to seventy-five years, some far beyond retirement age, continue to work in the informal sector to take care of family members or to supplement their pensions. Infection control measures went past the reality of social life in Jamaica. At the same time, the government made exceptions; for example, unvaccinated tourists were permitted to enter the country, even as officials called for mandatory vaccinations for all Jamaicans (some of the Jamaican population is known to be skeptical of vaccinations in general). Even with the end of border closures, COVID-19 continues to stifle the livelihoods of retired Jamaican returnees and their transnational families, especially due to the fear of getting sick while traveling. In this light, aspirations of mobility might dwindle the longer the pandemic lasts, as individuals continue to age and health concerns and considerations of safety play an ever larger role. However, aspirations to stay in touch with family and friends or to reconnect with social contacts in the homeland persist and are reconfigured into practices of virtual communication and exchanges.

Conclusion

The choice of a physical residence cannot be equated with reaching physical stasis. After living in Canada for decades, many women find it difficult to return to Jamaica permanently, although they retain a deep sense of home and belonging, which is strongly connected to their sociocultural identification as Jamaicans (Chamberlain 1998). The need to maintain a Jamaican identity persists in later life. Their practices and narratives reveal a multiplicity of cultural codes and symbols that go beyond the nation-state and highlight the multiple locations and temporalities of "home" that exist not only geographically but also mentally and emotionally. The emotional connections that Jamaican women uphold with their country of origin, as well as with various diasporic locales, help to create their perceptions of home, their identities, and their later-life geographies in a co-arranged symphony that renders home as both physical and metaphorical.

Throughout the life course, women have had to transform the ideal of home from one connected only to Jamaica to one bound by the expanse of their imagination, transcending the borders of Jamaica and North America alike. Retired Jamaican women's conceptualizations of a metaphorical home and physical residence are enmeshed in a broader social network of people, as well as in practical considerations that have served to embed them within multiple societies over time (Basch, Schiller, and Szanton Blanc 1994; Levitt and Schiller 2004). Decisions to remain in Canada or the United States expand discourses about migrants' eventual "final returns" to their country of origin at the end of the migration endeavor and put into question what "return" as a category in migration research truly means, especially with regard to migrants from the Global South.

NOTES

1. The most recent data, recorded for 1993–1999, showed 15,380 voluntary return migrants to Jamaica (Thomas-Hope, Knight, and Noel 2012).
2. All names of interlocutors are pseudonyms.
3. There is an important distinction between voluntary and involuntary return. Involuntary return, as in the forced return of deportees, is highly stigmatized in Jamaica and, for men and women, is associated with varying degrees of cultural isolation, loss of status, or lack of community acceptance (see Golash-Boza 2014).

REFERENCES

Alber, Erdmute. 2013. "Within the Thicket of Intergenerational Sibling Relations: A Case Study from Northern Benin." In *The Anthropology of Sibling Relations: Shared Parentage, Experience, and Exchange*, edited by Erdmute Alber, Cati Coe, and Tatjana Thelen, 73–96. New York: Palgrave Macmillan.

Amour, Rochelle, Janelle N. Robinson, and Ishtar Govia. 2020. *The COVID-19 Long-Term Care Situation in Jamaica*. London: International Long-Term Care Policy Network, Care Policy and Evaluation Centre, London School of Economics and Political Science. https://ltccovid.org/wp-content/uploads/2020/05/The-COVID-19-Long-Term-Care-situation-in-Jamaica-25-May-2020-1.pdf.

Appadurai, Arjun. 1996. "Global Ethnoscapes: Notes and Queries for a Transnational Anthropology." In *Recapturing Anthropology: Working in the Present*, edited by Richard G. Fox, 191–210. Santa Fe, NM: School of American Research Press.

Basch, Linda, Nina Glick Schiller, and Cristina Szanton Blanc. 1994. *Nations Unbound: Transnational Projects, Postcolonial Predicaments, and Deterritorialized Nation-States*. Basel: Gordon and Breach.

Bauer, Elaine, and Paul Thompson. 2004. "'She's Always the Person with a Very Global Vision': The Gender Dynamics of Migration, Narrative Interpretation and the Case of Jamaican Transnational Families." *Gender and History* 16 (2): 334–375.

Cassarino, Jean-Pierre. 2014. "A Case for Return Preparedness." In *Global and Asian Perspectives on International Migration*, edited by Graziano Battistella, 153–165. Cham: Springer International Publishing.

Chamberlain, Mary, ed. 1998. *Caribbean Migration: Globalised Identities*. London: Routledge.

———. 2017. *Family Love in the Diaspora: Migration and the Anglo-Caribbean Experience*. London: Routledge.

Clifford, James. 1997. *Routes: Travel and Translation in the Late Twentieth Century*. Cambridge, MA: Harvard University Press.

Coe, Cati. 2013. *The Scattered Family: Parenting, African Migrants, and Global Inequality*. Chicago: University of Chicago Press.

———. 2015. "The Temporality of Care: Gender, Migration, and the Entrainment of Life-Courses." In *Anthropological Perspectives on Care: Work, Kinship and the Life-Course*, edited by Erdmute Alber and Heike Drotbohm, 181–205. New York: Palgrave Macmillan.

Crenshaw, Kimberlé W. 2017. *On Intersectionality: Essential Writings*. New York: New Press.

Drotbohm, Heike. 2013. "The Promises of Shared Motherhood and the Perils of Detachment: A Comparison of Local and Transnational Child Fostering in Cape Verde." In *Child Fostering in West Africa: New Perspectives on Theory and Practices*, edited by Erdmute Alber, Jeannett Martin, and Catrien Notermans, 177–199. Leiden: Brill.

Easthope, Hazel. 2004. "A Place Called Home." *Housing, Theory and Society* 21 (3): 128–138.

Etzold, Benjamin, Milena Belloni, Russell King, Albert Kraler, and Ferruccio Pastore. 2019. "Transnational Figurations of Displacement: Conceptualising Protracted Displacement and Translocal Connectivity through a Process-Oriented Perspective." TRAFIG Working Paper 1. Bonn International Center for Conversion (BICC), Bonn.

Faist, Thomas. 2006. "Transnationale Migration als relative Immobilität in einer globalisierten Welt." COMCAD Arbeitspapiere–Working Papers 11. Centre on Migration, Citizenship and Development, Bielefeld. https://nbn-resolving.org/urn:nbn:de:0168-ssoar-413154.

Foner, Nancy. 1975. "Women, Work, and Migration: Jamaicans in London." *Urban Anthropology* 4 (3): 229–249.

Gall, Gerald L. 2013. "Québec Referendum (1995)." In *The Canadian Encyclopedia*. Historica Canada. Article published 21 August 2013; last modified 4 March 2015. https://www.thecanadianencyclopedia.ca/en/article/quebec-referendum-1995.

Gambold, Liesl. 2013. "Retirement Abroad as Women's Aging Strategy." *Anthropology and Aging Quarterly* 34 (2): 1953–1971. https://doi.org/10.5195/aa.2013.19.

Geertz, Clifford. 2003. *Dichte Beschreibung: Beiträge zum Verstehen kultureller Systeme*. Frankfurt: Suhrkamp.

Golash-Boza, Tanya. 2014. "Forced Transnationalism: Transnational Coping Strategies and Gendered Stigma among Jamaican Deportees." *Global Networks* 14 (1): 63–79.

Goulbourne, Harry, and Mary Chamberlain, eds. 2001. *Caribbean Families in Britain and the Trans-Atlantic World*. London: Macmillan Caribbean.

Hall, Stuart. 1990. "Cultural Identity and Diaspora." In *Identity: Community, Culture, Difference*, edited by Jonathan Rutherford, 222–237. London: Lawrence & Wishart.

———. 1999. "Thinking the Diaspora: Home-Thoughts from Abroad." *Small Axe* 6: 1–18.

———. 2001. "Negotiating Caribbean Identities." In *New Caribbean Thought: A Reader*, edited by Brian Meeks and Folke Lindahl, 24–39. Kingston: University of The West Indies Press.

Horst, Heather A. 2011. "Reclaiming Place: The Architecture of Home, Family and Migration." *Anthropologica* 53 (1): 29–39.

Horst, Heather A., and Daniel Miller. 2005. "From Kinship to Link-Up, Cell Phones and Social Networking in Jamaica." *Current Anthropology* 46 (5): 755–778.

Jamaica Information Service. 2020. "Stay-at-Home Age Limit Lowered to 65." https://jis.gov.jm/stay-at-home-age-limit-lowered-to-65/.

James, Kenneth, Desmalee Holder-Nevins, Chloe Morris, Denise Eldemire-Shearer, Jeneva Powell, and Hazel Laws. 2012. "Ageing in Place: Implications of Morbidity Patterns among Older Persons—Findings from a Cross-Sectional Study in a Developing Country (Jamaica)." *Australasian Journal on Ageing* 31 (3): 170–175.

Johnson, Lisa. 2020a. "Coronavirus, Social Boundaries and Food Security: Observations in Jamaica." In "Bordering in Pandemic Times: Insights into the COVID-19 Lockdown," edited by Christian Wille and Rebekka Kanesu. Special issue, *Borders in Perspectives* 4: 101–104. https://d-nb.info/1213094275/34.

———. 2020b. "Sehnsuchtsräume und Beheimatungsstrategien jamaikanischer Frauen in Montreal." In *Geographien der Grenze*, edited by Florian Weber, Christian Wille, Beate Caesar, and Julian Hollstegge, 301–315. Wiesbaden: Springer.

———. 2021. *Moves—Spaces—Places: The Life Worlds of Jamaican Women in Montreal. An Ethnography*. Bielefeld: Transcript.

Katz, Stephen, and Debbie Laliberte-Rudman. 2005. "Exemplars of Retirement: Identity and Agency between Lifestyle and Social Movement." In *Cultural Aging: Life Course, Lifestyle, and Senior Worlds*, edited by Stephen Katz, 140–160. Toronto: University of Toronto Press.

Labelle, Micheline, Serge Larose, and Victor Piché. 2019. "Caribbean Canadians." In *The Canadian Encyclopedia*. Historica Canada. Article published 3 May 2019; last modified 13 December 2021. https://www.thecanadianencyclopedia.ca/en/article/caribbean-canadians.

Lehmkuhl, Ursula, Hans-Jürgen Lüsebrink, and Laurence McFalls. 2015. "Spaces and Practices of Diversity: An Introduction." In *Of "Contact Zones" and "Liminal Spaces": Mapping the Everyday Life of Cultural Translation*, edited by Ursula Lehmkuhl, Hans-Jürgen Lüsebrink, and Laurence McFalls, 7–28. Münster: Waxmann.

Lemard, Glendene A. N. 2004. "Violence as a Global Health Challenge: A Case Analysis of Jamaica Using an Interdisciplinary Approach." PhD diss., University of Miami.

Levitt, Peggy, and Nina Glick Schiller. 2004. "Conceptualizing Simultaneity: A Transnational Social Field Perspective on Society." *International Migration Review* 38: 1002–1039.

Marcus, George E. 1995. "Ethnography in/of the World System: The Emergence of Multi-sited Ethnography." *Annual Review of Anthropology* 24 (1): 95–117.

Matsuoka, Atsuko, Marie Beaulieu, and Brigitte Kitchen. 2013. "Strengths and Flaws of Aging Policies in Canada / Les forces et les faiblesses des politiques du vieillissement au Canada." *Canadian Review of Social Policies/Revue canadienne de politique sociale*, no. 68–69: ii–xiii.

Ong, Aihwa. 1999. *Flexible Citizenship: The Cultural Logics of Transnationality*. Durham, NC: Duke University Press.

Papadopoulos, Dimitris, and Vasilis S. Tsianos. 2013. "After Citizenship: Autonomy of Migration, Organizational Ontology and Mobile Commons." *Citizenship Studies* 17 (2): 178–196.

Pauli, Julia. 2008. "A House of One's Own: Gender, Migration, and Residence in Rural Mexico." *American Ethnologist* 35 (1): 171–187. https://doi.org/10.1111/j.1548-1425.2008.00012.x.

Planning Institute of Jamaica. 2016. *Economic and Social Survey Jamaica*. Kingston: Planning Institute of Jamaica.

Plaza, Dwaine. 2001. "Ageing in Babylon: Elderly Caribbeans in Britain." In *Caribbean Families in Britain and the Trans-Atlantic World*, edited by Harry Goulbourne and Mary Chamberlain, 219–234. London: Macmillan Caribbean.

Schmidt Camacho, Alicia. 2008. *Migrant Imaginaries: Latino Cultural Politics in the U.S.-Mexico Borderlands*. New York: New York University Press.

Statista. 2021. "Jamaica: Age Structure from 2010 to 2020." Release date June 2021. https://www.statista.com/statistics/527154/age-structure-in-jamaica/.

Statistics Canada. 2017. *Canada [Country] and Canada [Country]* (table). *Census Profile*. 2016 Census. Statistics Canada Catalogue no. 98-316-X2016001. Ottawa: Government of Canada. https://www12.statcan.gc.ca/census-recensement/2016/dp-pd/prof/index.cfm?Lang=E.

———. 2019. *Canada's Population Estimates: Age and Sex, July 1, 2019*. Statistics Canada Catalogue no. 11-001-X. Ottawa: Government of Canada. https://www150.statcan.gc.ca/n1/en/daily-quotidien/190930/dq190930a-eng.pdf?st=9U6H6LGI.

Thomas-Hope, Elizabeth. 2006. "Maximizing Migration: Caribbean Return Movements and the Organization of Transnational Space." In *Returning to the Source: The Final Stage of the Caribbean Migration Circuit*, edited by Dwaine Plaza and Frances Henry, 167–187. Kingston, Jamaica: University of the West Indies Press.

Thomas-Hope, Elizabeth, Pauline Knight, and Claudel Noel. 2012. *Migration in Jamaica: A Country Profile 2010*. Kingston, Jamaica: International Organization for Migration.

United States Census Bureau. 2019. *American Community Survey 2019*. People Reporting Ancestry. https://data.census.gov/table?q=PEOPLE+REPORTING+ANCESTRY&t=Ancestry&d=ACS+1-Year+Estimates+Detailed+Tables&tid=ACSDT1Y2019.B04006&hidePreview=false.

PART II

Intergenerational Negotiations

CHAPTER 4

Aspiring to Retire

INTERGENERATIONAL CARE IN A GHANAIAN TRANSNATIONAL FAMILY

Cati Coe

Care in later life often involves kin-time. Kin-time is the sequencing and timing of kin-work, that is, the tasks and labor required to sustain a family over time (Stack and Burton 1993). The paradigmatic case is Carol Stack's research (1996) on how African American migrant women in the northern United States were called to return home to care for aging relatives in the South, sometimes mid-career, illustrating how kin-timing is more visible in situations of migration. As research on transnational families has shown (Deneva 2012; Coe 2013), the timing of kin-work may not always be synchronized across multiple life courses, and may be the source of tensions and conflicts that reconfigure the social identities of kin members. At the same time, transnationalism and translocalism offer other possibilities for negotiating kin-timing and performing kin-work. In this chapter, I discuss the cultural scripts that help people synchronize kin-time across different life courses, reconcile themselves to a particular fraught decision, or legitimate their denial of another's claim to their kin-work. The scripts at stake here involve the aspirations of retiring and the launching of a young person into adulthood in a transnational family from Ghana.

What I want to emphasize is that these cultural scripts are used to guide action, by the major participants, their relations, and their advisers. These scripts provide a sense of a good life and a feeling of moral personhood (Mattingly 2014). They are based on a commonsense of the kinds of material resources that will be available across the life course. They indicate the temporal conditions for aspirations, such as the timescales of preparation involved in pensions, education, or house construction and the temporality of the life course (explored further in the next section of this volume). These scripts are used to gather the relevant signals or information to evaluate kin-timing. Scripts are not necessarily fully conscious, but they can be invoked as idioms (in words and images) to convince others and oneself of what is appropriate. These scripts are shared within social networks and reinforced by important others, such as close friends and religious authorities.

In situations of conflict, flipping between scripts, using the discourses associated with one script or another alternatively, is common. Other research, particularly examining notions of romantic love, has documented this recombination of discourses. For example, Laura M. Ahearn (2001) shows how "newer" ideals of love and personal compatibility co-exist with "older" notions that marriage is determined by fate in Nepal. For example, a Nepalese woman mixes the two idioms of fate and choice in explaining her marriage: "We didn't dislike each other enough to break up. This is my fate, I said, see? . . . Well, for myself it was written that I would marry; if it hadn't been, I would have left him, see?" (110). One way to reconcile differing scripts is to mix them, which leads to the emergence of new discourses and the elision of the differences between the new and the old. Ann Swidler (2001) views this lack of consistency as a case of people's flexibility, in that "people move among cultural logics with ease or build personal edifices out of brick and mortar from polyglot cultural sources" (147). My own sense, instead, is that people are actively grappling with these scripts through their emotions, trying to shape a life with the help of these scripts. Those who experience more of a match between their aspirations and their reality are more likely to accept cultural scripts wholeheartedly and with ease. Crisis prompts more active negotiation of cultural scripts (Parish 2008; Swidler 2001). As people twist and turn between these scripts in their own lives, spinning them around and creating new combinations, they may generate what I have in other work with Erdmute Alber (Coe and Alber 2018) called inscriptions, practices and discourses that represent modifications and alternatives to cultural scripts. Thus, when aspirations do not match the existing scripts, people's emotions push them to dance between multiple scripts and even modify those scripts to create new directions for their lives.

This chapter examines the competing aspirations of an aging Ghanaian home health worker in the United States, who wanted both to retire to Ghana and to launch her young-adult daughter Berenice into successful adulthood in the United States. Over five years, the aging mother, whom I will call Millicent, struggled to reconcile these multiple aspirations, in which retirement was dependent on building a house in Ghana and successful adulthood on education and professional work in the United States. Different locations were associated with different aspirations, resources, and stages of the life course—Ghana with childhood and aging and the United States with working adulthood—prompting both the daughter's and mother's transnational migrations, often temporally out of step. Furthermore, various scripts about retirement and successful adulthood were mobilized through these negotiations. Later-life aspirations are not only individual projects at a particular stage of the life course but also inter-generational ones, with effects across the generations.

I met Millicent through my research on African home care workers in the United States, and we quickly became friends, mainly because of Millicent's warm personality (Coe 2019b). When I met her in May 2015, Millicent was in her sixties and wanted to retire from home care, a physically demanding job, which she had done for about twenty years in the United States. She simultaneously wanted to launch her daughter in her twenties into successful adulthood. Over the course of five years, she did retire, and that retirement entailed a return to Ghana. However, as a result of financial difficulties, she left retirement and returned to the United States to work. During this period, Berenice went back and forth between Ghana and the United States, at different times and separately from her mother. She currently remains unlaunched, her future unclear. My primary source of information was the mother, Millicent, with whom I had regular phone conversations and many visits, particularly while she was in the United States (2016–2018, 2020) but also in Ghana in 2015 and 2019. I met Berenice three times, twice in Ghana (in 2015 and 2019) and once in the United States (2017), but Berenice, knowing that her mother confided in me, was reserved with me. In these meetings, I was often placed in the role of an adult and counselor by her mother, expected to assist Berenice through moral encouragement and educational advice. Berenice was often sullen and moody in her mother's presence. Our roles precluded more open kinds of communication between us.

Cultural Scripts of Aging

As she struggled to figure out the best course of action for herself and her daughter, Millicent grappled with competing cultural scripts of aging, illustrating how care is bound up with cultural understandings of reciprocity and moral personhood (Hromadžić and Palmberger 2018; Rasmussen 2018; Sokolovsky 2009). In one cultural script, she was supposed to be responsible for her own future well-being, while helping her daughter grow up. This cultural script is dominant in the United States and is becoming more prominent in middle-class circles in Ghana. We could call it a Western model of aging, but it has been localized in Ghana, with slightly different permutations than accrue in the United States, because traveling models change across contexts (Behrends, Park, and Rottenburg 2014; Lamb 2016). The plan, at least among the Ghanaian middle class, is not to be fully self-reliant in retirement, but to be mainly independent in case the children cannot help or only help inconsistently. Several years ago, at a fellowship meeting for older adults in the Presbyterian Church of Ghana, I heard one older man encourage his fellow attendees, all older people, to plan ahead for their futures by saving. This model of self-care is most able to be carried out by a very small percentage of the Ghanaian population: retired civil servants, who receive a pension and are overwhelmingly male. Eighty percent of workers in Ghana work in the informal sector, and generally do not contribute to pensions (Dovie 2018). Pensions, pegged to a previous salary, are often a pittance because of inflation. High inflation has also meant that cash savings have historically not made much sense, whereas an investment in building a house is seen as more secure. However, a range of financial products, including life insurance, are increasingly being marketed in many African countries like South Africa and Eswatini, indicating the financialization of the

Global South and the reworking of kinship relations through insurance (Bähre 2012; Golomski 2015; Kar 2018). A master's-level study in Ghana in 1998 found that 26 percent of pensioners (i.e., retired civil servants) had undertaken investments or savings alongside their pensions (Nelson-Cofie 1998). As in the West, the cultural script of self-reliance is most able to be followed by those who receive state social protection, who are more likely to be male and more middle class.

Another route to self-reliance is building a house or two. A house allows an older person to live with few expenses and thus relatively independently. Furthermore, a house owner can be a patron to relatives, who can live in the house for free and, in exchange, provide labor for household chores (Van der Geest 1997). A second house or a portion of a house can also generate income through rent, or serve as the site of a business, particularly in urban areas with high rents. This is another version of the cultural script of self-reliance in which a house enhances the owner's social reputation, provides financial stability, and recruits the labor of others.

In another cultural script of aging, parents are supposed to do everything they can to support their children to be successful. The model parent, in this regard, is the impoverished mother who, abandoned by her husband, sold food on the street in order to send her children to school, and it is she who is seen as most deserving of her children's care as she ages (Coe 2011). As a result, an aging adult can rely on her children—whether fostered or biological—to care for her out of obligation for what she had previously done for them. This cultural script of interdependence is illustrated by a proverb, as told to me by one grandfather: "If your mother or father or someone looks after you while your teeth are coming in, when it comes to the time where his or her teeth are falling out, you look after him or her."[1] In practice, this cultural script entailed a migrant adult daughter or granddaughter moving back to the hometown to care for the old and very young while the other siblings supported the hometown household financially (Coe 2016). This cultural script has become the orthodoxy in Ghana but is increasingly perceived as dissatisfying and precarious—onerous on the adult children because of their inability to provide for their seniors due to unemployment or underemployment or, conversely, to forgo economic opportunities and return to the hometown in late middle age (Coe 2019a). Some adult children have denied care or provided it reluctantly because they felt that their parents—particularly fathers—did not take good care of them in their childhoods (Aboderin 2006). The children's lack of success is attributed to the parents' lack of care, thus freeing them from obligations. This also takes the form of witchcraft accusations: by hurting their relatives, as illustrated by their lack of success, older women can justifiably be denied care. In general, it is poorer people who rely on the cultural script of interdependent aging in Ghana, and it requires economically successful, reliable, and grateful children in order to be enacted across the generations. Thus, this cultural script works best during economic boom times, when parents' investment in children's educations leads to their upward economic and social mobility, such as in the decades before and after Ghana's independence and in the past twenty years.

Both the cultural scripts of self-reliance and of interdependence have a somewhat long temporal horizon for the person who would like care in later life. Both entail planning ahead, in which one invests in future care while one is capable of building a house, accumulating savings, or educating children. The scripts assume different kinds of resources will be available, in the sense of whether financial investments will grow over time (rather than declining in value due to high inflation), or whether middle-aged people will have greater access to resources than children or older adults because of their physical strength and labor. These scripts also involve different forms of trust: in the script of interdependence, in the willingness and ability of one's children to reciprocate; in the script of self-reliance, in the protection of assets by the state, traditional authorities (in the case of land), and financial institutions. These scripts are generated from past and contemporary experiences of the self and others and are used to plan ahead for the future.

The scripts entail different obligations to self and others. Obligations to support children have vastly expanded, from taking care of them while their teeth are coming in to supporting them through many years of education—until adolescence or young adulthood—and perhaps beyond. Care in old age entails a moral evaluation: in the script of interdependence, the older person cared for by their adult children must have taken good care of them, in part by being generous with the few funds they had, and raising moral human beings who want to reciprocate for their care, and the abandoned older person must have done something wrong in their youth—whether being infertile, having a disastrous marriage that caused a rift with the children, or neglecting their children. In the script of self-reliance, the older person invested money in buildings, businesses, insurance schemes, and savings accounts, thus demonstrating shrewdness, intelligence, and prudence with money, perhaps by withholding everyday support to those around them. The most successful aging adults have the resources to invest in both houses and people.

There is an expanding literature on the elusiveness of adulthood, which youth in Africa and other parts of the world struggle to attain (e.g., Durham and Solway 2017; Jeffrey 2010; Mains 2011; Masquelier 2005), but very little of that literature focuses on the intergenerational effects of such an elusive adulthood (for an exception, see Roth 2007). Aspirations in later life, as well as at other stages of the life course, are affected by these intergenerational dynamics and also have intergenerational effects (see also Whyte, this volume). An elusive adulthood can make it difficult for the parents of youth to retire. As Millicent aspired, to her own retirement and to Berenice's successful adulthood, she used both of these cultural scripts to guide her actions. However, neither quite worked in her situation, because of her lack of material resources. She thus experienced major internal conflict, as demonstrated by her alternation between these cultural scripts.

Besides flipping between various scripts, another strategy that Millicent used to pursue her aspirations was her access to and knowledge of two locations—Ghana and the United States—which offered different social and material resources. Transnationalism has often been used by working-class migrants to mitigate their status degradation in the country of migration (Coe 2020; Nieswand 2011), using a strategy similar to urban African migrants who "retire" to a life of farming in their rural hometowns to maintain their social-class status (Kroeker 2020). By bringing their resources into a place with a lower cost of living, migrants can assume or maintain a middle-class lifestyle. Millicent thus used transnationalism as a hedge against her few resources. However, this strategy also generated friction because different places were associated with different stages of the life course: the United States with working adulthood and Ghana with childhood and retirement (Coe 2012). The transnationalism of the mother's retirement—to Ghana—was in the opposite direction of her daughter's ideal trajectory in the United States, making the mother's and daughter's migrations temporally out of step.

Millicent's Retirement and Berenice's Adulthood

During the five years I have known Millicent, she actively struggled to reconcile two competing goals: to launch her daughter into successful adulthood, associated with education and a career in the United States, and to secure a retirement out of her own resources, which meant building houses in Ghana. Both the houses and her daughter seemed to function symbolically at times as extensions of Millicent's own self, to which she was emotionally attached. Both were public signs of Millicent's personhood. At times, construction seemed to provide more satisfaction, because it was more amenable to her direct control, but it also generated laments, anxieties, and humiliation as she was cheated in various ways (Coe 2019b). She often talked about both daughter and house with the same level of worry. Millicent grappled actively with the two cultural scripts of aging and care because neither model was coming to fruition. Lauren Berlant (2011) suggests that the objects of our desire might get in the way of our happiness, because they are founded on economic conditions that have become precarious. This case study suggests that people are able to detach from one aspiration, but only when another object of desire is available to take its place.

Millicent at Work in the United States, Berenice in School in Ghana

Millicent's own timing in the life course as being ready to retire was out of sync with her daughter's ongoing education. When I met Millicent, she was age sixty-two and hoping to retire soon. She worked as a home care worker in Maryland, in the United States. Caregiving is a physical profession, involving a lot of lifting, and Millicent was beginning to feel exhausted from the work. Many care workers suffer from back and knee injuries, although Millicent fortunately did not. Millicent measured her aging by her bodily strength as well as the age-determined eligibility for Social Security, the contributory pension plan available to U.S. workers (not just U.S. citizens) through the U.S. government. At the age of sixty-two, she could begin to collect Social Security, and the pension would be based on her low wages across twenty years of working in the United States. Unlike U.S. health insurance for older adults, which is not transnationally mobile, Social Security is relatively easily transferable to Ghana, through electronic bank transfers (Coe, forthcoming). Although Millicent could begin to collect Social Security at the age of sixty-two, if she waited to initiate it at the age of sixty-six, she could receive a larger monthly income. In order to retire from work in the United States, she felt she needed to build a house in Ghana. She had already completed one house in the rapidly expanding suburbs of Accra, which she hoped to rent out for additional income. In May 2015, she came to Ghana for an extended stay to oversee the construction of a second house.

At the same time, she was very concerned about the well-being of her daughter Berenice. Five years earlier, when Berenice was fifteen, Millicent had sent Berenice to junior secondary school in Ghana, allowing the school to put her several grades below her grade level in the United States. Millicent made this decision against the wishes of Berenice's father. She did so because of Berenice's educational difficulties in the United States, as well as because the parents' marriage was disintegrating. Sending a child back was a common threat among Ghanaian transnational parents, although it was carried out only in situations of a child's academic crisis or perceived delinquency and when a trusted caregiver in Ghana was available (Coe 2013). Divorce can also prompt a child's relocation to Ghana. Sending her daughter to Ghana allowed Millicent to work longer hours and as a live-in caregiver. Her inability to drive restricted the kinds of jobs she could assume; since many care workers refused live-in positions, her willingness to take a live-in job opened a wider range of employment possibilities.

At the age of twenty in June 2015, when I met her, Berenice was finishing secondary school in Ghana. Simultaneous with supervising the construction of her house, Millicent was arranging for Berenice to enroll in Scholastic Aptitude Test (SAT) classes in Ghana in preparation for her taking a test that would allow her to attend a highly reputable university in the United States. Millicent told me that she wanted Berenice to get a scholarship to a "good university" in the United States; she did not want her to go to community college, which she could do without taking the SAT (field notes, 21 June 2015). Millicent felt that because Berenice was a U.S. citizen by birth, it was her birthright to return to the United States. Ghanaian universities were difficult to get into, requiring high scores on the West African Senior School Certificate Examination (WASSCE), and the U.S. labor market did not value Ghanaian educational credentials, and so Millicent wanted her daughter to pursue higher education in the United States. Millicent's successes seemed embodied in the photo of Berenice standing on the completed foundations of the second house (figure 4.1).

Figure 4.1. In Accra, Ghana, June 2015. Photograph by Cati Coe.

Millicent and Berenice in the United States

After taking the SAT test in Ghana, Berenice came to join her parents in the United States in November 2015. This reunion prompted several months of conflict in the household. Although the parents had effectively ended their marriage and were not speaking with each other, they lived together in the same house out of economic necessity. Their modest house was under threat of foreclosure. After the economic collapse of 2008, they owed more on the house than it was worth. They were unable to resolve their financial disputes with each other to save the house from the bank's repossession, although not paying the mortgage on the house also reduced their expenses in ways that they appreciated: Millicent's husband essentially stopped working, and Millicent used the money she would have spent on housing in the United States to build a house in Ghana, securing her retirement there. Although Millicent was a U.S. citizen, and through her marriage had entitled Berenice's father, also from Ghana, to U.S. citizenship, she envisioned a return to Ghana when she could no longer work, as many other Ghanaian migrants did. Social Security payments would ensure a better quality of life in Ghana than in the United States.

When Berenice returned to the United States, she allied with her father against her mother, refusing to talk to her mother for several months. Millicent described an incident in which her pastor had come to the house one evening, from eight o'clock to midnight, and in front of him, Berenice had insulted her mother. Although Millicent appreciated the pastor's message that Berenice should obey her mother, she simultaneously resisted his advice that she respect her husband as the head of household (field notes, 3 January 2016). During that difficult winter, when her relationship with Berenice disintegrated, Millicent told me she wanted to call the police on Berenice for disrespecting her (but her friends warned her against doing so) and she wanted to kick her out of the house (but her friends told her that if her husband was a co-owner and wanted Berenice to stay, then Millicent did not have a legal basis to do so). In March 2016, Berenice began to reach out to Millicent, perhaps because her father was not helping with her daily expenses. Millicent paid for Berenice's hairdo, bought her clothes, and brought her to church, signs of their reconciliation. Berenice seemed to have recognized that her mother was necessary for her social personhood.

Berenice unfortunately did not do well on either the SAT or the WASSCE she had taken in Ghana, but she hid her test scores from her mother for a year, and Millicent had difficulty accessing them without her daughter's help. Her lack of knowledge slowed down the decisions about what to do for her daughter. Once she learned of the scores, Millicent decided to enroll Berenice in community college, but learned (in September 2016) that Berenice needed to complete the General Educational Development (GED) exam because she had not passed the WASSCE in Ghana. The GED is a proficiency test that those who do not complete high school can take to obtain a U.S. high school diploma. It is typically a more difficult route to acquire a diploma than attending high school and is less valued by employers. Over the following nine months, Berenice tried twice to pass the GED, but by May 2017, she had missed the cutoff score by a few points and Millicent seemed to have given up on the GED.[2]

Berenice shared Millicent's aspirations for her—that she become an independent adult—but their strategies for how to attain that goal often differed. Both of them changed their methods for attaining that goal fairly frequently, responding to the frustrations that they were facing. When I visited, Berenice was talking about returning to Ghana, comparing herself to her former secondary classmates who were completing university there and hoping her mother could send her to a prestigious private university known as Ashesi (field notes from visit, 13 March 2017). Millicent had now recalibrated her daughter's academic potential away from university and pinned her hopes on vocational education—mentioning nursing assistance and culinary arts. She had downgraded her sense of Berenice's capabilities. However, she was also amenable to her daughter's arguments: she was considering whether she could pay for a private university in Ghana on her Social Security earnings. A friend argued against this change in plans to Ghana, saying that if Berenice were to ever work in the United States, she would need a U.S. educational credential. Encouraging Millicent to mix interdependence with self-reliance, the same friend told her to focus on Berenice now that the house was finished, and give her two or three years of help, to get her on her feet. Millicent was eager for guidance from others, using her friends as examples to plan her own actions (see Parish 2008). She seemed sensitive to the social concern that her daughter's lack of success might reflect on her own lack of care. She needed to clarify to her daughter, herself, and others that she was not the cause of her daughter's academic disappointments, out of bitterness with the marriage, or that her financial well-being, as exemplified by her houses, came at the expense of her daughter's well-being. In other words, she needed to prove she was not a witch engaging in negative reciprocity, but a sacrificing mother engaged in balanced reciprocity.[3]

However, Berenice was not responding appropriately to a sacrificing mother. In September 2017, Millicent told me, Berenice told her that she was a "wicked woman" and that she "doesn't like her." Berenice told Millicent that she "likes other children more." Berenice accused her mother of cursing her, a veiled allusion to witchcraft, and Millicent replied that those who do not respect their parents are cursed. Millicent reported, "I wash my hands [of her]. I have suffered. I will let her go. I will go back to Ghana in January [2018], and live on my Social Security. Right now she is crippling me, with requests for clothes. I can't even buy food." Millicent told me that she told Berenice, "I am half dead; your father is half dead. But you are coming up." Thus, she felt that her capabilities to support Berenice were waning, while Berenice's abilities were increasing. Invoking the cultural script of interdependence, Millicent attempted to persuade Berenice into accepting that it was the right time in their respective life courses to switch roles as provider and receiver.

A Return to Ghana

Berenice's father surprisingly resolved Millicent's dilemmas by secretly taking Berenice to Ghana with him in December 2017, shortly before their house in the United States was repossessed by the bank (see Table 4.1 for a timeline). Although Millicent remained in contact with her daughter, her husband's action rendered her no longer responsible for her daughter's education, which stagnated without her support. Millicent was simultaneously worried about her daughter's future and relieved at having her daughter taken off her hands. As a result, after working in the United States for another year, she was able to retire to Ghana in January 2019. Three years' rent on the first house in Ghana, collected in advance, allowed her to complete the second house. However, when she returned to Ghana, she found the second house's construction was shoddy, with major sections requiring repair. She reconciled with her daughter, putting her into school for cosmetology, which she complained was an expensive course because it required so many supplies. She struggled to pursue her competing goals on her Social Security pension of USD 17,000. As a result, she returned to the United States to work nine months later, in September 2019. Many retiring migrants return to the United States to continue working or to access Medicare, the health insurance program for older adults, as they find themselves financially strapped or socially uncomfortable in Ghana. However, Millicent told me that she would not need to come back to the United States if it were not for her daughter. In the United States, she stayed on a friend's couch in her living room at a cost of USD 500 a month as she struggled to find full-time work. Her inability to drive made her employment less attractive to

TABLE 4.1

A TIMELINE OF KEY EVENTS IN A TRANSNATIONAL FAMILY

	2015	2017	2019–2020
Millicent	62 years old, working in home care in the United States	working in home care in the United States	66 years old, retired in Ghana in January 2019 but returned to the United States to work in September 2019
Berenice	20 years old, schooling in Ghana in June 2015, came to the United States in November 2015	Studying for alternative high school diploma In the United States / Returned to Ghana with her father in December 2017 / Living with father in Ghana; no schooling	24 years old, studying cosmetology in Ghana; back in the United States in November 2020
Houses	First house finished, second house foundation begun in Ghana	House in the United States lost to foreclosure	Second house roofed in early 2019
Pension	Millicent eligible at age 62, at reduced rate		Eligible for higher monthly income at age 66

clients, and she could find only weekend work until August 2020, when the pandemic made more people seek live-in home care, afraid of the risks of outbreaks in long-term care facilities.

A Postponed Retirement and Another Launching Attempt in the United States

Thus, Millicent postponed retirement again in order to help her daughter. When her mother returned to the United States, Berenice was now seemingly committed to a life course in Ghana. The timing between Berenice's and Millicent's life courses as well as their respective emplacement seemed awry: Berenice was still being launched into adulthood five years after I met her; Millicent was no longer retired, at the age of almost seventy, and remained working in the United States. When I spoke to Millicent in September 2020, she was thinking once more of bringing her daughter to the United States, because her daughter now wanted to become a nanny or housekeeper, but she was not sure how she could afford to support Berenice in the United States. Millicent had recently fallen on the pavement outside a store, requiring twelve stitches, and was feeling "tired" of working (field notes from phone call, 4 September 2020). Although she recovered, the fall reminded her that she was aging. She wanted to be in Ghana but had no concrete plans for a return.

When I most recently contacted Millicent, in December 2020, I was surprised to learn that Millicent's friend had rescued Berenice from Ghana the month before, bringing her to stay in her own house in the United States while Millicent remained working in a live-in job, the first she had found in many months and one that did not require much physical exertion. Millicent told me that the friend felt that Berenice was "wasting" her time in Ghana. Berenice left Ghana without completing her vocational degree in cosmetology. The friend was working on getting a diagnosis of a learning disability so that, in the short term, Berenice could be allowed more time during the GED test and, in the long term, be eligible for Social Security disability payments. Millicent told me excitedly about the occupations of her friend and her husband and the size of their house, as well as her friend's competence in handling the education of her own three sons, who were all "fine." Her friend had the economic and cultural capital of the middle class to navigate the complex bureaucratic hurdles and seek an official recognition of a learning disability. Without the friend's impetus, and a large enough place to host Berenice, Berenice would not have returned to the United States. Millicent paid for Berenice's plane ticket and gave her friend money for Berenice's maintenance. Berenice, for her part, was ecstatic to be back in the United States and, as a sign of her continued loyalties, spoke of bringing over her father from Ghana.

Other people can substitute for a parent if her life course is out of sync with that of her child. In particular, historically, among Ghanaian siblings, the oldest sibling often takes over the education and parenting of younger siblings when parents become unable to do so, whether because of death or retirement. However, this usually happens among full siblings, siblings of the same mother and father, because the conflicts between their parents tend to create rifts between half siblings. Berenice was the youngest of three children, born when Millicent was middle-aged, and the only child of her father. Berenice's two older siblings, the children of Millicent's first husband from Liberia, lived in Texas and California, far away from Maryland on the East Coast. Millicent had sent her first two children to live with their remarried father in Texas ("sacking them"), when they had disrespected her second husband, Berenice's father. One sign of her geographical and emotional distance from them is that her oldest daughter had had a child ten years ago, whom Millicent had never met. Her own estrangement from them no doubt led to their reluctance to take her place when she struggled to care for Berenice. However, when Berenice arrived back in the United States in November 2020, Millicent's son and his father traveled from Texas to welcome Berenice in the midst of the pandemic, indicating a possible willingness to begin caring for her. Millicent told me that Berenice was calling her brother every day on the phone. Thus, Berenice seemed to recognize in her brother another potential source of support. Although he was not in a position to be much of a benefactor, since he worked in a gas station, he sent his mother money occasionally. Others also tried to substitute for Millicent. In particular, a friend with greater cultural and economic capital has taken on the role of foster parent to Berenice. Valentina Mazzucato, Ernestina Dankyi, and Miranda Poeze (2017) have similarly noted the key role of benefactors who arrive, somewhat out of the blue, to help raise the children of transnational families.

Millicent's aspirations were reshaped by her and her daughter's life-course events. Her aspirations responded to events and adjusted accordingly, through the emotions of disappointment, anger, and advice from others. Millicent seemed mainly to be operating according to the script of self-reliance. Millicent was not relying on any of her children to help her when she was old. However, she was interested in helping her daughter to become independent and self-sufficient; failing to do so made her unworthy of respect from others. She was encouraged to help her daughter by her friends, who prodded her not to abandon her daughter despite her insulting behavior. In part, Millicent's reluctance with the script of interdependence was that her last-born did not seem to be capable of launching herself into a successful career, and thus would never be a source of support. Furthermore, her daughter was not grateful, and might never want to reciprocate for the care she had given her, because she would be permanently allied to the father from whom Millicent had bitterly separated. Yet, Millicent had to protect herself against charges of witchcraft regarding her daughter's inability to launch into successful adulthood. Invoking the script of interdependence, Millicent attempted to goad Berenice into accepting that it was time in their respective life courses to switch roles in their exchange of material resources. She flipped between the two scripts, trying to reconcile them and do both simultaneously, even as her own financial situation precluded doing so. Thus, Millicent thought she would have to be self-reliant, but she would be drained of the ability to do so by Berenice's life-course demands. It was as if she had to choose between two different investments in the future: her daughter's education or her own security, as represented in houses. Millicent grappled substantially with scripts of aging and care, as she tried to find ethical and emotional direction for her actions, in concert with significant others, such as friends and religious authorities.

Explored and Unexplored Options

Education does not have to be the sole pathway for adult success, and when one route fails, people may choose others that are deemed more likely to succeed. Berenice's possible marriage or motherhood was not being presented as an alternate route to economic security. I can only speculate on why, drawing on my wider knowledge of southern Ghana forged through my ethnographic research since 1997. One reason is that educational degrees are important in marriage markets in Ghana; social class differentiation is marked by class endogamy. Given Berenice's economic and educational prospects, potential suitors might also be suspect as wastrels. A second is that women are expected to be economically independent of their husbands, because men are not always responsible fathers. (One model of this within the family was Berenice's older sister, who was raising her child as a single mother.) Motherhood propels Ghanaian women in Ghana into economic activity, often into trading or other informal economic activities, because of the need to feed their children (Clark 1999). In any case, it felt as if those around Berenice saw only one trajectory for her: an immigrant pathway in which success is determined by migration to the United States and pursuit of an education and career there.

The first alternate script chosen for Berenice was vocational education, signaling that Berenice would not attain middle-class status in either Ghana or the United States (except through ownership of a boutique). Vocational education is a common strategy for the academically unsuccessful and working class in both the United States and Ghana, given the costs and barriers of university education. Cosmetology is an important occupation among Senegalese and other francophone West Africans in the United States, allowing female immigrants to make more money than their husbands (Babou 2008), although it is somewhat less common as an occupational niche among Ghanaians. The second script chosen, somewhat unusually by Millicent's friend, at least in my experience among the Ghanaian diaspora, was attempting state recognition of a learning disability and aspiring to permanent reliance on the U.S. welfare system.[4] In some ways, this pathway was a recognition of Berenice's difficulties with launching, since disability payments would launch her into adult poverty (albeit stable and possibly independent poverty) in the United States. The aspirations for Berenice were recalibrated and downgraded in response to changing circumstances, while Millicent's aspirations for retirement, in contrast, did not shift, but instead were simply deferred over and over again.

Millicent's aspirations for retirement were intertwined with her aspirations for Berenice's adulthood. She doubted that her daughter would be willing or able to help her when she needed care. Instead, the daughter seemed committed to interdependence with her father, who had done little to help her, in Millicent's eyes. Yet Millicent was acutely aware that, for Berenice's own successful future, she should be in the United States. She worried that she could not afford to support her there on her pension. For her own self-sufficient aging, she needed her daughter to be self-sufficient in adulthood.

Conclusion

Aside from Berenice's academic difficulties, perhaps caused by a learning deficiency as suggested by Millicent's friend and adopted by Millicent as a partial explanation of her daughter's troubles, and the end of Millicent's marriage, the major reason that these cultural scripts did not work was because of Millicent's low-wage work. As Elizabeth Cooper and David Pratten (2015) have noted, uncertainties are socially produced. The script of self-reliance functioned like a Gramscian hegemony, providing an outline for a moral life that only members of a certain social class could live up to, and thus attain respect and status for meeting a cultural ideal (Gramsci 1978; Williams 1990). This seems like a case of cruel optimism, in which pursuing the object of desire prevents one from attaining happiness (Berlant 2011). The scripts of middle-class life in Ghana, through which Berenice viewed herself, particularly in her dreams of attending Ashesi University like her former classmates, were not affordable to her mother, a care worker whose pension did not stretch very far. Given the mother and daughter's history of mistrust and conflict, they were not able to forge a new inscription of intergenerational care out of the ruins of cultural scripts that had worked for others in other circumstances, but which were not working for them.

Millicent seems to illustrate that retirement is a classist dream out of reach for a globalized working-class. Millicent tried to use transnationalism to overcome the limitations of her low-wage work. She was partly successful in this strategy: by losing a house to foreclosure in the United States, she was able to finish a house in Ghana, and she could afford to live on her Social Security payments in Ghana but not in the United States. Self-sufficient retirement, so long as it was in Ghana, seemed possible. Transnationalism was necessary, but not sufficient, to aspire in a working-class family. Millicent found supporting her daughter into successful adulthood during her retirement required continued transnationalism, prompting a new migration and a renewed period of work. An older adult needed to continue to pour her resources into supporting the next generation, and yet she did not feel assured that such care would be reciprocated should she require resources in the future. We observe their perseverance in trying to attain the object of desire, and considerable flexibility in switching between aspirations to structure their activities, when one aspiration seemed unattainable.

Millicent blamed neither herself nor society for these struggles, instead unleashing her anger on her daughter and ex-husband, further damaging these relationships. Her struggles illustrate the emotional cost of class-based cultural scripts of the life course, as an aging, low-wage migrant aspired to retire and raise her daughter to a successful adulthood simultaneously.

Acknowledgments

This research was funded by the Research Council of Rutgers University. I am grateful to my interlocutors for including me in their lives. The editors and the participants in the conference panel and small workshop from which this volume emerged provided incisive comments on earlier drafts of this chapter.

NOTES

1. Original in Akuapem Twi: "Sɛ wo maame anaa wo papa anaa obi a hwɛ wo na wo se yi aba de a, edu baabi hwɛ no na wei [*pointing to his teeth*] no ntutu."
2. The GED was revamped in 2014 to become more difficult. The pass rate in 2016 and 2017 was 79 percent and 80 percent, respectively (Gewertz 2018).
3. Millicent did not talk to me of these concerns about being accused, but she did actively accuse her husband's family of ruining him, and she was concerned about her daughter being possessed by an evil spirit as a result. As I have witnessed in other fieldwork in Ghana, lack of

success in life is often blamed on witchcraft, and mothers, as the prime suspect of the cause of their children's disability or mental illness, do everything they can to deflect blame and cast it on members of the father's family.

4. The U.S. state, even gutted through neoliberalism, offered more social protection than the Ghanaian state to older adults and the disabled. Although the Ghanaian state is much more of a developmentalist state, its resources are concentrated on the young who can contribute to economic development (Aboderin and Ferreira 2008; Doh 2012).

REFERENCES

Aboderin, Isabella. 2006. *Intergenerational Support and Old Age in Africa.* New Brunswick, NJ: Transaction.

Aboderin, Isabella, and Monica Ferreira. 2008. "Linking Ageing to Development Agendas in Sub-Saharan Africa: Challenges and Approaches." *Journal of Population Ageing* 1 (1): 51–73.

Ahearn, Laura M. 2001. *Invitations to Love: Literacy, Love Letters, and Social Change in Nepal.* Ann Arbor: University of Michigan Press.

Babou, Cheikh Anta. 2008. "Migration and Cultural Change: Money, 'Caste,' Gender, and Social Status among Senegalese Female Hair Braiders in the United States." *Africa Today* 55 (2): 3–22.

Bähre, Erik. 2012. "The Janus Face of Insurance in South Africa: From Costs to Risk, from Networks to Bureaucracies." *Africa* 82 (1): 150–167.

Behrends, Andrea, Sung-Joon Park, and Richard Rottenburg. 2014. "Travelling Models: Introducing an Analytic Concept to Globalisation Studies." In *Travelling Models in African Conflict Management: Translating Technologies of Social Ordering*, edited by Andrea Behrends, Sung-Joon Park, and Richard Rottenburg, 1–42. Leiden: Brill.

Berlant, Lauren. 2011. *Cruel Optimism.* Durham, NC: Duke University Press.

Clark, Gracia. 1999. "Mothering, Work, and Gender in Urban Asante Ideology and Practice." *American Anthropologist* 101 (4): 717–729.

Coe, Cati. 2011. "What Is the Impact of Transnational Migration on Family Life? Women's Comparisons of Internal and International Migration in a Small Town in Ghana." *American Ethnologist* 38 (1): 148–163.

———. 2012. "Growing Up and Going Abroad: How Ghanaian Children Imagine Transnational Migration." In "Transnational Migration and the Study of Children." Special issue, *Journal of Ethnic and Migration Studies* 38 (6): 913–931.

———. 2013. *The Scattered Family: Parenting, African Migrants, and Global Inequality.* Chicago: University of Chicago Press.

———. 2016. "Orchestrating Care in Time: Ghanaian Migrant Women, Family, and Reciprocity." *American Anthropologist* 118 (1): 37–48.

———. 2019a. "Beyond Kin Care? Institutional Facilities in the Imaginations of Elderly Presbyterians in Southern Ghana." *Africa Today* 65 (3): 69–88.

———. 2019b. *The New American Servitude: Political Belonging among African Immigrant Home Care Workers.* New York: New York University Press.

———. 2020. "Social Class in Transnational Perspective: Emotional Responses to the Status Paradox among Ghanaian Transnational Migrants." *Africa Today* 66 (3–4): 161–180.

———. Forthcoming. "The Contradictions of Transnational Care: Imaginaries and Materialities of Social Protection in Returns to Ghana." In *Going Back: An Anthropology of Return*, edited by Deborah Boehm and Mikaela Rogozen-Soltar. New York: New York University Press.

Coe, Cati, and Erdmute Alber. 2018. "Age-Inscriptions and Social Change: Introduction." *Anthropology and Aging Quarterly* 39 (1): 1–17.

Cooper, Elizabeth, and David Pratten, eds. 2015. *Ethnographies of Uncertainty in Africa.* Basingstoke: Palgrave Macmillan.

Deneva, Neda. 2012. "Transnational Aging Carers: On Transformation of Kinship and Citizenship in the Context of Migration among Bulgarian Muslims in Spain." *Social Politics* 19 (1): 105–128.

Doh, Daniel. 2012. *Exploring Social Protection Arrangements for Older People: Evidence from Ghana*. Saarbrücken, Germany: Lambert Academic Publishing.

Dovie, Delali Adjoa. 2018. "Utilization of Digital Literacy in Retirement Planning among Ghanaian Formal and Informal Sector Workers." *Interações: Sociedade e as novas modernidades*, no. 34: 113–140. https://doi.org/10.31211/interacoes.n34.2018.a6.

Durham, Deborah, and Jacqueline Solway, eds. 2017. *Elusive Adulthoods: The Anthropology of New Maturities*. Bloomington: Indiana University Press.

Gewertz, Catherine. 2018. "GED Passing Rates Rise, but Fewer Students Take Exam after Redesign." *Education Week Blog*, 21 February 2018. https://blogs.edweek.org/edweek/high_school_and_beyond/2018/02/GED_more_taking_but_fewer_passing_equivalency_exam_after_redesigned.html.

Golomski, Casey. 2015. "Compassion Technology: Life Insurance and the Remaking of Kinship in Swaziland's Age of HIV." *American Ethnologist* 42 (1): 81–96.

Gramsci, Antonio. 1978. *Selections from Political Writings 1921–1926*. Translated and edited by Quentin Hoare. New York: International Publishers.

Hromadžić, Azra, and Monika Palmberger, eds. 2018. *Care across Distance: Ethnographic Explorations of Aging and Migration*. New York: Berghahn Books.

Jeffrey, Craig. 2010. *Timepass: Youth, Class, and the Politics of Waiting in India*. Stanford, CA: Stanford University Press.

Kar, Sohini. 2018. *Financializing Poverty: Labor and Risk in Indian Microfinance*. Stanford, CA: Stanford University Press.

Kroeker, Lena L. 2020. "Moving to Retain Class Status: Spatial Mobility among Older Middle-Class People in Kenya." *Africa Today* 66 (3–4): 136–158.

Lamb, Sarah. 2016. "Traveling Institutions as Transnational Aging: The Old-Age Home in Idea and Practice in India." In *Transnational Aging: Current Insights and Future Challenges*, edited by Vincent Horn and Cornelia Schweppe, 178–199. New York: Routledge.

Mains, Daniel. 2011. *Hope Is Cut: Youth, Unemployment, and the Future in Urban Ethiopia*. Philadelphia: Temple University Press.

Masquelier, Adeline. 2005. "The Scorpion's Sting: Youth, Marriage and the Struggle for Social Maturity in Niger." *Journal of the Royal Anthropological Institute* 11: 59–83.

Mattingly, Cheryl. 2014. *Moral Laboratories: Family Peril and the Struggle for a Good Life*. Berkeley: University of California Press.

Mazzucato, Valentina, Ernestina Dankyi, and Miranda Poeze. 2017. "Mapping Transnational Networks of Care from a Multi-actor and Multi-sited Perspective." In *Situating Children of Migrants across Borders and Origins: A Methodological Overview*, edited by Claudio Bolzman, Laura Bernardi, and Jean-Marie Le Goff, 269–284. Dordrecht: Springer.

Nelson-Cofie, Akosua Mensima. 1998. "Maintaining the Costs and Care of the Elderly in Ghana: Will It Work?" Master's thesis, University of Ghana.

Nieswand, Boris. 2011. *Theorising Transnational Migration: The Status Paradox of Migration*. New York: Routledge.

Parish, Steven. 2008. *Subjectivity and Suffering in American Culture: Possible Selves*. New York: Palgrave Macmillan.

Rasmussen, Susan. 2018. "Intergenerational Relationships and Emergent Notions of Reciprocity, Dependency, Caregiving, and Aging in Tuareg Migration." In *Care across Distance: Ethnographic Explorations of Aging and Migration*, edited by Azra Hromadžić and Monika Palmberger, 55–75. New York: Berghahn Books.

Roth, Claudia. 2007. "'Tu ne peux pas rejeter ton enfant!': Contrat entre les générations, sécurité sociale et vieillesse en milieu urbain burkinabè." *Cahiers d'études africaines*, no. 185: 93–116.

Sokolovsky, Jay, ed. 2009. *The Cultural Context of Aging: Worldwide Perspectives*. Westport, CT: Praeger.

Stack, Carol. 1996. *Call to Home: African Americans Reclaim the Rural South*. New York: Basic Books.

Stack, Carol, and Linda M. Burton. 1993. "Kinscripts." *Journal of Comparative Family Studies* 24 (2): 157–170.

Swidler, Ann. 2001. *Talk of Love: How Culture Matters*. Chicago: University of Chicago Press.
Van der Geest, Sjaak. 1997. "Money and Respect: The Changing Value of Old Age in Rural Ghana." *Africa* 67 (4): 534–559.
Williams, Rory. 1990. *A Protestant Legacy: Attitudes to Death and Illness among Older Aberdonians*. Oxford, UK: Clarendon Press.

CHAPTER 5

Between Aging Parents There and Young Children Here

THE ASPIRATIONS OF LATE-MIDDLE-AGED PERUVIAN MIGRANTS IN SANTIAGO AS A TRANSNATIONAL SANDWICH GENERATION

Alfonso Otaegui

Late middle age—the period between the late fifties and early sixties—is a time when many reflect on life and its purpose. It is a point at which it makes sense to look backward and take stock of one's life. Migrants at this life stage are in a very particular position, as their lives have taken them to different places and experiences: for them, life as a journey is not merely a metaphor. How does living half of one's life in a foreign country shape aspirations in later life and reflections in late middle age? Is the stage that follows late middle age the end of mobility? These are some of the questions that may arise for those at this time of life. Besides, improved quality of life is redefining late middle age all over the world, and the prospects for the next life stage may seem more promising. Thus, it now makes sense to also look forward at this point in life.

Aging populations have created socioeconomic challenges for governments worldwide—related to employment, health care, loneliness, and other issues—as well as cultural changes around the experience of aging and intergenerational relationships.[1] Improved life expectancy and better quality of life have led to a more vital experience of aging, fostered by "active aging" policies that encourage older adults to stay in work and delay retirement (Ney 2005). The status of advanced age has changed in recent decades, with greater value attributed to youth (Bennett and Hodkinson 2012; Blaikie 1999), leading to a new ambivalence around age. When it comes to intergenerational relationships, in many countries middle-aged people have become a "sandwich generation," providing care to their parents and their children simultaneously (Chisholm 1999; Walton 2018). How do these changes in aging experience intersect with migration? How does being long established in the destination country affect the experience of late middle age? This chapter will address these questions through the case study of Peruvian migrants in Chile.

Chile has one of the older populations in Latin America, with a life expectancy of 80.5 years. Almost 3.5 million people—roughly one-fifth of the population—are over 60 years of age (Ministerio de Desarrollo Social y Familia 2017). Consequently, Chile has implemented public policies around active aging, and its discourse permeates everyday life. For instance, advertisements often include older adults doing activities that are usually associated with young people.

In the 2017 census, Peruvian migrants were the largest immigrant group in Chile, making up 25.2 percent of the migrant population (INE 2018, 8).[2] Waves of Peruvian immigration in the 1980s, 1990s, and 2000s changed the urban landscape in Chile, especially Santiago (Torres and Hidalgo 2009; Ducci and Rojas 2010), with the proliferation of Peruvian stores and restaurants (Bonhomme 2013; Imilan 2013). Peruvian migrants who arrived during those waves, and have lived in Chile for over two decades, are now approaching late middle age. They thus constitute a good case study to address our research questions.

Late-middle-aged Peruvian migrants claim to feel younger than they expected, and they act accordingly—working hard, delaying retirement—embodying the discourse of active aging. But is this a consequence of how discourse and policies on active aging have permeated everyday life in Chile, or is it a reflection of research participants' own moral values and work ethics? Moreover, because of the greater value attributed to youth and staying active, participants face a choice between claiming the authority of advanced age and claiming the status of retained youth. How do migrants experience this ambivalence toward age?

Questions on vitality and ambivalence toward age converge in the phenomenon of the "sandwich generation," which takes care of the older generation and honors their advanced age while also providing support to children and, in line with the active aging paradigm, aims not to become a burden in the future. How do migrants navigate the experience of having care obligations "upwards and downwards" (Walton 2021, 28), when their parents live in their home country and their children in the destination one?

This chapter addresses these questions through the study of the aspirations of late-middle-aged Peruvian migrants around work, everyday life, well-being, death, and even beyond death. It analyzes Peruvian migrants' discourses on vitality and dedication to work and their plans for retirement. Next, it discusses the diverse arrangements of this "transnational sandwich generation," as these late-middle-aged migrants provide good care to their parents in Peru, even though they do not want to receive care from their children in Chile. The chapter addresses this apparent contradiction and reflects on what they consider to be their life's purpose by exploring their migration stories and aspirations to a "good life" (Fischer 2014; Pauli, this volume). Sacrifice appears as a common trope underlying past stories and future projects. This notion seems to provide retrospective meaning to their lives and lays the foundation for an idea of legacy. The conclusion discusses the findings and argues that the "in-betweenness" (Bhabha 1996) of transnational migration can work as a metaphor to better understand late middle age.

This study is based on sixteen months of ethnographic fieldwork among Peruvian migrants aged forty-eight to sixty-nine years who have lived in Chile for about ten to thirty years.[3] Most research participants are upper-middle-class professionals with college degrees, while some are working-class migrants. I met them at the Latin American Church, a common point of reference for migrants in Santiago, which provides a space for expressions of popular devotion and also offers legal advice (Ducci and Rojas 2010, 107).[4] I joined a Peruvian Christian brotherhood and participated in regular meetings, masses, spiritual retreats, processions, and fundraising events. Through the brotherhood I was able to access other Peruvian social circles, such as business and city associations. Even though I conducted semi-structured interviews with twenty-five research participants (sixteen men and nine women), most insights come from participant observation and casual conversations.

The Experience of Aging: Between Retained Youth and Menacing Old Age

"I feel young, as if I were forty years old," says Estefanía, a fifty-seven-year-old bank employee who has lived in Chile for over half her life.[5] We have been talking for over an hour at her lovely two-story house in the south of Santiago. Every detail in the living room seems carefully chosen, which fits her elegant appearance. "People always think I am younger than I really am," she adds, as most participants do. Martín, a lower-middle-class security guard, said people think he is fifty-two, although he is actually sixty-five years old. Pablo, an upper-middle-class businessman, states he feels forty, even though he is sixty. The participants typically declare that they feel much younger than they are and that people around them believe them to be at least ten years younger. They also compare themselves to their parents and grandparents at the same age and find themselves much more vital and active than how they recall those people. "Forty years ago, I was twenty, and my father was my current age—he looked so much older.[6] He would not go out, except for family meetings. I go out a lot, but I don't know if my children see me now the way I used to see my parents then," says Mariano, a sixty-two-year-old notary who has lived for twenty-five years in Chile.

In conversations with participants on their experience of age, a standard trope is the unexpected vitality they feel and how this translates into work and social life (and which matches my observations during fieldwork, attending innumerable social meetings, dinners, and parties). "I always have meetings and appointments—last Friday it was the birthday of a sister-in-law, on Saturday the birthday of Daniela from the Peruvian Club, and Sunday the birthday of my daughter Virginia. On Monday [it was] another compadre's birthday. On Tuesday, I went to Concepción for work, and I returned yesterday, Thursday evening," says

Esteban, a sixty-four-year-old businessman. He arranged the interview at the Latin American Church, an hour before the Holy Friday procession. Rather than eager participation in a university study, the meeting is a concession, a space made in his tight schedule for a fellow brother. He is just so busy every day of the week.

Commitment to work and family seems to be the basis of self-worth for research participants. According to participants' recollections, their migration stories usually consist of a succession of better jobs (the literature on migration in Chile presents a more nuanced picture instead. See, for example, Stefoni et al. 2017, Contreras et al. 2013, and Bonhomme 2021, on the hardships of migrants trying to access the labor market in Chile). Esteban describes how he came to Chile in the late 1980s, how he managed to reach the privileged position he occupies today, and how his success results from his efforts. He concludes, smiling proudly, "My daughters say I am a workaholic." Esteban does not utter this term in a negative tone, nor is he the only one to describe himself with that word. Lower-income participants describe themselves in similar terms. Take Ana, a sixty-one-year-old domestic worker who raised her two children alone in Chile. Her story resembles that of many other lower-income Peruvian women: she came alone in the 1990s; she started working as a live-in domestic worker; and a couple of years later she was able to bring her children from Peru and to work as a live-out domestic worker (cf. Stefoni and Bonhomme 2014). "She cannot even handle holidays," says her forty-three-year-old daughter, laughing. "She gets anxious after two weeks of not working, she would even sell her holidays!"[7] For the participants, vitality equates to hard work. This also informs how they view retirement.

Perspectives on Retirement

Almost none of the participants picture themselves as retired. "Not working? I would die!" says Esteban, the sixty-four-year-old businessman, assertively. They might officially retire, but will not give up working. Ana, the sixty-one-year-old domestic worker and single mother, recently retired, but still works three eight- to ten-hour shifts every week. "Not working? I would get bored," says Ignacio, a sixty-one-year-old warehouse manager. Dedication to work not only is the basis of self-worth or an expression of vitality. It also responds to a more mundane aspect of everyday life: boredom. So it is with Roberto, a fifty-nine-year-old factory manager. He is second-in-command at a textile factory. After a long day of work, he gets home at around six o'clock. His grown-up children live independently, and his wife is still at work at that time. He used to get bored, so, about three years ago, he bought a car and started to work as an Uber driver a couple of days a week. "In this way, I will have finished paying for the car in a couple of years," he says. "In those hours I do something, I work a little more."

Although vitality plays a role in such discourses on retirement, the pension system in Chile is a conditioning factor. Indeed, it provides a sound basis for what is claimed to be the decision to never stop working. The Administradoras de Fondos de Pensiones, or AFP, is a capitalization system run by private-sector pension funds. Workers must contribute a fixed percentage of their salary toward a fund.

A private AFP invests the money and makes it grow. Once the worker retires, this sum—which varies based on the contributions made—provides a salary. This system has been severely criticized, especially in recent years. Participants know their pensions will not allow them to live according to their expectations. They knew this long ago, when they first moved to Chile in their late thirties, without a working life that would be long enough to build up a good retirement fund. On top of this, some participants did not save money for the long term or buy an apartment. Instead, they put their children first. Francisco, a fifty-seven-year-old janitor, sent his extra money back to Peru to pay for his children's studies. Roberto, the fifty-nine-year-old factory manager who occasionally drives an Uber, invested all his money in educating his children at the top educational institutions in Chile. Neither has an apartment of his own; they still rent. However, neither regrets these decisions. They prioritized the next generation over their own future.

Early Signs of Advanced Age

Participants claim at first to feel an unexpected vitality for their age. However, in more extended conversations, they admit that they have started to notice early signs of frailty, such as high blood sugar, diabetes, hypertension, or fatigue. Some participants feel less energetic at social events. "'Before, I could stay up to 3:00–4:00 A.M., now it is midnight, and I am already yawning," says Estefanía, the fifty-seven-year-old bank employee. Esteban, the sixty-four-year-old businessman, reveals that meetings with old friends are shorter, as they all feel tired.

In recent years, these late-middle-aged men and women have managed to prevent the frailties of old age from harming their active lifestyles by eating less fried food or reducing sugar intake, among other things. Some are more careful with spicy Peruvian dressings. Others have noticed early signs of aging in their lower resistance to the usual sources of stress. To battle high blood pressure, some participants have had to quit coffee—which they find very difficult because it affects their work performance—start taking medication, or doing cardio exercises.

These experiences of aging seem to contradict the participants' discourse on vitality. Many resolve this contradiction by evoking the dichotomy between body and spirit and claiming to have retained their youth despite the body's natural decay. For example, Javiera, a fifty-three-year-old domestic worker, says, "In my spirit, I feel young, but when it comes to the body, my little bones ache."[8]

Early signs of advanced age can threaten participants' identity as workers and providers. Teresa, a fifty-three-year-old in-house domestic worker, sends money to pay for her mother's cancer treatment in Peru. "Sometimes I feel the *achaques* [ailments resulting from old age]—my hand hurts—but it is better not to think about age and to keep working [to support my mother]," she says stoically. Ignacio, the sixty-one-year-old warehouse manager, is starting to experience what might be the early symptoms of Alzheimer's: he has started to forget things. He is mainly concerned about his performance at work: "I am worried that it might affect how people see me at work, that they might see this [forgetfulness] as a lack of interest in work."

Participants follow typical active aging narratives. They equate staying active and working to staying young. They measure their self-worth based on how much they dedicate themselves to work and even take pride in being called workaholics. They cannot think of themselves in the future, not working, or picture themselves as older adults. This inability is not surprising, as most have very active lives and are almost as busy as they have always been. The age-related frailties they experience, though acknowledged, are manageable. In a way, these late-middle-aged workers are halfway between retaining youth and entering a menacingly quiet old age. Taking age as socially constructed and subjectively felt, they are certainly no longer young, but nor are they yet "older adults," as their parents seemed to be at this age.

Where does the aura these late-middle-aged migrants possess, of "active aging," come from? Dora Sampaio (2020), in her work with return migrants in the Azores, highlights the effect that transnational mobility has on the understanding of aging. Migrants returning from the United States compare themselves to the local nonmigrant population, revealing a different mind set toward aging. Returnees claim to pay greater attention to their health than locals do, worry about becoming a burden on their children, and display a rigorous work ethic. Sampaio (2020, 11) suggests that this shift toward active aging is influenced by their time in the United States, which produces hybrid formulations of aging subjectivities.

Two decades in Chile, with its active aging policies and neoliberal way of life, could be a plausible reason for the participants to adhere to the active aging narrative. However, their migration stories reveal another cause: the ethic of hard work, which they have practiced since they were young and still living in Peru, and which continued during their journey to Chile and subsequent settlement. Participants value themselves as workers and providers, and to keep working as hard as ever means to keep being who they are. Thus, the attitude that underlies this apparent "active aging" is not a new one: it results from the persistence of this longtime identity. Besides, as members of the sandwich generation, they must provide for their parents and children, which requires even more effort.

Intergenerational Relationships: Between Aging Parents and Dependent Children

The contrast between the two kinds of intergenerational relationships experienced by members of the sandwich generation sheds light on their perspectives toward the future. Peruvian migrants assume caring for their parents as a natural responsibility, as fulfilling a reasonable expectation. Yet they reject the possibility of turning into recipients of care provided by their children.

Vincent Horn, in his analysis of the literature on transnational families, synthesizes older adults' situations into four categories: the "stayers," the "transnational travelers," the "late-in-life family joiners," and the "ones aging abroad" (2019, 25–34).[9] These categories, though preliminary and fluid, for the most part well describe the situations of the parents of the research participants: the "stayers" who have remained in Peru, the "transnational travelers" who move back and forth between Peru and Chile for a couple of months a year, the "late-in-life family joiners" who come to live in Chile at an advanced age and are supported by their migrant children, and "the ones aging abroad." This last category does not fit the participants' parents but fits the participants themselves. Many have spent half of their lives in Chile, some even longer.

Esteban's parents fit the first and largest category, the "stayers." Esteban, the upper-middle-class businessman, and his brothers can afford to travel to Lima to visit them often. They have arranged for people to take care of their aging parents. One of his brothers lives in Chile, while the other returned to Lima for work some years ago. The three brothers tried to convince their parents to come to Chile, but they refused, stating that their networks and lives are in Peru. Their mother told them: "You three and my grandchildren, you all work, who am I going to stay with?"[10] Esteban seems satisfied and at peace with the care provided to his parents.

This air of duty fulfilled is not at all apparent in Teresa's case. The fifty-three-year-old domestic worker is employed at a house in Vitacura, an upper-class neighborhood in Santiago. Like many live-in domestic workers, she works fourteen hours a day, from seven in the morning to ten at night. She has a single day off on the weekend. Teresa has thought of going back to Peru more than once, as her mother has breast cancer. On one visit home, looking at her ill mother and her single son, she almost decided to stay. But Teresa has no job in Peru and no one to support her. Her brothers are there, with her mother, but she does not trust them to provide good enough care. "They are there, but they are men," she says. She wanted to return to Peru two years ago, but the priest at her church convinced her otherwise, reminding her that, in Santiago, at least she could work and send money to support her family.

Only one case, that of Gerardo's parents, fits the category of "transnational travelers."[11] Gerardo is a forty-nine-year-old biochemist. His parents have always been in a good financial situation, so he has never had to send remittances. His parents frequently visit on family occasions, such as the births of Gerardo's daughters and nieces—Gerardo's sister migrated to Chile before him. His parents have Chilean ID cards, which allow them to come more frequently and stay longer than with a tourist visa. They stay in Santiago for two or three months at a time and then spend two to three months in their hometown of Arequipa in Peru.

Roberto's parents and Estefanía's parents are examples of "late-in-life family joiners." In both cases, the children invited their parents to come to Chile when the latter passed the age of seventy. Roberto's mother passed away a couple of years after arriving, while his father died more recently. Estefanía's mother also died some years after arriving. Her father, aged eighty-eight, is still alive and is mainly cared for by Estefanía and her sister Romina, both of whom are childless. He sees his other daughters, who also live in Chile, less often. Neither Roberto nor Estefanía has any family members remaining in Lima. Roberto's siblings have all migrated to Chile, while Estefanía's two brothers live in the United States and Japan.

A clear sense of duty toward their parents is apparent among these Peruvian migrants. When retracing their stories, from their early years in Peru to coming to Chile and their initial struggles, they convey the respect and gratitude they feel toward their parents. For example, Pablo, the sixty-year-old businessman, recalls how hardworking his mother was, despite having no formal education. "She would prepare meals and sell them to companies, or [to the public] on special occasions such as national holidays," he says. "With all her efforts, she was able to raise the three of us to become professionals," he adds proudly, as he and his two siblings all have college degrees. In other cases, this sense of duty transforms into constant worry. Teresa talks to her widowed mother by videocall every night: "I am always checking on her. Through the camera, I see her. I call her every day."

Participants display great respect for older adults for their age and experience. Estefanía's father is treated with reverence at meetings of the Brotherhood of the Lord of Miracles. Many members of the brotherhood state, during formal speeches, what an honor it is for this former member to be present. At the celebration of Arequipa's anniversary, the Arequipeños association in Santiago gave Sister María, a seventy-eight-year-old nun, an award recognizing her decades of providing support to migrants at the Latin American Church. The traditional status of advanced age is unquestioned when it comes to their parents' generation.

The participants dedicate a great deal of effort to taking care of their parents. They explicitly show respect for the experience and authority of older adults, whether their own parents or others. It is thus astonishing to hear these late-middle-aged Peruvian migrants state very firmly that they do not want their own children to take care of them in the future, so as to avoid burdening the next generation.

A possible explanation for that apparent contradiction is that caring for aging parents is tiring, and Peruvian migrants want to spare their children the experience. It requires a lot of logistical and financial effort, even apart from the emotional stress when a parent's health declines, or when they feel unable to provide the care they would have wanted for their parents. Yet the migrants convey a sense of duty and even pride for the care they provide to their parents, so the argument of not wanting their children to experience this effort seems insufficient.

However, that explanation also offers a clue, as participants focus on their children as a way of subliminally talking about themselves. As the following section shows, by neglecting themselves and sacrificing themselves for others, late-middle-aged Peruvian migrants are fulfilling their own life purpose.

Janus's Vantage Point: The Two Gazes of Late Middle Age

The participants of this study are at a life stage in which it makes sense to look backward and forward at the same time. In ancient Roman mythology, Janus is the god of transitions and duality. Ancient statues represent him with two faces looking in opposite directions. This vantage point serves as an appropriate metaphor for the aspirations of late-middle-aged Peruvian migrants. Having reached this point in their lives, these migrants have a long past to look back on, but they do not yet feel as though they are at the end of the road. Just as they are sandwiched between older parents and young children, they are between two stages of life: a claimed retained youth and looming old age. And, a common thread appears when looking in both directions: an aesthetics of sacrifice.

Looking Backward: All the Sacrifices We Made

Conversations on aspirations and life stories as migrants inevitably lead to reflections about the past and the present. Both casual discussions and semiformal interviews on their life stories turn into exchanges on life's purpose. When addressing this subject directly and explicitly, replies are quite normative and dwell on family and Christian devotion, which is no surprise given that most participants belong to Peruvian Christian brotherhoods. However, when reading between the lines of interviews or conversations about life-changing events—migration journeys, complicated health problems, the death of a relative—an aesthetics of sacrifice reveals itself.

Two migration stories illustrate this point. Roberto, the fifty-nine-year-old factory manager, came to Chile in 1997. He had had a hard time in Peru during the late 1980s and early 1990s, amid a constant economic crisis that left him perpetually unemployed or sub-employed. His wife received a job offer in Chile and migrated six months before him. He had to stay alone in Peru taking care of their two little boys. "It was tough to live like that, the distance, the children away from their mom," he says. He finally came to Chile by bus, with the children, but was stopped at the border. He lacked some documents he needed to exit Peru with his sons, and he had no money even for a hotel room. Some locals helped him with accommodation and food, and he finally managed to get to Santiago. The first years were challenging: uncertainties about staying or going back, getting used to the food, finding a school for the children, finding a stable job for himself. With a great deal of effort, he and his wife managed to achieve a good life. Later, all his siblings also migrated to Chile.

Javiera, the fifty-three-year-old domestic worker, also recalls early hardships: the discrimination her children suffered in Chile due to their skin color, their accent, their mother's job and appearance, and how difficult it was to fit in (cf. Tijoux 2007, 2013).

Twenty years later, both migrants describe their current situation as a satisfactory outcome of their struggles. Roberto is happy that his two sons are professionals. Javiera is proud that her eldest daughter got a college degree and even bought an apartment before her death, while her son has his own small air-conditioning company. Their stories make sense to them as a sacrifice for their children. That sacrifice becomes, retrospectively, their own life's purpose. Their children are living proof that all the effort was worth it.

Settled in the Present

The present is also full of sacrifices, as participants' repeated and proud references to their workaholism indicate. Their current situation is the result of their decades in Chile, an experience that also informs their aspirations toward the future, such as to return to Peru after retirement.

Aspirations by themselves are not enough to achieve a good life, as such projects are made possible—or are limited—by concrete opportunities (Fischer 2014, 208; see also Amrith, Sakti, and Sampaio, this volume). In Chile, Peruvian migrants found opportunities for an economically stable life. This was true for both upper-middle-class and working-class participants. The former had college degrees and, in general, better opportunities—such as a position in a firm—while the latter came to look for low-paying jobs, such as in-house domestic work, cleaning, and so forth. In both cases, participants were able to provide for their families in Chile and back in Peru, albeit to different degrees and occupying different socioeconomic strata. Surprisingly, most participants declare that they had not planned to stay in Chile for as long as they did when they migrated. Rather than "settling" in Chile, they realized that they had "dis-adapted" to Peru after a couple of years. A short visit to Peru revealed to them that they could no longer deal with simple annoyances of everyday life, such as the chaotic traffic in Lima, or some messiness here and there. Life in Chile was more organized, but they missed their home country and their families. Decades later, leaving aside those who can afford to travel back regularly, most participants conclude that, nowadays, missing Peru is less hard, mainly due to two factors: communication technologies and the wide availability of Peruvian products.

Even though participants declare they have stayed in touch with their families in Peru since the advent of cheap phone calls (Vertovec 2009, 55), they emphasize how much easier it is now, with smartphones. WhatsApp videocalls allow them to have close, visual contact with their relatives, while Facebook allows them to exercise copresence through the live streams of communal events such as birthday parties and religious processions (Otaegui, 2023) (figure 5.1).

Most participants recall struggling to adapt to the local food in their first years. Nowadays, besides the large number of Peruvian restaurants (Imilan 2013), most Peruvian products can easily be found in specialized stores. Considering also the Christian brotherhoods honoring Peruvian icons and the Peruvian business and city associations, it can be said that many Peruvian experiences are re-created in Chile. In a way, it is easier to live in Chile as a Peruvian migrant now than it was three decades ago.

With communication technologies, and the availability of Peruvian products and traditions, it is easier for the participants to stay in their destination country. The necessary trade-offs for a good life are fewer now, or are at least more manageable, to the point that no participant, with one exception, declared that he or she wants to return to Peru after retirement. The future seems to be somewhat vague in the participants' imaginations, concerning not only their retirement plans but life itself.

When asked how many more years they think they will live, or how these years might be, the answers are uncertain, fuzzy—as fuzzy as the age categories they use to define themselves. Estefanía, the fifty-seven-year-old bank employee, replies:

Figure 5.1. Here and there: Peruvian migrants live streaming the Lord of Miracles celebration in Santiago (Chile). Photograph by Alfonso Otaegui.

"Perhaps ten more years. In my family, people do not live long." Javiera, the fifty-three-year-old domestic worker, has never thought of how long she would live. "That's up to the One above us [God] to decide," she states. She would like to live fifteen more years. "I would not like to be old and depend on other people, on my children," she says.

Death seems not to be their biggest worry. When speaking about death and when it will come, the participants accept it as a natural fact of life. As is usually the case among older adults (Duque 2019, 2022; Miller et al. 2021; Garvey and Miller 2021), participants are more worried about a possible loss of autonomy in their last years rather than death itself. This loss of autonomy would mean turning into a burden. The aspirations of these Peruvian migrants, however, transcend their own future and even reach the next generation.

Looking Forward: Sacrifice and Legacy

When these late-middle-aged migrants reflect on their lives, backward and forward, the aesthetics of sacrifice permeating the discourse is coupled with a desire to leave something behind. In most cases, this translates into the well-being of their children. As noted previously, some Peruvian migrants have no property, as they decided to invest instead in their children's education. Most participants see education as a tool for advancing in life, which will enable their children to become resilient and independent. Elena, a forty-nine-year-old nurse, confesses: "I only ask God two things: that I may die without pain and that [by the time I die] my daughters do not need me anymore. With those two things, I would be fulfilled." Elena states that her daughters still need her, as they are only eighteen and twenty-one years old. Elena herself lost her mother when aged twenty-two years. She knows how hard it is and finds reassurance in knowing that she has provided her daughters with a good education: "With that tool, one can move forward." Such statements are common among both upper-middle-class and lower-middle-class Peruvian migrants. Martín, the sixty-five-year-old security guard, saves a little money every month. His daughter, who lives in Peru and has had mental health issues, wanted to go back to university. Martín decided to fund her education and told her: "I will not leave you money [as an inheritance], but at least I will leave you a brain [i.e., education]."

These migrants see their own realization in their children's success, whether this means college degrees, proper jobs, or owning property. Their children are the legacy that justifies a life of sacrifice. However, some things do not pass on to the next generation. These late-middle-aged Peruvian migrants share with their Peruvian parents the devotion to Peruvian Christian icons. They learned it from their grandparents and parents, and lived it in Peru, through processions and celebrations. Their children, raised in Chile, do not share this devotion. Their migrant parents attribute it in part to Chile being a "much less devoted" country and accept it with almost stoic resignation. In a way, Peruvian migrants have also sacrificed the continuity of certain traditions.

Perhaps the most illustrative example of this aesthetics of sacrifice toward their children to avoid being a burden, coupled with a resignation toward loss of tradition, is the choice of cremation. In Catholicism, paying respect to the dead is very important. Several participants recall going to a cemetery in Peru to honor their grandparents or even family members they had never met. Despite burial being more traditional, most participants have come around to the idea—some quite recently—that they would prefer to be cremated. In a way, this is another sacrifice they make for the sake of their children.

Two significant explanations appear in conversations with migrants who prefer cremation as the means of disposing of their bodies. The first relates to the practicalities of being a migrant. Repatriation of a deceased migrant for burial to Peru presents many difficulties. Liliana, a sixty-one-year-old accountant, recalls the story of her sister who passed away in the United States. The bureaucracy of moving a corpse to another country was a nightmare, so Liliana finally decided to let the body rest in the United States. Repatriation is also extremely expensive.

The second reason relates to the discontinuity of traditions. Mariano, the sixty-two-year-old notary, acknowledges this, combining resignation with nostalgia. "Families used to go to the cemetery to put flowers on their dead ones," he says. "But that [tradition] is lost, they start to forget you . . . what would be the point [of a burial]? Even I go to the cemetery less often when I visit Peru." Mariano sees it as a natural change with new generations: some customs just fade away. He is starting to consider cremation, so his children can spread his ashes if they want. He wants to release his children from the duty of going to the cemetery. Elena, the forty-nine-year-old nurse, has no doubts: "I want cremation. It is the most pragmatic for my daughters, so they can forget about going to the cemetery and laying down flowers."

There is a sense of not being a burden to their children, coupled with accepting that their children will not continue these traditions. There is also something about cremation and the portability of funeral urns that make it poetically fitting for migrants: it is a movable burial for movable people. The story of Marcos, a fifty-six-year-old call center manager, illustrates this point. His mother lives in Peru. His wife and son live in Chile. When discussing the future, death, and what will happen after, he firmly states: "Cremated. Half of me will be here; the other half will be there." Marcos made this decision only three years ago. "I used to say that I wanted to be buried in Peru." he explains. "But then, my son said that I was only thinking about myself and not about the son wanting to see his father." That was enough for Marcos to decide on cremation and dividing his ashes across his two countries: the country of his mother and the country of his son.

Conclusion

Late-middle-aged Peruvian migrants not only have settled for a long time in Chile. In a way, they hope also to settle for a long time in the present moment, in the stage of life they currently occupy. They are not only a transnational sandwich generation, with aging parents in Peru and young children in Chile, they are also late-middle-aged individuals trying to hold on to youth before old age comes for them. Anchored in the present, their aspirations for the future appear fuzzy and advanced age seems to be admired only when it applies to their parents. Despite the ambivalence of their aging experience, their condition as migrants is useful as a means to conceptualize late middle age.

Even when late-middle-aged Peruvian migrants discuss their aspirations for later life, these are never concrete plans for real moments in the future. Participants state that they will not retire, or that they will continue working even if they retire. They do not want their children to take care of them in their last years or even after death, and they present cremation as a sensitive choice toward their children. However, these statements should not be taken as decisions, or as visions of the future. After all, it will be another fifteen to twenty years before it becomes apparent whether they hold to their word or not. Instead, these aspirations are declarations about the present.

The participants focus on the present, which is why the future appears blurred beyond it. It is not that far beyond, but is blurry anyway. Their conversations about the future are deeply rooted in the present. In this present, these proud wage earners can keep being who they are. In this present, these late-middle-aged Peruvian migrants feel enthusiastic, hardworking, and even powerful: after all, two generations depend on them. As a sandwich generation, they successfully support both their parents and children. The work this requires makes their lifestyle fit the active aging narrative—and even the "successful aging" narrative (Lamb 2017), with its emphasis on productivity—by the book. Yet, as previously discussed, their lifestyle also reflects a long-term ethic of hard work. Participants experience a much greater degree of vitality than they expected, compared to their memories of parents and grandparents. Though certain undeniable frailties show that old age is coming for them, their remaining vitality, and its material consequences in terms of work and ability to provide, is proof for them of their claimed youth. Yet, this relationship between claimed youth and menacing old age does not lack ambivalence.

The ambivalence toward the experience of aging—between claiming the traditional authority of advanced age and claiming the status of retained youth—is not merely a matter of subjectively felt vitality. This ambivalence is heavily informed by close contact with the older generation. The participants provide care to their parents and value and respect them for their age, but they do not want to take that place themselves in the near future. Participants support their children, but do not want their children's support when the time comes. Their identity (and self-worth) profoundly depends on their working life, and is on the verge of workaholism, so they cannot afford to become passive care receivers. They respect and revere their parents, but are afraid of being in their place one day. It is not fear of being old per se. It is the fear of losing autonomy, becoming dependent, turning into a burden, that worries them more than death.

Their condition as migrants shapes their life stories and consequently their experience of aging: from the sacrifice narrative and dedication to work to support their families back in Peru, to the factual justification for delaying retirement, to the resignation that their children will not continue certain traditions and the need to arrange for their parents' care abroad (or migrating in later life), among others. The option of cremation is perhaps the clearest manifestation of their desire not to burden the next generation and exemplifies their acceptance that customs change with migration. Their life—even their afterlife—is marked by mobility.

Russell King and his colleagues remark that, while "migration is a relatively unambiguous phenomenon . . . ageing is a much more . . . slippery process to define and conceptualise" (2017, 183). Perhaps using the "relatively unambiguous" process of migration as a metaphor can help us better understand the fuzzy nature of late middle age. It can be conceptualized as a migration journey between two stages in life (see also Amrith, this volume). It is a middle point that is well past the first half, a suitable vantage point for the two gazes of Janus.

As with many migrants, the lives of late-middle-aged Peruvians in Santiago is informed by experiences of being in-between. They live between two countries, two generations (their Peruvian parents and their Chilean children), and two different life stages (retained youth and looming old age). They live between providing care (to their parents) and not wanting care (from their children), and between a continuing legacy (through their children, who have a promising future) and one that will not continue (their religious devotion will not pass on to the next generation).

Carolina Stefoni and Macarena Bonhomme highlight how the concept of "in-betweenness" (Bhabha 1996) helps to understand the experience of migration: many migrants live in a "third space," between two worlds, their origin country and the destination country, and struggle with belonging and identity (Stefoni and Bonhomme 2014, 83). This metaphor is helpful also to conceptualize the experience of late middle age. It is a third space in the life course: no longer youth, not yet advanced age. These late-middle-aged adults hold on to their own identity as (young) active workers without fully accepting that they are somewhere in-between, closer to the next stage, of advanced age. The only certainty lies in the present, where they can keep being who they were and continue their narrative of sacrifice. The future that lies ahead is a place where they hope never to settle, with its threats of passivity, dependency, and an unproductive life. Like Janus, they look both ways, but sometimes it seems one of the faces—the one toward the future—has its eyes shut.

Acknowledgments

I want to thank all the participants of the "Aspiring in Later Life" workshop at the Max Planck Institute for the Study of Religious and Ethnic Diversity for their valuable comments on this subject and the Anthropology of Smartphones and Smart Ageing team for their continuous feedback throughout fieldwork and writing. I am also very grateful to Megha Amrith, Victoria K. Sakti, and Dora Sampaio, who provided me with insightful comments and useful critiques on a previous version of this chapter. Last but not least, I want to express my deepest gratitude to all research participants who made me feel like a brother and offered me a glimpse into their vibrant and complex lives as Peruvian migrants in Chile. All remaining errors or shortcomings are my own responsibility.

Notes

1. Globally, the population older than sixty years will double from 11 percent to 22 percent between 2000 and 2050 and reach two billion people (WHO 2014).

2. According to the data gathered up to 31 December 2020, Peruvians are now the second-largest immigrant group (16.3% of the migrant population in Chile), surpassed only by Venezuelan migrants (30.7%) (INE 2021, 15).

3. This research was funded by the Center for Intercultural and Indigenous Research (CIIR)—grant ANID FONDAP15110006—and was conducted within the Anthropology of Smartphones and Smart Ageing, a global comparative project, coordinated by Daniel Miller at University College London.

4. Around two-thirds of migrants live in the metropolitan region. Menara Guizardi and Alejandro Garcés (2014) call "methodological Santiaguism" the bias of most migration studies in Chile, which focus solely on Santiago. This chapter does not pretend to describe the experience of all Peruvian migrants in Chile, or even in Santiago.

5. All participants' names have been changed and their professions modified as well. These changes do not affect the integrity of the data. All participants' quotes were originally in Spanish. English translations are ours.

6. Mariano uses the word *mayor* in Spanish. *Mayor* means "older" when applied to "adult," as in "older adult," and does not necessarily have a negative connotation. The word *viejo*, or "old," has a pejorative connotation when applied to people.

7. "Selling holidays" means working for double pay during holidays, instead of taking regular paid holidays.

8. See King et al. (2017) for a critical review on the literature on this Cartesian division applied to aging.

9. According to Horn (2019) transnational family studies usually focus on parental relations and have only recently addressed relationships between other members, such as older parents.

10. The literature on transnational families shows that, in some cases, following reunification older parents complain that their migrant children do not provide enough emotional support (cf. Lamb 2002 on migrants from India).

11. According to Horn's literature review (2019), "transnational travelers" usually applies to grandmothers traveling to the receiving country to help their children care for newborn babies (cf. Goulbourne and Chamberlain 2001).

REFERENCES

Bennett, Andy, and Paul Hodkinson, eds. 2012. *Ageing and Youth Cultures: Music, Style and Identity*. London: Berg.

Bhabha, Homi K. 1996. "Culture's In-Between." In *Questions of Cultural Identity*, edited by Stuart Hall and Paul du Gay, 53–60. London: Sage.

Blaikie, Andrew. 1999. *Ageing and Popular Culture*. Cambridge: Cambridge University Press.

Bonhomme, Macarena. 2013. "Cultura material y migrantes peruanos en Chile: Un proceso de integración desde el hogar." *Polis, Revista Latinoamericana* 12 (35): 63–84.

———. 2021. "Racismo en barrios multiculturales en Chile: Precariedad habitacional y convivencia en contexto migratorio." *Bitácora Urbano Territorial* 31(I): 167–181. https://doi.org/10.15446/bitacora.v31n1.88180.

Chisholm, June F. 1999. "The Sandwich Generation." *Journal of Social Distress and Homelessness* 8 (3): 177–191.

Contreras, Dante, Jaime Ruiz-Tagle, and Paulina Sepúlveda. 2013. "Migración y mercado laboral en Chile." *Serie Documentos de Trabajo N° 376*. Facultad de Economía y Negocios Universidad de Chile. Santiago.

Ducci, Maria, and Loreto Rojas. 2010. "La pequeña Lima: Nueva cara y vitalidad para el centro de Santiago de Chile." *EURE, Revista latinoamericana de estudios urbano regionales* 36 (108): 95–121.

Duque, Marília. 2019. "Dependence Is the New Death." *Anthropology of Smartphones and Smart Ageing Blog*, University College London, 13 March 2019. https://blogs.ucl.ac.uk/assa/2019/03/13/dependence-is-the-new-death-by-marilia-duque/.

———. 2022. *Ageing with Smartphones in Urban Brazil: A Work in Progress*. London: UCL Press.

Fischer, Edward F. 2014. *The Good Life: Aspiration, Dignity, and the Anthropology of Wellbeing*. Stanford, CA: Stanford University Press.

Garvey, Pauline, and Daniel Miller. 2021. *Ageing with Smartphones in Ireland: When Life Becomes Craft*. London: UCL Press.

Goulbourne, Harry, and Mary Chamberlain, eds. 2001. *Caribbean Families in Britain and the Trans-Atlantic World*. London: Macmillan Caribbean.

Guizardi, Menara, and Alejandro Garcés. 2014. "Estudios de caso de la migración peruana 'en Chile': Un análisis crítico de las distorsiones de representación y representatividad en los recortes espaciales." *Revista de geografía Norte Grande* 58: 223–240.

Horn, Vincent. 2019. *Aging within Transnational Families: The Case of Older Peruvians*. London: Anthem Press.

Imilan, Walter. 2013. "Restaurantes peruanos en Santiago de Chile: Construcción de un paisaje de la migración." *Revista de estudios sociales* 48: 15–28.

INE (Instituto Nacional de Estadísticas). 2018. *Características sociodemográficas de la inmigración internacional en Chile Censo 2017: Síntesis de resultados, noviembre 2018*. Santiago, Chile: INE.

———. 2021. *Estimación de personas extranjeras residentes habituales en Chile al 31 de diciembre de 2020*. Santiago, Chile: INE.

King, Russell, Aija Lulle, Dora Sampaio, and Julie Vullnetari. 2017. "Unpacking the Ageing–Migration Nexus and Challenging the Vulnerability Trope." *Journal of Ethnic and Migration Studies* 43 (2): 182–198. https://doi.org/10.1080/1369183X.2016.1238904.

Lamb, Sarah. 2002. "Intimacy in a Transnational Era: The Remaking of Ageing among Indian Americans." *Diaspora* 11 (3): 299–330.

———, ed. 2017. *Successful Aging as a Contemporary Obsession: Global Perspectives*. New Brunswick, NJ: Rutgers University Press.

Miller, Daniel, Laila Abed Rabho, Patrick Awondo, Maya de Vries, Marília Duque, Pauline Garvey, Laura Haapio-Kirk, Charlotte Hawkins, Alfonso Otaegui, Shireen Walton, and Xinyuan Wang. 2021. *The Global Smartphone: Beyond a Youth Technology*. London: UCL Press.

Ministerio de Desarrollo Social y Familia. 2017. *Síntesis de Resultados Casen 2017: Adultos Mayores*. Santiago, Chile: Gobierno de Chile, Ministerio de Desarrollo Social y Familia. http://observatorio.ministeriodesarrollosocial.gob.cl/storage/docs/casen/2017/Resultados_Adulto_Mayores_casen_2017.pdf

Ney, Steven. 2005. "Active Aging Policy in Europe: Between Path Dependency and Path Departure." *Ageing International* 30 (4): 325–342.

Otaegui, Alfonso. 2023. *Ageing with Smartphones in Urban Chile: The Experience of Peruvian Migrants*. London: UCL Press.

Sampaio, Dora. 2020. "Languages of Othering and Cultural Hybridity: Transnational Cultures of Ageing in the Context of Return to the Azores." *Ageing and Society* 41 (6): 1289–1307. https://doi.org/10.1017/S0144686X20001373.

Stefoni, Carolina, and Macarena Bonhomme. 2014. "Una vida en Chile y seguir siendo extranjeros." *Si somos americanos: Revista de estudios transfronterizos* 14 (2): 81–101.

Stefoni, Carolina, Sandra Leiva, and Macarena Bonhomme. 2017. "Migración internacional y precariedad laboral. El caso de la industria de la construcción en Chile." *REMHU, Revista Interdisciplinar da Mobilidade Humana* 25 (49): 95–112.

Tijoux, Maria Emilia. 2007. "Peruanas inmigrantes en Santiago: Un arte cotidiano de la lucha por la vida." *Polis, Revista de la Universidad Bolivariana* 18: 1–12.

———. 2013. "Niños(as) marcados por la Inmigración Peruana: Estigma, sufrimientos, resistencias." *Convergencia: Revista de ciencias sociales* 61: 83–104

Torres, Alma, and Rodrigo Hidalgo. 2009. "Los peruanos en Santiago de Chile: Transformaciones urbanas y percepción de los inmigrantes." *Polis, Revista de la Universidad Bolivariana* 8 (22): 307–326.

Vertovec, Steven. 2009. *Transnationalism*. London: Routledge.

Walton, Shireen. 2018. "The Sandwich Generation: Mobile Views from Multicultural Milan." *Anthropology of Smartphones and Smart Ageing Blog*, University College London, 17 March 2018. https://blogs.ucl.ac.uk/assa/2018/03/17/the-sandwich-generation-mobile-views-from-multicultural-milan/.

———. 2021. *Ageing with Smartphones in Urban Italy: Care and Community in Milan and Beyond*. London: UCL Press.

WHO (World Health Organization). 2014. *Ageing*. Geneva: WHO. http://www.who.int/ageing/en/.

CHAPTER 6

Whose Aspirations?

INTERGENERATIONAL EXPECTATIONS AND HOPES IN EASTERN UGANDA

Susan Reynolds Whyte

"I'm back from Kampala," said Jaja with a straight face, as she slowly hobbled back from the latrine, leaning heavily on her stick. She could still manage those twenty meters and ironically call the move to relieve herself a trip to Kampala. That afternoon, we were sitting where she always sat, on the step of her house, talking about a real journey she had taken six months earlier. One of her grandsons, Kato, had carried her on a motorbike to his home, about ten kilometers away, where he and his brothers and their wives had cared for her for some months. Jaja had her own house on the land of her late husband, surrounded by the homes of her sons' children, who, with their wives and families, provided everyday help. But Kato, a daughter's son, took her away for a long visit because he and his mother believed Jaja was not well cared for at her home. They declared: "Bedbugs were swarming like white ants, taking her blood." Jaja herself said that the trip was more about running away from bedbugs than visiting the homes of her daughter's sons. But she was full of praise for them and their wives. They served her with heaps of food. "They could even come at night to take me to one of their houses to eat." But while she was still enjoying freedom from bedbugs, someone came to say that her brother's daughter had died. Her grandson carried her on his motorbike to the burial, where she stayed some days to mourn and then returned to her own home. "The bedbugs had taken a rest, but after a short time they returned in strength. They are still biting, but I am here."

Jaja was well into her nineties, and like other very elderly people I have been following, she was becoming less and less mobile.[1] The old and frail depend on their sticks, but even more, they depend on a configuration of potential caregivers who sometimes move them, as Kato moved Jaja, and very often move themselves to care for old relatives.[2] It is these moves and locations, together with the sociality and material things that have significance in conditions of poverty, that I explore in this chapter. Mobility of caregivers and receivers is both physical and social. In what follows I will suggest that the aspirations of old people in this part of eastern Uganda must be understood within this shifting configuration of relatives, through whom, and with whom, they try to make a livable, if not a good, life. Old people's desires and hopes are intertwined with the aspirations of their relatives, sometimes in happy congruence and sometimes not. Arjun Appadurai's (2004, 2013) perspectives on imagining and anticipating the future are useful, but his suggestions about the capacity to aspire must be rethought in connection with aspiration in later life.

The setting where I work is one of high fertility, so families are large and potential caregivers are many. Jaja had borne eight children; although only three were still living, they had left many descendants. But resources are small—Bunyole (Butaleja District) is rural and poor. Livelihood depends on farming and small business and "distributive labor," that is, on working to be distributed *to* by those with more means (Ferguson 2015). Yet receiving support is not easy where few people have regular salaries or jobs from which they can retire on a pension. Especially younger people leave to seek work in Uganda's larger towns, but most are struggling ("gambling" as they say) trying to earn enough to survive in the city. There is not much international migration from this area, so mobility is within the country, the region, and the district. For some elderly people, movement is to a grandson's home, a neighborhood funeral, or just to the latrine.

Uganda has only recently, and with donor support, introduced a program of senior citizen grants. This very modest payment of UGX 25,000 (USD 6.70) a month, paid quarterly to people aged eighty and older, has so far only happened once in Butaleja District. Although it should have been repeated in September 2020, the elderly are still waiting. The amount is small, but cash in hand means a lot in conditions where jelly for dry skin and sugar for tea are so appreciated. One old friend recounted that while he and others were waiting in line to receive the money, they were told that President Yoweri Museveni had sent a message to all the old people that they should eat and enjoy the money that had been brought to them. "So, most of the old people took the president's advice to just eat and enjoy from their money. Some old people drank too much alcohol and died!" I never confirmed that people splurged the grant on alcohol, but many, including that old man, indulged in buying meat—a taste of what the good life could be. Old Jaja, famous for her love of meat, blurted out when we were talking about her friend who used to be fat, "May God give us life! We shall eat that life!," while showing how she would tear the meat, pulling it sideways to rip it and chew with her few teeth.

What is the life that old people hope for in their remaining years? To explore that question, I draw loosely on a distinction made by Appadurai (2013) in his work on the future as cultural fact. He suggests that three kinds of thinking about the future be considered: imagination, anticipation, and aspiration. Imagination connotes a vision of the future. Anticipation points to the expectation of something probable. Aspiration directs hope and ambition toward something desired. This approach to expectations and hopes links to a growing body of work on ideas of a good old age in radically different settings (Lynch and Danely 2013; Lamb 2017; Hromadžić and Palmberger 2018). Themes addressed in that work resonate with those that concern Jaja and others in eastern Uganda. They are not inspired by the goals of healthy or active aging, espoused by public health authorities in wealthier countries. As Sarah Lamb (2017) and contributors have shown, the obsession with "successful aging" is widespread, but far from universal. Instead, my interlocutors aspire to "comfortable aging," something that is a struggle for many. The themes that Meika Loe (2017) unfolds from her research with very old people in upstate New York are also found in eastern Uganda: interdependence, accepting vulnerability and limitations, coming to terms with mortality. They play out differently in a setting with little security beyond that provided by intimate others, with poor yet expensive health care, and with a constant lack of cash (see also Wolter, this volume). But fundamentally they are central to anticipation and aspiration.

Imagining Pasts and Futures

On what basis do we imagine the future? Appadurai (2013) asserts that it is mostly on the basis of past, and I would add present, experience. The people of Bunyole share a past when life was informed by an ideal of patrilineal kinship and virilocal marriage. Sons were allocated land by their fathers, and they brought wives to make homes there, with the consequence that parents grew old with their sons, daughters-in-law, and sons' children nearby. Daughters were mobile; they moved away to their husbands, though they maintained continuing links with their parental homes. It was never entirely like that and has become less so with time. Shortage of land and a rapidly growing population meant that some men moved away to find land in other districts, a practice that has become more and more common. Divorce was always a possibility; women left their husbands and moved back to the homes of their fathers and brothers until they moved on to another man. Yet in recent decades, partnerships have become less and less firm, with daughters staying for long periods in their parental homes and sons' partners coming and going. Weak marriage ties have long characterized southern Africa (Pauli and Van Dijk 2017); in recent decades, partnership instability is also increasing in Uganda, while the frequency of formal marriage declines (UBOS 2017, 72). What is significant in Bunyole is that the imagined topography of an old couple surrounded by the homes of their sons' families is an image that still lingers in people's minds and holds to a certain extent. Even when the patrilineal virilocal ideal is not realized, the location of children and grandchildren makes a kind of kin topography that is fundamental for understanding the past and imagining the future. Appadurai (2013, 288) wrote that community, family, and personal archives of memory are more important than state or bureaucratic archives in forming people's sense of locality. Those images of children and grandchildren located nearby or farther away trace maps for possible futures. But they are maps that can shift; as family members moved around in the past, so may they also in time to come.

Sitting in the shade of her magnificent cashew tree, an elderly woman named Judith explained that she had borne eight girls and two boys. "I wanted three or four boys, but God did not give. The wife of my first son made it good, though.

She had seven boys and one girl. Boys will expand the home. They will build houses all around here," she said, motioning toward the compound where the houses of her two sons stood near her own. "If the land is not enough, the boys will buy more." Remembering the large home in which she herself grew up, and counting the number of her grandsons, Judith imagined a future when the vicinity of her home would be crowded with the houses of her sons' sons and their wives. Today there is a shortage of land, but people in their eighties and nineties, like Judith, do not worry so much about that, as middle-aged parents do. They are of a time when the average completed fertility rate was about eight, and they envision a future surrounded by the houses of many descendants.

For many old people, it is not just the number of children but their children's success in life that forms the basis for imagining the future. Schooling is important in the minds of many. A couple of years later, I visited Judith again, and we talked about her marriage: "My mother's brother [who brought her up] did not let me marry the man I wanted. I had met a rich and well-educated man who wanted to pay bridewealth and marry me properly in church. If I had married him, I would have been powerful, and my children would have gone to school. But my uncle made me marry a friend of his, who was not interested in educating our children—except for the one son who studied and became a teacher. It was my daughter's son who graduated from university. I even went to Kampala for the celebration, and I danced and ululated."

The son who became a teacher built a brick house for his parents, and another for his wife and children. Even though he stays at the school where he teaches, his family lives right next to Judith, and he earns enough to help with her medical expenses. These days, education does not guarantee a job; many young people, even with university degrees, never achieve the security of a regular salary. In the past, schooling was more significant as a step toward employment, and this is reflected in Judith's ruminations and her imagination of a future when graduates like her daughter's son will provide support for the family.

The archive of the past shows that old people were supported materially by at least some descendants, whether they had much schooling or not. The image of an old person in a cluster of the homes of sons and their families remains an ideal. But the experience of more recent decades is that an unmarried daughter may inhabit one of the houses or that the son does not live in his house full-time, though some of his children may stay with their grandparents. On this basis, old people imagine a future in their own home, where family members live nearby, and someone supplies a little money.

Anticipating the Expected

Anticipation concerns the near future, and it focuses on something specific that is definitely expected, likely, or at least quite possible. Those few elderly people who received the first distribution of senior citizen grants anticipated the next payout covering another three months. They had plans for how they would spend the money. Most thought of buying special eats: meat and *matoke* for making the steamed plantain dish that is a bit of a luxury in this part of Uganda. An elderly woman named Rosa, with whom I spoke about prospects for the next distribution, anticipated taking her trusted daughter-in-law to help collect the money, since her nephew had stood in line for her the first time and taken most of it.

Old people anticipate the arrival of a relative who has promised to visit. When Jaja spied an airplane around the time she knew I was coming, she happily told others that it must be bringing me. They plan for visitors and try in advance to organize a meal. Once Jaja scolded me for passing her home often without stopping; she made me promise to come the next day and gave explicit instructions to her grandson Henry, who lived next door. When I arrived, they had killed a chicken for me and my companion in anticipation of our visit. Elderly people look forward to celebrations, including the various phases of burials and funerals, which every old person attends unless truly immobile. These are the small events of everyday life that involve some kind of mobility—of themselves or others.

The great event that elderly people anticipate is death—their own and that of other old people. It is omnipresent in Bunyole, where people are buried at home and funerals are the most important of rituals, bringing together hundreds of mourners. The final immobility of a person mobilizes people from near and far as news goes out by word of mouth, handwritten messages, and radio announcements about the death and the time of burial. The body is laid out in the house of the deceased and people enter to view it, wailing on three notes and calling out their loss. Those closely related sleep several nights at the bereaved home, where a funeral fire is kept burning. In everyday life, anticipation of death is not hidden (see also Gill, this volume).

People, particularly old people, talk openly of their own demise and that of others (see also Van der Geest 2002a). Jaja once told her daughter Veria to send a message to her other daughter, Agatha: "Is she waiting for me to die before she brings that goat she promised?" Often elderly people leaving a funeral or looking at a recent grave remark, "He/she left me with a big debt [*ebbanja*]," that is, an obligation—to die as well. Or "He/she has gone to keep a place for me." A common greeting, "How are the bones" may elicit a smile and the response "They want to go down," that is, they are tending toward the grave. An old person feeling exhausted might say, "The bones will be a bundle of dry grass," metaphorically implying a corpse that is light and dry. The realism of such remarks is sometimes lightened by humor, as Jason Danely (2017) found among the very old in Japan. Irony and wryness seem to reflect an acceptance of the inevitable. The difference is that, in Bunyole, laughing about death is not restricted to the elderly. Songs for dancing and drinking often have an "eat, drink, and be merry" theme with call phrases and responses about the grave:

> "If you find your friend, laugh with her. The grave will eat the bones."
> "Where does your nose point? Down. That's where we're going."
> "The bones will rot. The body is for maggots."
> "Let us drink, you yourself drink! Will it be like this when we are inside the grave?"

While reminders about death are common and general, they are also specific, as when people give instructions about where they want to be buried. This happens when there is any possible doubt, for example, when men have been living in town or when women have no firm husband on whose land they could be buried. Other people also directly express their anticipation of a very old person's imminent death. On one visit, I had brought a new mattress for Jaja. It was lying near us, still in its plastic wrapping, rolled up and tied with a rope, when an old friend and neighbor stopped to greet her. She immediately spotted the new mattress and congratulated Jaja for it. "But how long do you have to enjoy that mattress?" she asked, then added: "Of course, it will be nice that you are laid out on a good mattress when mourners come."

A few years earlier, Jaja herself anticipated the death of her daughter Anna, who was about seventy at the time. We were sitting with her in the usual place when her granddaughter Mercy arrived on a bicycle: "Anna is very sick and sends word that she wants to be buried next to her father." My first reaction was that we should get Anna to the hospital; perhaps her life could be saved. Jaja immediately ordered that someone should clear the cotton plants near her husband's grave and remove the firewood that another daughter had stored in the house, so that Anna's body could lie there. Sadly, her anticipation proved right. Anna survived for another two weeks, after hospital treatment proved useless. She was brought to her mother's house, where she lay unconscious for several days while mourners gathered outside, waiting for word before they started wailing. At her burial, the priest remarked, perhaps in sympathy with Jaja: "A wise woman dies before her children, but Jaja is still here." Jaja lived on, but her condition slowly declined and her needs for care increased. Toward the end, two of her children were openly anticipating, almost asserting, that her husband should come for her. And he did. Jaja died three years after her daughter Anna.

Adult children foresee the day when they will stage a funeral for their parents. If they never built a good house for them, those who have the means try to do so before the end, so they will not be shamed when mourners come. The anticipation of an old person's death puts the behavior of his or her children in sharp relief. Have they made every effort to ease the last years and months of life? When death is anticipated, the virtues and vexations of intimate others (Whyte 2022) are illuminated.

Aspiring to a Good Life?

When we asked very old people about what makes their life good and what they hoped for, the immediate answer was often: Nothing is good. We hurt, we have become useless, we move with difficulty. They recounted details of bodily loss, but often with forbearance and sometimes with humor. Self-deprecating, lighthearted remarks were a way of expressing, even performing, reduced aspiration. Jaja's joking announcement that she had returned from Kampala as she tottered back from the nearby latrine is a good example. When my assistant Rose recently visited

Judith, she admired Rose's coronavirus mask. "It would be good for old people. We would feel comfortable if no one could see the big gaps in our mouths where our teeth have fallen out." An elderly man named Hasahya, too, remarked that his mouth was folding in because he was losing his teeth. He added: "The termite mound re-creates itself every year, but for us, life diminishes year by year."

While caregivers tried to provide medicine for acute problems like malaria or bouts of diarrhea, the old people were resigned to their general decline. One man, Samwiri, had become very shaky since the last time we visited, but he said there was nothing much that could be done about it. Another, Yokosofati, who only leaves his bed in the late afternoon to sit in the shade, declared that his health was not going to get better, but he had adapted to it. Even when he is given medicine, it only works briefly. But he liked listening to the radio and chatting with visitors. Going to a private clinic was expensive, and the government health units gave poor service. Rosa told us that last time she went to the hospital, the receptionist asked why she came to waste medicine that could be used to treat still useful young people. (I once heard an old lady recount a similar story to her equally old crony, and they both laughed about it.) Rosa did not think it was amusing; she declared she would not go back to the hospital after that insult. She accepted that she had to walk slowly and rest between steps; at least she could manage to attend funerals in the neighborhood.

Appadurai (2004) wrote that the capacity to aspire is unevenly distributed. Those who have some resources, who have experienced that they can realize something they hope for, are more capable of aspiration. Appadurai was thinking about political and economic inequality and about certain kinds of aspiration such as community action to improve life conditions. Still, his observation may be applied in another way. The capacity to aspire is also unevenly distributed over the life course. Younger people's aspiration capacity depends in part on the chances and experiences that characterize their social and economic position. But they are also capable of aspiring because of their youth, their bodily capital, and the years ahead of them. As people become frailer, and more dependent on others, their horizons of aspiration diminish. In Bunyole, increasing loss of mobility meant that even attending funerals, going to church, or visiting others were hard. People could no longer hope to participate physically in a wider social world. Except for occasions when they were carried to stay with other relatives, they spent their days at home (see Obrist 2016). Those who could move a little followed the rhythm of the sun, shifting from the shade of the mango tree to that of the tamarind and back to the shadow of the house. Many of the desires my oldest friends expressed were modest indeed; yet they all had some aspirations.

For the feeblest, like Jaja, comfortable aging was about good things to eat. Asked what would improve her life, Jaja's response was brief: meat, sugar, tea leaves, and soap. Jaja's love of meat was legendary. She herself laughed about it. When we brought her a kilo, she always called for a knife, cut it in chunks, and counted the pieces so she knew how many there should be when it came back from the hearth

Figure 6.1. Jaja and a great-granddaughter cutting meat and counting the pieces. Photograph by Susan Reynolds Whyte.

(implying that she would catch the cooks if they took any) (figure 6.1). Once she tried to hurry her granddaughter to prepare the meat, comparing herself to a hungry carnivore: "A hyena doesn't sleep with something smelly" (i.e., it devours the meat immediately before it goes bad).

Beyond pork and tea with excessive sugar, Jaja wanted freedom from bedbugs and a lamp to keep sorcerers away at night. It was her grandson's wife and neighbor, Mary, who wanted a thermos flask for her, so she could be away from Jaja for longer, knowing that the old lady had warm tea. She added that there was nothing much that could be done to improve granny's life in her remaining years, except to provide the necessities and make her comfortable where she is, until she joins her husband.

Even though special things to eat were the first things that some mentioned as characterizing the good life, there were always other dimensions. A fundamental desire, call it an aspiration, was to live out the final years at home. You should be surrounded by relatives, who will feed and care for you; there should be grandchildren to send for water. You should die at home, where you will be buried. It is better to die in the right place to avoid the costs of transporting a corpse.

Those men who have worked elsewhere mostly move back to the land of their fathers when they are no longer able to keep on with their jobs. Some have tried to maintain a house on their rural land so that they have a place waiting. Even men without children, or without contact to their children, returned to stay near their brothers and brothers' children. Of four such men I know, one was brought back mortally ill to be cared for by his family (Whyte 2022), while the others returned from jobs to stay in houses on the land of their fathers, where they could eat the food cooked by the wives of their brothers and brothers' sons. In one of those instances, the brothers joined together to build a house for the childless man, confirming that the aspiration to spend the last years at home is shared and supported by close relatives.

For women, going home or being at home is more complicated (Whyte 2005). Ideally, they should grow old and be buried at the home of their husband and sons. Alternatively, they may age or be buried at their father's home, as was Jaja's daughter Anna. Yet the place where a woman should spend her twilight years may not be the place where some relatives feel she is best cared for. There may be different opinions about location, and old women communicate their own wishes, sometimes indirectly. Jaja has two living daughters, both married. Veria comes regularly to visit Jaja, bathe her, and wash her clothes. Agatha, who lives in a neighboring district, took Jaja to stay with her, in part to relieve her sister. She kept Jaja for four months and cared for her well. But then Jaja began to act strangely; she became possessed (*ohusamira*) and her dead husband spoke through her, telling her to go home and clean his grave. Something similar happened when another old lady was taken to Kampala to stay with her son's family. The son's wife was a health worker and cared for her assiduously; her daughters came to visit her in the city. Yet when she began to remove her clothes, act possessed, and speak wildly about going back home, everyone agreed that she could not stay. In both these cases, the virtuous caregivers who took the old women to live with them said that it was shameful for them to be keeping them away from their homes when they were behaving oddly and drawing attention to the situation. Their embarrassment coincided with the wishes of their charges to go home to where their husbands were buried.

One of the cultural sensibilities that affects the movements of old people and their caregivers is *obuhwe*, the modesty that should obtain between in-laws of adjacent generations. A woman should not stay in the house of her married daughter; she and her son-in-law avoid each other. When Jaja became possessed while visiting her daughter in the next district, people remarked that it was extra-shameful because she was at her in-laws (although she was staying in a separate house). Therefore, devoted daughters care for their old mothers by visiting them, leaving their husbands and children for a day or a week to travel to where their mother stays. In some cases, daughters take turns going to care for their mothers. A son's wife can do it, or even better a grandson's wife, but the best person to bathe and nurture a weak old woman is a daughter.

For very old people, the good, or at least livable, life is with children and grandchildren, if not their own, then those of their siblings. Having many children is valued, especially by that generation, and old people are happy to mention the number of their offspring. Hasahya, now in his eighties, confided that people envied him because of his many children and grandchildren. What is important, however, is not just numbers, but the success and well-being of children, their resources and ability to help. People aspire for children, sons or daughters, who earn and show love with money and gifts. Although younger people realize that it is harder to educate and thus improve employment chances for many children, the older ones seemed to think that more children increased the possibility that at least one or two would make good. The way these elderly men and women talked about their children, with pride, satisfaction, or disappointment, shows how they aspire for and through them.

Unlike most of the other elderly people I followed, Hasahya still had children in school, since he got many more children late in life with a much younger wife. He was disappointed that the daughter who should have continued to secondary school had just run off. "All my hope was in that girl. I thought she would be able to help the family in the coming years. My daughters have married into poor families who cannot help me [by paying bridewealth or in other ways as in-laws should]." He lamented: "All my boys are very unserious, and the big ones are helpless. And I have never seen daughters-in-law as indifferent as mine. Even if I was sitting under that jackfruit tree, dying of hunger, they would never bring me anything to eat." Now Hasahya's aspirations have shifted to his thirteen-year-old daughter, whom he considers very clever. He says that he knows he may not live to see her finish school, but hopes that if she makes it in life, she might be able to support the family when he is gone. As Hasahya made clear, aspirations for children were not only that they should make good for their own sakes but also that they should succeed so as to help their old parents and the rest of the family.

Yokosofati's aspirations on this count seemed closer to realization. When the COVID-19 pandemic and lockdown hit, his eldest son decided the time had come to leave his construction job in Kampala. He declared he wanted to settle down to farming and help his father accomplish his plans. His other sons, too, lived next to him and helped him. With his debilities, Yokosofati was too weak to lead his family, but he took comfort in his children: "What I have not been able to accomplish in my home, my sons will finish it."

The aspirations of younger people are to find a mate, or mates, to have children and grow a home, and to create links with other families through affinity. Finding partners is thus about widening the social world. My old friends aspired for their children and grandchildren to get partners and increase the family's network of in-laws. Their own aspirations to marry were long past. Yet they and their relatives joked about it still. When a visiting brother-in-law said playfully to Samwiri that he was bringing more daughters from his clan, Samwiri laughed and said, yes, he should bring them, that girls of his clan make the best wives. And then, sighing, he added that if only he could regain his strength, he would dig and raise the bridewealth. When we brought gifts of cosmetic jelly and old women smeared it on their dry skin, they bantered with their relatives: "Look at me, shining and beautiful. Soon men will be bringing cows!" Samwiri and his first wife had never held a church wedding, something that many desire, but few achieve. Now she was hunched with age, but laughed when her sister tried to straighten her up and said teasingly, "How will you look in a wedding dress if you stoop like that?" Playing with impossible dreams, making fun of what can never come to pass, was a way of acknowledging lost aspirations and accepting their loss.

The Aspirations of Caregivers

To say that the aspirational horizons of frail old people constrict is not to say that they have no wishes and hopes. It is to recognize that they are less able to accomplish things on their own and that the aspirations of their caregivers affect them more keenly. Sometimes the desires of both parties converge; sometimes they diverge. Whose aspirations? The aims of those who provide and those who receive care must be considered together. The ambitions and desires of caregivers are fundamental in a situation like this.

As old people become less mobile, their lives are informed by contingency in that they are dependent on the aspirations and happenstances of their intimate others. Developments in the lives of caregivers affect those reliant on them. Those who are disabled become fixed; their needs for care are fairly constant, albeit with fluctuations. But many of those who should help them are unstable; their life courses are dynamic as they pursue their own hopes and deal with untoward events. The rhythms of caregivers and care receivers are not in sync. Jaja hoped that her great-granddaughter Jenifer would stay on with her and not marry until after she died. But Jenifer fell pregnant and left her for a man. Then Jaja's granddaughter Mercy separated from her partner and moved in with Jaja. Particularly when the caregiver is young and facing vital conjunctures (Johnson-Hanks 2002), the situation of a very old person must be readjusted. Since women are usually the ones who perform the daily tasks of care, their responses to changing partnership and maternity situations affect efforts toward a comfortable life directly. But the shifting locations of men are also consequential.

Yokosofati was pleased that the aspirations of his eldest son brought him home from the city to live near his father. Samwiri, in contrast, regretted that two of his sons had taken their families to stay far away where they were working. He was worried that they had bought land near Kampala and shifted there with all their children and wives. He said that during this whole COVID-19 period, he had not seen them. The oldest son's well-built house near home was now abandoned. Samwiri did not think that things would get any better now that his sons had built very far from him. And his health was getting worse by the day. "But if they keep sending help especially for treatment, I will have to learn to live in the current situation I am in." In an earlier conversation, Samwiri had recalled how he and his first wife had pursued their own dreams. They farmed jointly, grew cotton for cash, planned together, built a good house, bought more land, and had many children. Now he saw his sons aspiring for their own lives in ways that made him feel diminished. Even though there were plenty of grandchildren in his home, the fact that his two eldest sons were not there to carry on moderated his aspirations to see his home grow in their hands. But at least his sons' jobs "outside" meant they could send money for the expensive medical treatment of his many maladies.

Sometimes aspirations of caregivers are congruent with the desire for "comfortable aging." The wish for a good house, with a corrugated iron roof, may be achievable through care of a better-accommodated old person. A woman named Stella had left her husband long ago and moved back to her parents with her children, staying in a small, vacated house in the compound. After her father died, she cared for her mother in Bulaya House, a roomy structure that her brother had built from his earnings in Europe. After the old lady died, Stella stayed on in that solid house. In the same way, those providing most daily care for Jaja took over her house when she died.

The material aspirations of caregivers, and their life projects of education, work, and building their own families, are not the only desires that affect their engagement in the care of debilitated old people. An important desire is to be recognized as a dutiful relative in caring for an old person. Just as Lawrence Cohen (1998) wrote of northern India, families are ashamed if their old parent appears neglected. This is not to say that people are only motivated by the wish to look virtuous. Many sincerely wish to do what they can, but they also want to be seen to be doing it. In a rural setting where neighbors know and talk to one another, criticism circulates readily (Whyte 2022).

A recent incident is telling. Rose went to visit Jaja and heard how her trouble controlling her bowels was putting off the wives of her grandsons (see Van der Geest 2002b). No one wanted to sleep with her in her stinking house. One declared that she would not clean her: "Granny was not barren, she has daughters who should wash her. I have my own people whose feces I must clean." Jaja asked Rose to bring the water warming in the sun and bathe her, a request that Rose welcomed as an indication of closeness, having known Jaja for many years. But Mary, the wife of her grandson Henry, who lives next to Jaja, said she would manage and refused to allow Rose to do it: "How would people look at us?" In other words, the caregiver aspires to be acknowledged by others as virtuous, smelly as care may sometimes be. Allowing a visitor to provide intimate care, even though she is a friend of the family, would be shameful. As Brigit Obrist (2016, 111) found in Tanzania: "Neighbours, friends and tenants sometimes assist with advice, comfort, or practical help. Asking them for more intimate involvement would be considered shameful, not only for the older person but also for his or her close kin."

Family members aspire to stage a worthy funeral when an old person dies, in part because the ceremony reflects on the entire lineage. But even before the person dies, providing obvious care is noticed by others. Bulaya House was a concrete testimonial to a son's concern, one that redounded to his credit even after his mother died. Insuring that a weak elderly father or mother is clean and well dressed brings respect and self-respect. Here, too, humor sometimes highlights what is at stake. Once when we were visiting Judith, she glanced around at her daughters-in-law and grandchildren and announced: "My children are getting tired of me.

I better get a share of land from my brother and move there." Everyone smiled because it was well known how attentively they cared for her. Even when she went to mourn, her grandchildren followed her, bringing hot food in a covered container and fresh water in a thermos flask. No one would ever imagine that her family was tired of her.

Conclusion

The people I have been following are in their eighties and nineties. They were losing their health and mobility. Few would describe their lives as good, yet all enjoyed and hoped for small comforts. Aside from desiring modest requirements of food, housing, and nurturing care, they aspired to life with intimate others, on whom they were dependent for help and company. Those intimate others were mobile in different ways, attempting to realize various life projects. So, the hopes and expectations of the very old were heavily contingent on the moves and aspirations of their younger kin.

Adult children and grandchildren had their own concerns and plans and constraints; as they pursued their aspirations for livelihood and building a home, they did not necessarily prioritize the wishes and needs of their debilitated elders. There were conflicts among potential caregivers about who should care how; some felt the burden was too heavy. Yet there were many examples of intimate others who aspired, among other things, to be recognized and respected as caring for their old and frail elders. Despite inconveniences and difficulties, most younger people feel obligation and affection for their older relatives, feelings that are realized in more and less sufficient care. Although their aspirations may differ, they are mutually entailed.

The concepts of imagination and anticipation help us to grasp later-life aspirations both more generally and more specifically. Insofar as imaginations of the future are based on past and present experience, they are shared to a great extent. The adult children of today's old people experienced how their parents cared for their grandparents. They have in common a past where values and practices of mutuality obtained. This helps to explain why ideals of respect and care for elderly relatives are so readily expressed, even if they are not realized. They are broadly imagined. In contrast to this general orientation to the future, anticipation is more specific and time-bound. It brings the likely near future close into the present and calls forth action. It relates to events and specific situations—the arrival of a grandchild for the school holidays, the meat to be cooked for Christmas. Old people anticipate their deaths, as do their younger relatives; the day is not known, yet all appreciate that the time is approaching. But an anticipated situation may have very different implications for different parties, which is why the study of aging should include the appreciation of generational relations. Aging is not only something individuals experience; nor is it just a matter of how cultures and societies construe it. It is best understood in terms of mutually shifting configurations.

The intergenerational perspective on aspirations is essential in conditions where state or welfare institutions do not provide support to old people, and where individuals do not have capital to insure their own welfare. It adds a relational and contingent dimension to what might otherwise be an individualistic or collectivist view of future orientations in later life. Aspirations are reciprocally shaped. The desires of an old person often require efforts from a younger relative. The aspirations of a child or grandchild may include the satisfaction and appreciation of an elderly relative. Or they may mean a relegation of responsibility to another relative. In any case, aspiring has intergenerational implications.

Acknowledgments

I gratefully acknowledge the Velux Foundation for support to the project "Aging as a Human Condition: Radical Uncertainty and the Search for a Good (Old) Life" and my colleagues on that project for continuing conversations. Research in Uganda was approved by the Uganda National Council of Science and Technology. Thanks to the editors of this volume and anonymous reviewers for encouragement and suggestions. My deepest appreciation goes to the old people and their families in Bunyole who have welcomed me into their homes over the years.

NOTES

1. Since 2017 I have repeatedly visited seven old people and their families, with support from the project "Aging as a Human Condition," funded by the Velux Foundation. They live in a part of Bunyole, where I have been doing ethnographic work for many years. On these visits I was accompanied alternately by Kekulina Namuyonga and Rose Danya (the "we" in my accounts). I am grateful to Keku and Rose for help in translating and continuing discussions about aging in Bunyole.

2. Sequence of intergenerational moves in Jaja's later years:
February 2018. Her daughter Anna is brought home to die.
March 2018. She goes to stay with a daughter's son, Kato, and his brothers and their wives.
April 2018. She travels to the funeral of her brother's daughter and then returns home.
May 2019. She goes to stay with her daughter Agatha in another district.
September 2019. She returns to her home and is cared for by her granddaughter Mercy and great-granddaughter Jenifer, who stay with her between their partnerships.
March 2021. Her daughters Veria and Agatha come to be with her as she dies at home.

REFERENCES

Appadurai, Arjun. 2004. "The Capacity to Aspire: Culture and the Terms of Recognition." In *Culture and Public Action*, edited by Vijayendra Rao and Michael Walton, 59–84. Stanford, CA: Stanford University Press.

———. 2013. *The Future as Cultural Fact: Essays on the Global Condition*. London: Verso.

Cohen, Lawrence. 1998. *No Aging in India: Alzheimer's, the Bad Family, and Other Modern Things*. Berkeley: University of California Press.

Danely, Jason. 2017. "Foolish Vitality: Humor, Risk, and Success in Japan." In *Successful Aging as a Contemporary Obsession: Global Perspectives*, edited by Sarah Lamb, 154–167. New Brunswick, NJ: Rutgers University Press.

Ferguson, James. 2015. *Give a Man a Fish: Reflections on the New Politics of Distribution*. Durham, NC: Duke University Press.

Hromadžić, Azra, and Monika Palmberger, eds. 2018. *Care across Distance: Ethnographic Explorations of Aging and Migration*. New York: Berghahn Books.

Johnson-Hanks, Jennifer. 2002. "On the Limits of Life Stages in Ethnography: Toward a Theory of Vital Conjunctures." *American Anthropologist* 104 (3): 865–880.
Lamb, Sarah, ed. 2017. *Successful Aging as a Contemporary Obsession: Global Perspectives*. New Brunswick, NJ: Rutgers University Press.
Loe, Meika. 2017. "Comfortable Aging: Lessons for Living from Eighty-Five and Beyond." In *Successful Aging as a Contemporary Obsession: Global Perspectives*, edited by Sarah Lamb, 218–229. New Brunswick, NJ: Rutgers University Press.
Lynch, Caitrin, and Jason Danely, eds. 2013. *Transitions and Transformations: Cultural Perspectives on Aging and the Life Course*. New York: Berghahn Books.
Obrist, Brigit. 2016. "Place Matters: The Home as a Key Site of Old-Age Care in Coastal Tanzania." In *Ageing in Sub-Saharan Africa: Spaces and Practices of Care*, edited by Jaco Hoffman and Katrien Pype, 95–114. Bristol, UK: Policy Press.
Pauli, Julia, and Rijk van Dijk. 2017. "Marriage as an End or the End of Marriage? Change and Continuity in Southern African Marriages." *Anthropology Southern Africa* 39 (4): 257–266.
UBOS (Uganda Bureau of Statistics). 2017. *Uganda Demographic and Health Survey 2016: Key Indicators Report*. Kampala: UBOS; Rockville, MD: ICF International.
Van der Geest, Sjaak. 2002a. "'I Want to Go!' How Older People in Ghana Look Forward to Death." *Ageing and Society* 22: 7–28.
———. 2002b. "The Toilet: Dignity, Privacy and Care of Elderly People in Kwahu, Ghana." In *Ageing in Africa: Sociolinguistic and Anthropological Approaches*, edited by Sinfree Makoni and Koen Stroeken, 227–244. Aldershot, UK: Ashgate.
Whyte, Susan Reynolds. 2005. "Going Home? Burial and Belonging in the Era of AIDS." *Africa* 75 (2): 154–172.
———. 2022. "Virtues and Vexations: Intimate Others Caring for Elders in Eastern Uganda." In *Imagistic Care: Growing Old in a Precarious World*, edited by Cheryl Mattingly and Lone Grøn, 187–206. New York: Fordham University Press.

PART III

Living in the Present

CHAPTER 7

Before It Ends

AGING, GENDER, AND MIGRATION IN A
TRANSNATIONAL MEXICAN COMMUNITY

Julia Pauli

The song "Un poco más," written by Mexican composer Álvaro Carrillo in the first half of the twentieth century, is still very popular in Mexico. When I started fieldwork in Pueblo Nuevo, in rural Mexico, in the mid-1990s, many people knew its lyrics by heart. The romantic song expresses the quest for a bit more time before love ends. I was astonished when almost twenty years later, in 2013, "Un poco más" was again mentioned during interviews with several generations of women in Pueblo Nuevo. Between 1995 and 2013, Pueblo Nuevo had changed substantially. In 1995, the vast majority of villagers would migrate only within Mexico. By the turn of the century, many migrated to the United States on a temporary basis. With the transnationalization of village life, new forms of consumption emerged, most visibly in impressive new houses built with the money the migrants remitted. Despite these changes, when in 2013 I asked women of different ages what they considered a good life to be, the women did not mention material wealth or conspicuous consumption. Instead, they hoped for stability, that things would stay as they are, just a little bit longer, just *un poco más*. The women were well aware of the fragility of their well-being. Endings pervaded their lives. They had suffered from and witnessed accidents, separations, poverty, sickness, death, and injustice. From these lived experiences, their own and others', they concluded that well-being was more than to have longings and to overcome losses. To be well, they told me, one had to appreciate the very moment that one was living. Soon it could be over. The women's views on well-being and good life surprised me. Seeing new cars, houses, washing machines, and television sets all over the village, I had expected more materialistic, aspirational, and future-oriented answers. From previous interactions, I knew that the women did emulate and desire the new styles and objects of transnational consumerism, hoping to get ahead, *adelantarse*. Still, this was not what they answered when I asked them about the good life. In this chapter, I trace the women's present-focused conception of well-being and relate it to other temporal categories of "the good life." I ask how their experiences and imaginings of endings frame their wish to prolong the present.

Well-being is a rather new theme in anthropology (Appadurai 2013, 293; Jiménez 2008a; Lambek 2008). The concept and related categories like happiness or "the good life" are key dimensions in political philosophy, development studies, and economics. In anthropology, until 2008, well-being had not been "the focus of explicit attention" (Jiménez 2008b, 2). With the publication that year of the seminal volume *Culture and Well-Being* (edited by Alberto Corsín Jiménez) this has changed, and an anthropology of well-being has been taking shape.

Not surprisingly, anthropology's take on the subject is ethnographic and comparative, highlighting the relativity of the concepts depending on the cultural, political, and social contexts of its usages. Contrary to economic approaches to well-being that stress and measure mainly material aspects, anthropologists underscore the importance of aspirations: "To understand the good life, wherever it may be found, we must take seriously not only material conditions but also people's desires, aspirations, and imaginations—the hopes, fears, and other subjective factors that drive their engagement with the world" (Fischer 2014, 5). Future making through aspirations is thus a central lens through which many anthropological studies try to understand people's sense of a good life. In comparative research on how German middle-class shoppers and Guatemalan coffee and broccoli farmers pursue happiness, Edward F. Fischer (2014, 2) thus observes: "Perhaps the good life is not a state to be obtained but an ongoing aspiration for something better that gives meaning to life's pursuits." According to Fischer, this striving for the good life can be analytically separated into two domains: a core, of adequate material resources, physical health and safety, and family and social relations, and the qualitative elements of well-being, which Fischer labels as more "subjective domains": aspiration and opportunity, dignity and fairness, commitment to a larger purpose (Fischer 2014, 5, 207–10).

While there is also work on the political dimensions of well-being (Appadurai 2013; see the contributions in Jiménez 2008a), most anthropological studies focus on Fischer's "subjective" dimensions. Michael Jackson (2011, xii) grounds his analysis of well-being in his observation that aspirations are the result of a sense that something is missing, leading to the conclusion that "there is more to life than what exists for us in the here and now." This longing beyond the present can be nostalgic and past-oriented: "At times we imagine that the lost object was once in our possession—a loving family, an organic community, an Edenic homeland, a perfect relationship" (xii). It can also be directed at the future: "At times we imagine that what we need lies ahead, promised or owed but as yet undelivered, unrevealed, or unpaid, not yet born" (xii).

While future making and nostalgic longing are thus common in the anthropology of the good life and well-being, an appreciation of the present is relatively rare in such studies. An exception is Michael Lambek's (2008) essay on well-being. There, Lambek describes a friend of his in Mayotte, northwest of Madagascar, living a content life as a carpenter and a performer and teacher of Sufi music. When the friend has to give up independent carpentry and work as a wage laborer with very little time left for his music, "his well-being radically decline[s]" (130). Well-being, Lambek argues (128), is thus an art of living, making the best of things in the face of considerable impediments.

In what follows, I scrutinize this art of living in the very present, also relating it to nostalgic longings and future aspirations. Jackson (2011, xi) has observed that "well-being is, therefore, one thing for the young, another for the old, and varies from place to place, person to person." To address some of the variations of well-being, I compare the lives and views on well-being of women from three different generations. I use the term *generation* (Alber, Van der Geest, and Whyte 2008) here as a genealogical classification, comparing a daughter, a mother, and a grandmother: Adriana, who in 2013 was in her twenties; her mother, Alma, then in her forties; and Alma's mother, Regina, in her sixties.[1] I suggest that for an understanding of future aspirations, nostalgic longing for the past, and a content sentiment of the present, it is important to situate these "structures of feeling" (Williams 1977) in the wider contexts of time, generations, and the (female) life course. The lives of women of different generations are complexly entangled, rendering it difficult to focus only on later life and older women. The interconnections become especially visible when looking at marriage and migration (Montes de Oca Zavala, Molina Roldán, and Avalos Pérez 2008, 220–235). Thus, to understand aspirations in later life, I also scrutinize how younger women frame well-being, asking how different generations of women inform and reflect on each other.

A Transnational Mexican Peasantry

Located about three hours away from Mexico City in the valley of Solís in the Estado de México, Pueblo Nuevo is in many ways typical for rural Mexican communities shaped by national and international migration. In about eighty years, the livelihoods of villagers have changed from subsistence-oriented land cultivation of maize and beans into a mixed economy of remittances and agriculture. National and transnational migration has framed and formed the lives of all families in Pueblo Nuevo. In 2013, roughly half of all adult men (aged fifteen years and older) had migrated to U.S. destinations. Most of them invested in the building of remittance houses in the *estilo del norteño*, or North American style (Lopez 2015, 51). Once a "traditionally looking" Mexican village of one-story houses made from adobe bricks, Pueblo Nuevo has changed considerably in appearance since the building of remittance houses. While in the 1990s there was still a lot of space between houses, today most available spots for building a house have been taken. A comparison of census data from 1997 and 2013 shows that the number of North American–style remittance houses has increased substantially (Pauli and Bedorf 2016, 2018). In 1997, 27 percent of the houses (or 44 out of 163) were built in North American style with money from U.S. migration. Sixteen years later, there were 128 new houses permanently inhabited and another 49 new remittance houses not permanently inhabited. Like many Mexican communities experiencing substantial transnational migration, these empty houses, or *casas vacías* (Lattanzi Shutika 2011, 68–90; Sandoval-Cervantes 2017), were most often meant as retirement homes for their absent owners. In addition to these two types of finished remittance houses, there were many more unfinished remittance houses in all stages of construction.

Gender frames the migration dynamics in Pueblo Nuevo. As in other Mexican regions, many more men than women from Pueblo Nuevo migrate internationally (Boehm 2016; Haenn 2020). None of the women whose lives and hopes I am discussing here has ever migrated to the United States. Both Alma and Regina migrated for a brief few years to Mexico City; Adriana never left the valley of Solís. Nevertheless, their lives were formed and framed by transnational migration. They had seen their husbands, fathers, sisters, brothers, sons, and daughters leave and return. To classify their role in the migration process, one could describe them as "stayers." Compared to migrants, stayers have received less attention in migration research (for exceptions, see Brettell 1986; Cohen 2002; Haenn 2020; Smith 2006). Their temporal horizons (Amrith 2021), aspirations, and ideas of well-being often remain unknown (Boccagni and Erdal 2021).

For migrants and stayers alike, the newly constructed houses built with the remittances from the absent migrants stand for the good life. In a paradoxical way, these remittance houses connect nostalgic longings and future aspirations. By building a remittance house in their home village, the absent owners hope to preserve their attachment to the village. In their nostalgic view, the village has become an idle and peaceful place not touched by change (Pauli and Bedorf 2018). During their absence and upon their return to the village, migrants long for what they imagine as a more harmonious village past. At the same time, the architecture and materiality of remittance houses differs strongly from local forms of house construction (Boccagni and Erdal 2021; Lopez 2015). The new forms of construction materialize future-oriented ideas of living and a good life. Remittance houses are thus the main reason why the appearance of rural Mexico has changed so profoundly (figure 7.1).

The very limited opportunity structures in rural Mexico further complicate this paradoxical construction of the good life. Employment beyond agriculture is hardly available in Pueblo Nuevo and other rural Mexican areas. To make a living and own a house, people have to leave and migrate. Similar to the largely disappointed expectations of the Zambian Copperbelt workers described by James Ferguson (1999), aspirations of Pueblo Nuevo migrants can hardly ever be fulfilled. To have a house in the village, migrants cannot live in the village. This situation leads to "frustrated freedom" (Fischer 2014, 155–156) and "cruel optimism" (Berlant 2011; Sandoval-Cervantes 2017). The desire for well-being has become an obstacle to the migrants' well-being (Berlant 2011, 1). Sarah Lynn Lopez also notes this problematic aspect of remittance houses. She observes that discourses on the migrants' building of houses and belonging in their areas of origin are generally future-oriented and optimistic: "Remittance space is largely about building aspirations, desires, and hopes into the Mexican landscape" (Lopez 2015, 171). But she argues there is in

Figure 7.1. The entrance gate of a rural Mexican household, decorated with the license plates of absent family members working in the United States, 2013. Photograph by Julia Pauli.

fact a more hidden layer of meaning, which requires research that pays more attention to the "inherent paradoxes and contradictions of remittance space" (171). An awareness of these troubling consequences of migrants' aspirations might also be an explanation for the way in which the women valued the present when I asked them about their ideas of the good life.

Since 1995, I have repeatedly returned to Pueblo Nuevo for fieldwork (Pauli 2000, 2008, 2020). A planned field stay in November 2020 had to be postponed to 2022 due to the global COVID-19 pandemic. During the ongoing pandemic, I kept connected with the village through social media, especially WhatsApp. The information collected through these means, however, does not have the same complexity as data collected through in-person fieldwork. Therefore, the analysis offered here is mainly based on ethnographic data collected in person, thus participant observation, supplemented by life and migration histories and repeated ethnographic census collections (Pauli 2000, 2013, 2020).[2]

Before Leaving: Adriana's Wish to Stay Home

Adriana and I were taking a walk through Pueblo Nuevo. It was a rainy Sunday in March 2013. Pointing to various houses in different states of construction, Adriana told me the stories of their absent owners. A woman, followed by two small children, greeted us on her way to the local store. Adriana smiled at her and told me that she feels sorry for her. "You know, we were friends in high school," Adriana explained.³ The information surprised me. Twenty-five-year-old Adriana seemed much younger than the tired-looking woman who had just passed us. "She is a bit older than me, though, late twenties," Adriana said, "and she is the mother of five children." Adriana's friend and her family were living in two small quarters on her husband's family compound. The husband had tried several times, unsuccessfully, to get into the United States as an undocumented migrant. "This is exactly what I try to avoid," Adriana said. "There is no point in marrying when you have to live a life like this." All she wanted was to stay a bit longer, "un poco más," in her parents' house: "I like the way I live." She emphasized that she was not against marriage or having children. Maybe later in life. Currently, she maintained, she did not want to leave home. She started to hum the melody of "Un poco más."

I met Adriana in 1996. During my first yearlong fieldwork in Pueblo Nuevo between 1996 and 1997, Adriana was one of the girls in the ballet class I taught at the village school (Pauli 2000). At the age of eight, she was a shy, skinny girl very similar to all other girls in the village. Sixteen years later, Adriana was in many ways not like other women of her age. Most of them were married and had several children. Economically, her peers depended on the incomes of their husbands. Adriana was not married and had no children. She was working as a supervisor of teachers for the local school administration. She and her father were the main breadwinners in the household where she lived. Her younger brother was also living in the household, working as a farmer and migrant. When she had completed high school, Adriana's parents decided to finance her further education with earnings from the father's migration. She became a teacher. In a cultural setting like Pueblo Nuevo, where marriage is still compulsory for women, this was an unusual path for a young woman.⁴

Adriana's view on the good life, actually *her* good life, provides a first insight into why some women in Pueblo Nuevo not only aspire for the future, or long for the past, but also want to prolong the present. First, Adriana realized what she would lose if she left her parental home. Her sense of an ending of the good life was informed by her knowledge of many unhappy relationships around her. Adriana knew how difficult life could be for young women in their mothers-in-law's households. Many daughters-in-law suffered and hoped to move into a remittance house built by their absent husbands, so they could leave their mothers-in-law's houses (Pauli 2007a, 2008, 2013). Instead of suffering from economic hardship and humiliations in a mother-in-law's household, Adriana enjoyed her life in her parents' household. She earned her own income and had a say in how it was spent. Second, Adriana compared her life with the life of her high school friend. She was aware of the good in her good life and the bad in her friend's bad life. These two forms of comparison—the more general one with women her age in the village and a more specific one with her friend—reinforced her conviction that she was already living a good life.⁵ Adriana's view was in tension with the existing gender norms and roles in the village that expected women to marry and have children. To prevent becoming an outsider, Adriana said, she might marry one day. By 2021, however, Adriana had not married or left her parental home, still enjoying her single good life.

Adriana's mother, Alma, also wanted to hold on to the moment. Wishing to prolong the present, Alma shared some interesting similarities with her daughter's view. Both women compared their lives with the lives of other women. These comparisons helped them to understand why they valued their own present. Alma's cherishing of the moment, however, was not based on the valuation of unusual living circumstances. Instead, her wish for a bit more time, a bit more of the present, stemmed from her fear of losing the ones she loved.

Before Losing: Alma's Hope for the Well-Being of Her Parents

Alma emphasized that she was content with her life. "This is how I want to live the remaining thirty years of my life," she told me. We had been talking about changes in the village, remarking on new houses and improvements of infrastructure, such as paved roads, electricity, and water. Our conversation took place in March 2013, a couple of days after I had gone for the walk with Adriana. We were drinking coffee in Alma's kitchen. Although her husband, Antonio—forty-nine years old and four years older than she—had migrated to the United States, the couple had not built a fancy remittance house. Instead, they had invested the money in improving their adobe brick house. They had built a bathroom, a living room, and new bedrooms. They also bought kitchen utensils, a new television set, a telephone, and a computer. Comparing her house to some of the very fancy remittance houses in the village, Alma told me that the price the absent owners had paid for such luxury was excessive. "You know," she said, "some of them got involved with the cartels. Others are even missing, probably dead." She was referring to a group of men from Pueblo Nuevo who went missing some years earlier. Their families had searched for their bodies in morgues across northern Mexico, unsuccessfully. Like her daughter Adriana, Alma compared her life with that of her peers. She concluded that it is better to value what one has and not to always want more. Unlike many other men in the village, Antonio, Alma's husband, was reluctant to migrate to *el norte*. He was a respected and hardworking man. Many migrants entrusted him with the care of their fields during their absences. This did not lead to a high income, but the family was able to survive. Only after Alma had a severe car accident and the family desperately needed the money to pay the hospital bills did Antonio migrate, without documents, in 2001. He was arrested at the border and spent some months in a U.S. prison. After this traumatic experience, he waited several years before migrating again, this time with papers and following the work invitation of his brother, who had established himself as a businessperson in Virginia.

I asked Alma what she thought is a good life. With a sigh, she told me that she hoped that God would let her parents live a little bit longer so that they could enjoy one another's company. She wanted to have "just a little bit more time with them." Again, the song "Un poco más" came up. Alma was worried that environmental pollution might affect the health of her parents and of other older villagers. One of the most polluted rivers in Mexico, the Río Lerma, flows through the Solís valley, causing anxiety and physical illnesses among the valley's inhabitants. Alma was also concerned about the effects of family conflict and crisis on her parents. She described how much her parents suffered when their daughter Yolanda, who was living in the United States, left again after a visit home. "They are crying," Alma said. "It is very painful. They do not know if they will ever see her again. If the family will ever be united." When Yolanda was home, the family tried to do everything to make the moment last. They organized barbecues, cooked and ate together, and visited friends and relatives. But the art of living together despite the knowledge of its ending was undermined by family conflict. One of Alma's sisters was jealous, feeling their parents were preferring her sisters to her. She had stopped visiting them. Alma hoped that the conflict would end. "It is too much for my parents to have to endure," Alma told me. "I do not want to lose them."

Alma's way to hold on to the moment and value the present resembled her daughter Adriana's view insofar as both women realized what they could lose. Where Adriana feared losing her independence and her home, Alma was afraid of losing the company of the ones she loved: her husband, if he were to get involved with the cartels to build her a fancy house; her parents, if they were stressed too much because of health problems and family crises. The women's appreciation of the present was also an embodiment, a physically felt sentiment, of their anxieties about the future. Alma and Adriana reached their understanding of what was of value in their lives through comparison with the lives of others. This enabled them to cherish the way they lived their lives. Aspiring only for the future or longing for the past could jeopardize this everyday contentment.

Alma and Adriana differed in how they viewed the role of God. Both women were of the Catholic faith. Adriana hardly mentioned God at all, while Alma credited God for giving and taking time and lives. For Alma, it was up to God whether her (good) present life continued. Another difference between Adriana and Alma related to aging and the body. Alma had experienced severe physical pain. Her accident had brought her near death. Since then, she closely observed her body, seeing its aging but also its resilience. This bodily awareness also informed the way she saw her parents' aging and their illnesses. She knew that their (good) time together could rapidly end. This perception resembled the view of her mother, Regina.

Before Letting Go: Regina's Desire for Control

After having listened to Adriana and Alma, I asked Regina if she would also talk with me about her ideas on the good life. She agreed and invited me to have a late breakfast, *un almuerzo*, with her. Between tortillas and hot chocolate, she told me about her health problems, her marriage, and her financial worries. Social security and pensions were almost nonexistent in rural Mexico. Older people survived on a mixture of kin support (often remittances), work, and temporary state subsidies. Since the mid-2000s, the state-run Oportunidades program was also active in Pueblo Nuevo.[6] My 2013 census indicates that state support for older people nevertheless remained minimal (Pauli and Bedorf 2018). When their grandson Manuel, who was living with them, was still attending school, Oportunidades granted Regina and her husband, Angel, a small allowance every two months. When Manuel quit school, the payments stopped. From then on, the couple only received a food basket every two months. Income from work and remittances from a daughter supplemented the food basket. Angel, sixty-seven years old, still produced and sold traditional adobe roof tiles. Sixty-one-year-old Regina sold her homemade tamales, a poplar Mexican street food made of corn, to pupils at the village school during their breaks. Her feet were hurting when she walked. Regina would have preferred to stop selling tamales but needed the money. Of her five daughters and one son, only her daughter Yolanda sent money regularly from the United States. Her other migrant daughter, Candela, hardly ever remitted; she also seldom returned to Pueblo Nuevo to visit her parents. In their youth, Regina and Angel had migrated to Mexico City for work, but since returning to the village when they were in their thirties, they never left again. They lived close to their daughter Alma in a modest house built with funds from a previous federal housing program.

Apart from economic worries, health problems related to aging were also occupying Regina. A few years earlier, a doctor diagnosed her with asthma.[7] With the help of her son, she was receiving treatment. From time to time, Regina got strong headaches, especially when she had walked too much and her feet were aching. "With age one loses strength," she told me, "but there is still some strength left. I am still in control." She hoped that with God's help her control over her life would last a bit longer, at least "un poco más."

Although Regina's life was not easy, she was nevertheless content with it. Reflecting on the death of her widowed mother-in-law, Isabel, she described what it meant to lose control of one's life. This comparison generated insights into what could be lost. Isabel's death was embedded in a long-term conflict between Isabel's youngest daughter, Leticia, and Isabel's eldest son, Angel, Regina's husband. For many years, Isabel was living in a house adjacent to her son Angel. On a daily basis, the couple and Isabel shared with, and supported, each other. When Isabel was sick, Regina cared for her. Isabel's daughter Leticia, upon her marriage, had left Pueblo Nuevo and moved to a different village in the valley of Solís. At the age of eighty, Isabel was diagnosed with cancer. When it became evident that Isabel's health was deteriorating, Leticia took her mother to live with her, without consulting Angel and Regina. A short time later, Isabel died in Leticia's house. Angel and Regina were infuriated and felt appalled. Leticia, as the youngest daughter, had the cultural obligation to care for the mother. Following the rule of ultimogeniture, she would inherit Isabel's house in return for this care (Pauli 2008; Pauli and Bedorf 2016). "But when did Leticia come to care? Only at the very end!" Regina told me with bitterness. "She should have left Isabel in our care and in her house. She would have lasted a bit longer." Regina was convinced that the move out of her house was against Isabel's will. But Isabel had lost control. Regina concluded that it was crucial to keep control over one's life. This was the essence of the good life, she explained to me. With a wink, she continued that she and her husband had taken care of the problem of inheritance, care, and ultimogeniture: "We have made our will with a solicitor. We will not tell our children who inherits what. They should all care for us. And not only at the very end." Thinking through what had happened to others and comparing this to her own life, Regina came to a positive evaluation of her present life, despite all the challenges and hardships she faced. Regina hoped that this present life would last a bit longer. Her practice of comparing and evaluating was similar to her daughter's and granddaughter's reflections on the present.

Comparison with others can also motivate future aspirations. One desires something someone else already has. This type of emulation stimulated the boom in house constructions in Pueblo Nuevo. The wish of these women to prolong the present, however, differed from these forms of future-oriented aspirations and comparisons. Emulation did not motivate the women's holding on to the moment. Rather, the opposite. The women wanted to prevent and not emulate something. Depending on their generation and age, what they wanted to prevent varied. In accordance with her stage in the life course, Adriana questioned the norm of compulsory marriage and patrilocal residence, instead enjoying her well-being as an unmarried, economically independent woman. Middle-aged Alma was more aware of life's fragilities than her daughter Adriana. She hoped that, with the help of God, sickness and death could be kept at bay, at least a little bit longer. Regina, finally, had accepted that sickness and death were part of her life. But she was afraid of losing control. She wanted to prevent illness from taking over her life. It was thus not an imagined future good that led the women to cherish the present. Quite the contrary, it was the reflection on what could be worse or lost that prompted them to appreciate the present.

Regina's narrative, however, was a reflection not only on what could be lost but also on what she had gained. Regina compared herself not only to other women. She also contrasted her momentary life with that of her husband, concluding that her current marital circumstances were much better than in the past. Similar to the reasoning of other older women in the community, Regina's reflections on her marital present were thus also a way of thinking through the different phases of married life.

Tranquility, Finally

With a twinkle, Regina told me that, for some time now, she was in control of her and her husband's lives. This gave her a deep sense of satisfaction. Over the years, we had repeatedly talked about her husband's addiction to alcohol. Many times I had seen Regina fearfully worrying about her husband's health and the family's economic survival. After a physical breakdown several years earlier, her husband had stopped drinking. Since then, she said, life had become so much calmer, "mucho más tranquillo." There were no more fights between them about her husband's whereabouts and how he spent their money. Instead, the couple enjoyed being together, having nice dinners without alcohol, visiting family, or just sitting in front of their house and greeting the neighbors passing by. Due to his long-term addiction, her husband's health had deteriorated. Although Regina was struggling with health issues herself, she nevertheless felt stronger than her husband. To show me that she was now in charge, she commented that remittances were always sent to her, never to her husband. Yolanda, the remitting daughter, knew that her mother, and not her father, was now responsible for household decisions.

Other women in their sixties and seventies who talked with me about aspirations and well-being also mentioned tranquility, *tranquilidad*, as something they had finally achieved in their lives and wanted to hold on to. Many women stressed how much they had suffered during the earlier years of their marriages, enduring too many insecurities, pains, and fears. Domestic violence was (and still is) common in the village (Pauli 2000, 2007b), and many women had suffered from physical and psychological abuse. In several interviews during the 1990s and 2000s, Clara, Adriana's other grandmother and Regina's *comadre*,[8] had told me about the decades-long abuse she had suffered at the hands of her husband, who had beaten her and had cheated on her. She had repeatedly considered leaving him. It was thus a surprise when, on my return in 2013, Clara, now in her sixties, greeted me in an upright position and with a big smile on her face in front of her eldest daughter's impressive remittance house. Her husband, now in his seventies, was standing next to her but appeared broken. He was bent over, apparently with strong back pain. Clara addressed him as "viejito," the diminutive for an elder man, telling me that her "viejito" had lost all his power. With an almost wicked smile, she looked him in the eyes and told him that he did not need to worry, as she was now taking care of everything. He only smiled vaguely. Clara was clearly enjoying her late-won control over her and her husband's lives, hoping that this state of affairs would last long.

The tranquility many women in later life experienced in Pueblo Nuevo was related to their social embedding and the changes in their marriages. At the beginning of married life, women felt very lonely and were subjected to mistreatment by their husbands and affines, especially their mothers-in-law (Pauli 2000, 2008). Over the years, that often changed. With the birth of children, women steadily built an increasingly larger social network of children, *comadres*, and neighbors (Pauli 2000). The networks of older men, in contrast, were much smaller. Remitting children almost always sent their remittances to their mothers to collect at the local Western Union branch. Many daughters were very outspoken in their support of their older mothers, stressing that they had seen and committed to memory the multiple pains their mothers had had to endure in their marriages. Clara's daughter had included a beautiful, large room for her mother in her remittance house but no room for her father. In addition to the support and care older women received from daughters, *comadres*, and neighbors, most women in their sixties and seventies were also in better health than their husbands. Older women thus had more strength and social support than their husbands to manage the everyday challenges of older age, enabling them to take over decisions previously controlled by their husbands.

Finally, women in their sixties and seventies also contemplated the hopes and aspirations of younger women. These considerations mainly related to marriage. There was no consensus among older women of when a woman was entitled to what kinds of aspirations. Some older women like Regina told me that younger women, for example, her granddaughter Adriana, had lost the ability to endure hardship. For Regina, well-being and the good life were not a given but had to be achieved through many years of hard work and the endurance of humiliation and struggle. To her, Adriana's unwillingness to marry and move out of her parental home was a sign of weakness. By contrast, Clara welcomed that younger women had become more demanding, not tolerating everything anymore. One of Clara's daughters was divorced. To be divorced is still very rare in rural Mexico (Willis 2014). Clara supported her daughter's decision to aspire for a life on her own and leave behind the constraints of an unhappy marriage. Why wait all your life for the good life, she asked me, if maybe you can have it earlier? Clara's wish to prolong her present, her hard-won tranquility, extended into an aspiration for the well-being of other women's lives, especially her daughters'.

Conclusion

Aspirations often motivate transnational migration. Migrants and stayers hope that through migration their living circumstances will improve (Cohen 2002). Women of all ages staying in Mexican villages like Pueblo Nuevo do not passively wait for the return of their migrating husbands or sons (Haenn 2020; Sandoval-Cervantes 2017). Instead, they actively build their future by building remittance houses, "houses of their own" (Pauli 2008). However, after more than twenty years of transnational migration from Pueblo Nuevo, it is now time to ask what happens when the building of the remittance house is finally finished and most of the desired consumption objects have been bought? I suggest that the valuation of the present—which, to my surprise, was the dominant temporal horizon (Amrith 2021) in my talks with women in Pueblo Nuevo about the good life—may also be interpreted as a new phase in the migration process (see also Otaegui, this volume). It is a phase following the fulfillment of some aspirations. In this phase, the goal is less about acquiring than it is about keeping what is there. Knowledge about potential losses, based on one's own experiences and the comparison with and evaluation of the lives of others, intensifies this appreciation of the present.

While the fulfillment of material aspirations helps to explain some of the sentiments to prolong the present, it does not take age and generation into account. Comparing women of three different generations shows that, despite their shared wish to hold on to the moment, the reasoning behind these "structures of feeling" (Williams 1977) varies among them. Jackson (2011, xi) rightly points out that the well-being of the young differs from the well-being of the old. Adriana's well-being and her cherishing of her present is also a provocation against local norms. Her father's income from migration enabled Adriana to live this life. She is proud of her vitality and her accomplishments. Regina is not as energetic as her granddaughter. Her art of living in the contemporary is calmer and more accepting of life's pains and troubles. Middle-aged Alma is in between her mother and her daughter. Her effort to have a good life in the company of loved ones accepts the impediments of life while still trying to overcome them.

Further, there is also variation within generations. Adriana, the youngest woman, clearly differs from most women her age in Pueblo Nuevo. Women in their twenties and thirties in Pueblo Nuevo are seldom satisfied with their lives. A migrating husband is often their only hope for a better future. Adriana, in contrast, is independent of a migrating husband. Although her case is unusual, I suggest that her desire for autonomy foreshadows changes in gender roles already well underway in Mexico, especially in urban areas (Esteinou 2014; Willis 2014). Increasingly, women decide to stay single, like Adriana, or opt out of marriage by divorce, like one of Clara's daughters (Davidson and Hannaford 2023). Older women discuss these changes. Some, like Regina, criticize younger women's aspirations for early well-being, stressing that to reach tranquility and well-being it takes time and hard work. Others, like Clara, welcome the changes, encouraging younger women to go ahead in their search for a better life. The art of living (Lambek 2008) and the wish to prolong the present before it ends are thus reflections about one's own life and the lives of others like granddaughters, daughters, mothers-in-law, parents, or husbands.

The women's wish to prolong the moment, *un poco más*, before it ends, is also their way to navigate through the multiple insecurities of their lives. With no social security to speak of and meager, unsteady incomes, women of all generations face existential uncertainties (Hänsch, Kroeker, and Oldenburg 2017). Awareness of one's own aging and increasing bodily fragility, experienced more often by older women, however, enhances the urgency to cherish what the moment offers. Women in later life in Pueblo Nuevo gain satisfaction from still being in control. This satisfaction is comparable to the feelings expressed by residents of a geriatric institution for abandoned elderly on the outskirts of Lima, Peru, who stated, after preparing and sharing a delicious meal, "'Es lindo ver que todavía podemos': it is rewarding to see that we still can" (Zegarra Chiappori 2019, 63). The aspiration to (still) be capable and in charge, in this very moment, weighs more than any future dream for the older women in Pueblo Nuevo, to stay like this only a little bit longer, only *un poco más*.

Acknowledgments

My deep gratitude goes to the inhabitants of Pueblo Nuevo for the many years of their support and insights. I very much thank Megha Amrith, Victoria K. Sakti, and Dora Sampaio for inviting me to their workshop "Aspiring in Later Life" in November 2020 at the Max Planck Institute for the Study of Religious and Ethnic Diversity in Göttingen. Their and the other participants' comments were most helpful in revising the essay. Many thanks also to Caroline Jeannerat for editing the chapter's language. For the ongoing exchange on migration, aging, and belonging, I very much thank Erdmute Alber, Franziska Bedorf, Bettina Beer, Cati Coe, Maren Jordan, and Dumitrița Luncă. Michael Schnegg's constructive criticism has much improved the argument of the essay, for which I am very thankful.

NOTES

1. To protect the anonymity of my interlocutors, I have changed personal information that is not crucial for my argument.
2. Most of the data analyzed here was collected within the project "Ageing in Transnational Space: Processes of (Re)migration between Mexico and the USA," funded by the German Science Foundation (grant SCHN 1103/3-1), from 2010 to 2013, with Michael Schnegg and me as project leaders. Michael Schnegg, Franziska Bedorf, and Susanne Lea Radt participated in data collection in 2010 and 2013.
3. The account here and elsewhere in the chapter is based on field notes and interview data that I translated from Spanish into English.
4. Research on single women in societies where marriage is normative is still rare (Lamb 2018).
5. Recently, more attention is being paid to comparison as a central way of knowledge production in anthropology (Schnegg and Lowe 2020).
6. The program has since ended.
7. Regina's asthma might also be the reason why she almost died from a COVID-19 infection in late 2020. Her daughter and granddaughter cared for her at home.
8. The Mexican *compadrazgo* system has emerged from the Catholic practice of godparenthood. However, unlike in Europe, where the most important relationship is that between godparent and godchild, the most important relationship in the Mexican *compadrazgo* system is that between the godparents (classified as *comadre* and *compadre*) and the parents of the child (Schnegg 2007).

REFERENCES

Alber, Erdmute, Sjaak van der Geest, and Susan Reynolds Whyte. 2008. *Generations in Africa: Connections and Conflicts*. Münster: Lit.
Amrith, Megha. 2021. "The Linear Imagination, Stalled: Changing Temporal Horizons in Migrant Journeys." *Global Networks* 21 (1): 127–145. https://doi.org/10.1111/glob.12280.
Appadurai, Arjun. 2013. *The Future as Cultural Fact: Essays on the Global Condition*. London: Verso.
Berlant, Lauren. 2011. *Cruel Optimism*. Durham, NC: Duke University Press.
Boccagni, Paolo, and Marta B. Erdal. 2021. "On the Theoretical Potential of 'Remittance Houses': Toward a Research Agenda across Emigration Contexts." *Journal of Ethnic and Migration Studies* 47 (5): 1066–1083.
Boehm, Deborah. 2016. *Returned: Coming and Going in an Age of Deportation*. Berkeley: University of California Press.
Brettell, Caroline. 1986. *Men Who Migrate, Women Who Wait: Population and History in a Portuguese Parish*. Princeton, NJ: Princeton University Press.
Cohen, Jeffrey H. 2002. "Migration and 'Stay at Homes' in Rural Oaxaca, Mexico: Local Expression of Global Outcomes." *Urban Anthropology and Studies of Cultural Systems and World Economic Development* 31 (2): 231–259.
Davidson, Joanna, and Dinah Hannaford. 2023. *Opting Out: Women Evading Marriage around the World*. New Brunswick, NJ: Rutgers University Press.
Esteinou, Rosario. 2014. "Intimacy in Twentieth-Century Mexico." In *Intimacies and Cultural Change: Perspectives on Contemporary Mexico*, edited by Daniel Nehring, Rosario Esteinou, and Emmanuel Alvarado, 35–55. Farnham, UK: Ashgate.
Ferguson, James. 1999. *Expectations of Modernity: Myths and Meanings of Urban Life on the Zambian Copperbelt*. Berkeley: University of California Press.
Fischer, Edward F. 2014. *The Good Life: Aspiration, Dignity, and the Anthropology of Wellbeing*. Stanford, CA: Stanford University Press.

Haenn, Nora. 2020. *Marriage after Migration: An Ethnography of Money, Romance, and Gender in Globalizing Mexico*. New York: Oxford University Press.

Hänsch, Valerie, Lena L. Kroeker, and Silke Oldenburg. 2017. "Uncertain Future(s): Perceptions on Time between the Immediate and the Imagined." *Tsantsa*, no. 22: 4–17. https://doi.org/10.36950/tsantsa.2017.22.7342.

Jackson, Michael. 2011. *Life within Limits: Well-Being in a World of Want*. Durham. NC: Duke University Press.

Jiménez, Alberto Corsín, ed. 2008a. *Culture and Well-Being: Anthropological Approaches to Freedom and Political Ethics*. London: Pluto Press.

———. 2008b. "Introduction: Well-Being's Re-proportioning of Social Thought." In *Culture and Well-Being: Anthropological Approaches to Freedom and Political Ethics*, edited by Alberto Corsín Jiménez, 1–32. London: Pluto Press.

Lamb, Sarah. 2018. "Being Single in India: Gendered Identities, Class Mobilities, and Personhoods in Flux." *Ethos* 46 (1): 49–69. https://doi.org/10.1111/etho.12193.

Lambek, Michael. 2008. "Measuring—or Practising—Well-Being?" In *Culture and Well-Being: Anthropological Approaches to Freedom and Political Ethics*, edited by Alberto Corsín Jiménez, 115–133. London: Pluto Press.

Lattanzi Shutika, Debra. 2011. *Beyond the Borderlands: Migration and Belonging in the United States and Mexico*. Berkeley: University of California Press.

Lopez, Sarah Lynn. 2015. *The Remittance Landscape: Spaces of Migration in Rural Mexico and Urban USA*. Chicago: University of Chicago Press.

Montes de Oca Zavala, Verónica, Ahtziri Molina Roldán, and Rosaura Avalos Pérez. 2008. *Migración, redes transnacionales y envejecimiento: Estudio de las redes familiares transnacionales de la vejez en Guanajuato*. Mexico City: Universidad Nacional Autónoma de México, Instituto de Investigaciones Sociales; Gobierno del Estado de Guanajuato.

Pauli, Julia. 2000. *Das geplante Kind: Demographischer, wirtschaftlicher und sozialer Wandel in einer mexikanischen Gemeinde*. Hamburg: Lit.

———. 2007a. "'Que vivan mejor aparte': Migración, estructura familiar y género en una comunidad del México central." In *Familias mexicanas en transición: Unas miradas antropológicas*, edited by David Robichaux, 87–116. Mexico City: Universidad Iberoamericana.

———. 2007b. "Zwölf-Monats-Schwangerschaften: Internationale Migration, reproduktive Konflikte und weibliche Autonomie in einer zentralmexikanischen Gemeinde." *Tsantsa*, no. 12: 71–81.

———. 2008. "A House of One's Own: Gender, Migration, and Residence in Rural Mexico." *American Ethnologist* 35 (1): 171–187. https://doi.org/10.1111/j.1548-1425.2008.00012.x.

———. 2013. "'Sharing Made Us Sisters': Sisterhood, Migration and Household Dynamics in Mexico and Namibia." In *The Anthropology of Sibling Relations: Shared Parentage, Experience, and Exchange*, edited by Erdmute Alber, Cati Coe, and Tatjana Thelen, 29–50. New York: Palgrave Macmillan.

———. 2020. "Rethinking the Ethnographer: Reflections on Fieldwork with and without Family in Mexico and Namibia." In *Being a Parent in the Field: Implications and Challenges of Accompanied Fieldwork*, edited by Fabienne Braukmann, Michaela Haug, Katja Metzmacher, and Rosalie Stolz, 39–60. Bielefeld: Transcript.

Pauli, Julia, and Franziska Bedorf. 2016. "From Ultimogeniture to Senior Club: Negotiating Certainties and Uncertainties of Growing Older between Rural Mexico and Urban Chicago." In *Migration, Networks, Skills: Anthropological Perspectives on Mobility and Transformation*, edited by Astrid Wonneberger, Mijal Gandelsman-Trier, and Hauke Dorsch, 47–66. Bielefeld: Transcript.

———. 2018. "Retiring Home? House Construction, Age Inscriptions, and the Building of Belonging among Mexican Migrants and Their Families in Chicago and Rural Mexico." *Anthropology and Aging* 39 (1): 48–65. https://doi.org/10.5195/aa.2018.173.

Sandoval-Cervantes, Iván. 2017. "Uncertain Futures: The Unfinished Houses of Undocumented Migrants in Oaxaca, Mexico." *American Anthropologist* 119 (2): 209–222. https://doi.org/10.1111/aman.12864.

Schnegg, Michael. 2007. "Blurred Edges, Open Boundaries: The Long-Term Development of a Peasant Community in Rural Mexico." *Journal of Anthropological Research* 63 (1): 5–31. https://doi.org/10.3998/jar.0521004.0063.103.

Schnegg, Michael, and Edward D. Lowe, eds. 2020. *Comparing Cultures: Innovations in Comparative Ethnography.* Cambridge: Cambridge University Press.

Smith, Robert C. 2006. *Mexican New York: Transnational Lives of New Immigrants.* Berkeley: University of California Press.

Williams, Raymond. 1977. *Marxism and Literature.* Oxford: Oxford University Press.

Willis, Katie. 2014. "Intimate Citizenship and Social Change in Contemporary Mexico." In *Intimacies and Cultural Change: Perspectives on Contemporary Mexico*, edited by Daniel Nehring, Rosario Esteinou, and Emmanuel Alvarado, 13–33. Farnham, UK: Ashgate.

Zegarra Chiappori, Magdalena. 2019. "Growing Old in the Margins in Lima, Perú." *Anthropology and Aging* 40 (2): 60–66. https://doi.org/10.5195/aa.2019.234.

CHAPTER 8

Disrupted Futures

THE SHIFTING ASPIRATIONS OF OLDER CAMEROONIANS LIVING IN DISPLACEMENT

Nele Wolter

All human beings look ahead, make plans, and hope, dream, and aspire to a future of living a "good life." Especially when one is younger, shaping the future seems particularly important: designing seemingly never-ending education paths, planning families (or not), and creating images of oneself in a world of contradictions. As one grows older, the path ahead seems shorter and more predictable. Retirement has already been, or soon will be, reached; family projects are complete; and one is facing the last stage of life, during which nothing unexpected is expected and one hopes to age successfully and in good health. Western notions of growing old "successfully" are marked by attributes like a strong and healthy body, self-determination, and independence, and where aging people may, for instance, attend fitness courses and live on their own into old age (see Lamb, Robbins-Ruszkowski, and Corwin 2017). In this conception, retiring means, not sitting at home and "waiting" for death to come, but being active and mobile and getting the best out of the last stage of life. This can include retiring away from home in a more "age-friendly" society, either temporarily or permanently, a trend that has emerged among European retirees in the past decades (see, e.g., Gustafson 2001; King, Cela, and Fokkema 2021; King, Warnes, and Williams 1998; Oliver 2007; Williams et al. 2000). Sarah Lamb, Jessica Robbins-Ruszkowski, and Anna I. Corwin expand this perspective, arguing, "Cross-culturally, we find other perspectives on what it is to age well" (2017, 5). They point to the necessity of looking beyond the stage of old age or retirement to understand that "our very ideas about what it is to be a normal, valued, and successful human being over the life course arise out of and are shaped by powerful cultural-historical, political-economic conditions and discourses" (17).

However, older age certainly does not mean that people do not make plans for the time ahead. During my fieldwork among aging internally displaced persons

(IDPs) in Bafoussam, Cameroon, in 2019, I frequently met research partners who told me about the intentions and aspirations they had held for later life. These plans had been disrupted by the political turmoil that began in 2016 and ended in a civil war–like situation that persisted until the time of my writing in 2022. Separatists and government troops have engaged in continuous fighting in the English-speaking Southwest and Northwest regions, which caused massive displacement, affecting an estimated 575,000 people (UNOCHA 2021), most of whom have fled to the francophone parts of the country. The most common destinations of these IDPs are mainly, but not solely, bigger cities like the capital Yaoundé, Douala, or Bafoussam, where they usually draw on existing social networks and hope to find accommodation and sources of income, among other things.

Confronted with this new environment, my interlocutors often found themselves in precarious situations that differed from their previous living conditions in a number of ways. Apart from scarce financial resources to pay for everyday commodities, such as food, body care products, clothes, and school fees and education materials for children and grandchildren, they experienced permanent pressure to find an appropriate place to live. The scarce housing available in Bafoussam, as in other cities of Cameroon, alongside weak financial situations, often forced my interlocutors—like most IDPs—to live with a large number of persons in the smallest of spaces. Harry[1] and his family, for instance, lived in a two-bedroom apartment intermittently occupied by up to twenty-two people. These extremely demanding circumstances in everyday life barely left room to think about the future. To some extent, for many IDPs the dream, and hope, was to return to their former homes in the anglophone regions and continue living their former lives. As it became more and more obvious that the war and displacement would be protracted, and there was no sign that they would be able to return in the near future, new plans had to be made for the time yet to come. This protraction points at the importance of the temporal dimension in migration and displacement, particularly when the past, present, and future are inextricably interwoven and determine the status quo of a migrated person (see also Pauli, this volume).

This chapter delineates how older IDPs in Bafoussam realign their future lives in contrast to, or based on, the aspirations they had before they were displaced. Building on in-depth interviews and participant observation in Bafoussam between November 2019 and March 2020 among twelve displaced families (including one individual awaiting family reunion), I outline the subtle entanglements of intra-familial ties and the temporal connections that affect the decisions of older Cameroonians to stay where they are, to move on to new places, or, finally, to return to their homeland. On the one hand, the different biographies reveal that shifting aspirations in later life are inevitably linked with social relations that change or intensify throughout the life course of my interlocutors. On the other hand, they demonstrate how temporalities play an important role in overcoming uncertainties in the already uncertain situation of displacement.

Shattered Present, Disrupted Futures: Time, Hope, and the Future during Displacement

A wider perspective on Cameroon's history is important to understanding the violent upheavals and conflict between separatists and the government in recent years. When the German Empire lost the Kamerun colony in 1916, the region was divided into British Cameroon and French Cameroon by a League of Nations mandate. While French Cameroon became independent in 1960, British Cameroon gained independence after a referendum in 1961. Its northern part joined Nigeria, and the southern part (including today's Northwest and Southwest regions of Cameroon) voted to join the newly established Republic of Cameroon.

When, decades later, in 2016, teachers and lawyers started demonstrating against the marginalization of the Cameroonian anglophone minority in the Northwest and Southwest regions, no one could have imagined that the effects of the protests would last for years to come. What started as peaceful marches against the government's replacement of English-speaking teachers, lawyers, and judges by their francophone colleagues turned into the most violent conflict the country had faced since independence. Secessionist groups, consolidated as the Amba Boys, started trying to separate the anglophone regions from the rest of the country and announced the Federal Republic of Ambazonia in October 2017.[2] Since then, ongoing clashes between government troops and separatists, particularly in the rural parts of the English-speaking regions, have terrorized large parts of the anglophone population. Numerous violations of human rights by both parties have been recorded, such as the killing of people, the use of torture, sexual and gender-based violence, extortion, and the burning of whole villages. Hundreds of thousands of children, women, and men have escaped the two regions, either to neighboring Nigeria or to francophone Cameroon (see, e.g., UNOCHA 2021).

While the majority of the displaced in Nigeria are in refugee camps (UNHCR 2021), most of those who stayed within the national borders found accommodation with family or friends or in temporary shelter, such as rented apartments or houses. For displaced families, staying in these makeshift homes often goes along with other struggles in day-to-day life. While children and adolescents are usually sent to school to resume their interrupted education, adult and older IDPs are usually busy making a living and reestablishing themselves in a new environment. Due to the weak job market throughout the country, finding employment is usually very challenging for the displaced. Most try to find work in informal markets, something quite common in Cameroon and other sub-Saharan countries (Benjamin et al. 2020). However, looking for a job in an urban setting is usually a new experience for many IDPs, as most come from rural areas or smaller towns in the English-speaking regions and often worked in the agricultural sector prior to displacement.[3] For this reason, many IDPs are focused primarily on everyday life and finding work. Shaping the future, or how "to anticipate the following day" (Bryant and Knight 2019, 9), is subordinated for most of them.

More than two decades ago, Saulo B. Cwerner argued that "human migration has been largely understood as a phenomenon intimately associated with *space*, more precisely as a process unfolding *in* space" (2001, 7; emphasis in original). Since then, more attention has been paid to the intersection of migration and time, not only in migration studies but also within anthropology (see, e.g., Appadurai 2013; Dalsgård et al. 2014; Munn 1992; Stock 2019), to highlight and analyze how time and temporality frame social life within different contexts of migration and im/mobility. Although it has been widely acknowledged that the past, present, and future are inextricably entangled, ethnographic research, and research on the future specifically, remains scarce, with some important exceptions (e.g., Bryant and Knight 2019; Kleist and Jansen 2016; Pine 2014).

In the context of migration, and particularly if looking at involuntary migration or (internal) displacement, notions of the future are often linked to feelings of hope, despair, uncertainty, and other similar emotions, perceptions, and sentiments about when migrants hope to return to their home regions, or to uncertainties about their future status as asylum seekers, due to immigration restrictions. Accordingly, the future of a migrant often depends on conditions in the present: conditions that are usually determined not by the migrants themselves, but by political decisions, legal principles, or the end to a war, and that can endure for long periods of time. Though these periods may be indefinite, this does not mean that attitudes toward, and notions of, the future remain the same, as has been impressively demonstrated by Cathrine Brun's (2015) research on Georgian IDPs experiencing protracted displacement. Brun shows that the hope of return is the main impetus for IDPs to keep up with their lives during displacement, which she refers to as a period of "protracted uncertainty" (20). Furthermore, Brun highlights that hope, as a collective discourse around return (30), has a "changing nature [and] must be seen in relation to the social status in which many IDPs find themselves" (31). Eventually, Brun makes clear that the hope to return changes from being "uncertain to unforeseeable" (31; referring to Lefebvre 2002), and even though it does not completely vanish over time, it changes how people design their present lives and orientations toward the future.

While Brun looks at hope and the future in the context of internal displacement and return, Nauja Kleist (2017) describes hope on the African continent as a driver of mobility, of the search for a better life elsewhere on the continent or beyond. She suggests that "hope constitutes a fruitful analytical framework in which to link questions of political economy and mobility regimes with analyses of the collective social imaginaries and aspirations which imbue migration projects" (1). Like Brun, Kleist conflates hope with uncertainty, but also highlights how hope can counter uncertainty by focusing on "potentiality and anticipation rather than fear and doubt" (2). She argues further that one of the specific features of hope is its relation to the future (10), which is conveyed during economic and political crisis, or linked with protracted conflicts (Kleist and Jansen 2016), to give only some examples. According to Kleist and Stef Jansen (2016), the different sorts of crises have long existed, but frame our present lives through their "intensified uncertainty and unpredictability" (376) caused by the rapidly changing, global, "uncontrollable dynamics where distant events have unforeseen local consequences" (375). Therefore, looking at the manifold crises that have occurred in the past decades and continue to emerge at present, I suggest that hope, in local and global contexts, unfolds shifting dynamics with regard to the future.

Like hope, aspiration can be seen as a driver of migration (Carling and Collins 2018; see also Carling and Schewel 2018), when migrants strive for a better life or want to get away from bad living conditions. Even in the context of forced migration or displacement, aspiration can also be a consequence of the migration process: when people decide to change their plans for the future based on their current temporary situations, which may then be prolonged. Looking at both aspiration and hope as drivers of mobility reveals the temporal character of migration. Jørgen Carling and Francis Collins argue, in a similar manner to Kleist and Jansen, that "aspiration and desire are part of a semantic field which relates the present or actual with the future or potential" (2018, 918), or as Elisabeth Scheibelhofer puts it, "Aspirations are a two-sided coin as they simultaneously address the present and the future" (2018, 1000). As Scheibelhofer further argues, in the context of migration, aspirations might change over time due to "biographical changes such as employment, migration, having children and retirement" (1000). Thus, her argument strengthens the perspective that older people's future aspirations not only may change in response to certain life events but can differ from those of younger adults in relation to different experiences, or to experiences that the latter have not experienced due to their shorter lives. As my empirical data shows, (forced) migration and displacement affects life plans at all life stages, including for older people, and can disrupt previous aspirations that are changed to entirely different plans that affect different generations within a family. This is in opposition to the common assumption that, in older age, people do not modify their life-course patterns.

Though aspirations may relate to certain (shifting) situations or events in life, it is nevertheless important to highlight here that "aspirations . . . are not situational but rather enduring through the life course" (Scheibelhofer 2018, 1000) and thus, as I will show, always respond to individual life trajectories. Aspirations are not situational, but they are also never an intrinsic factor but socially and culturally embedded and dependent on power relations and degrees of poverty, among other things (see Amrith, Sakti, and Sampaio, this volume; Whyte, this volume).

Hoping to Return, Aspiring to Move On: Narratives of Changing Hope and Shifting Aspirations

In 2019, I lived for four months in Bafoussam, the capital of Cameroon's West region, where I had conducted research before, and met regularly with eleven displaced families and one displaced man. The family members included not only the members of a nuclear family but also extended family spanning generations, among them, grandparents, grandchildren, cousins, in-laws, and other relatives, and sometimes friends and neighbors who were living with my interlocutors. Some of the displaced I interviewed did not come to Bafoussam first, but had lived elsewhere, where they had struggled due to the lack of a social network or high living expenses. The number of persons living in a household varied in size over time: sometimes other IDPs moved in and stayed for a while, until they found a place of their own, or relatives would come to visit and stay for several weeks or months. The family members ranged in age from three to ninety-two years and included male and female interlocutors equally. Though children were an integral part of family life, and I interacted a lot with them during my visits, I conducted interviews only with adults, as the content of the interviews was assumed (and indeed proved) to be very sensitive due to the often violent, traumatic experiences of my research partners.

Many of the IDPs I interviewed were suffering from economic deprivation and in precarious situations. However, despite the economic hardships most had gone through, none depended on governmental or humanitarian assistance, which was, in any case, barely available in Bafoussam at the time. Moreover, all of them could rely, if necessary, on a stable social safety net, with support from children or other relatives, as well as from friends, former colleagues, or neighbors.

Bafoussam, a city of approximately 350,000 inhabitants, has relatively good infrastructure, with several hospitals, numerous bilingual schools, a dense network of mainly Catholic churches, and three large markets and other places from which to purchase items for daily use. However, like many other bigger cities in Cameroon and other countries in sub-Saharan Africa, Bafoussam is not in a position to accommodate numerous labor migrants and city dwellers, and the job market does not offer nearly enough work opportunities. There is hence a lot of illegal housing and informal labor. The inflow of IDPs has put further pressure on the city administration and on Bafoussam's inhabitants.

I planned to return to Cameroon some months after my first phase of fieldwork to continue working with the same families. But the coronavirus pandemic thwarted my plans, and until the time of writing, I could not continue with on-site research. Instead, I turned to digital fieldwork and stayed in close contact with my interlocutors using instant messenger applications like WhatsApp or Telegram, the telephone, or other communication applications like Skype. I used WhatsApp and Skype for further interviews and to catch up with the lives of my research partners over quite a long period and in a more detailed way than I could have achieved with text messages. Although the pandemic certainly had a strong impact on how I conducted my research, it was barely mentioned during my remote conversations with IDPs and supposedly played only a minor role in their lives. Their main focus was the conflict in the Northwest and Southwest regions, and the hope that it would end one day, just as it had been during my research stay. For this reason, the pandemic does not play a considerable role in the following case studies.

DISRUPTED FUTURES

Figure 8.1. Nelson doing his daily exercise in Bafoussam. Photograph by Nele Wolter.

NELSON

I met Nelson one day after church, where the representative of the IDPs in the church community had introduced him to me. At the time we met, he was sixty-nine years old and living alone in a small, rented one-bedroom house located on the outskirts of Bafoussam. Either we met at church and talked after the service or I visited him in his little house, where we usually sat outside, talking and eating fruit and cucumber, while he showed me his books or other belongings that his wife had sent to him during his protracted stay in the francophone West region. Sometimes I joined him when he was doing "his sport," as he called it, and together we would walk around his neighborhood (figure 8.1). Despite his age, he went on walks every day for up to three hours, no matter how intense the sun was during the dry season or how the rain poured during the rainy season.

He showed me places he frequently visited, introduced me to neighbors, and told me the names of the schools we passed, where he went to buy his provisions, and where one could buy the best food. Apart from his sport, going to the market, or attending church on Sundays, Nelson told me that he did not meet many people in Bafoussam. Once or twice a week, two of his children who were at school in Bafoussam, but lived with friends of the family, visited him and helped him around the house. At times, he would talk to his landlady, who lived next door. But that was about it.

He had two wives, the first of whom lived in his rural home village. The second one lived in Bamenda, the regional capital of the Northwest. His first wife had had five children, all of whom were grown up and lived in different places in the francophone part of the country. He only talked about them when I asked explicitly, but then spoke in detail, giving their names and professions and describing what they were like. He told me that he had not seen his first wife for about two years and some of his children for even longer. With his second wife, who was younger than the first, he had two children, aged seventeen and nineteen years. Both children had lived in Bafoussam to attend school even before Nelson escaped Bamenda. His second wife worked as a nurse at a state hospital in Bamenda, and Nelson told me that they had applied for her transfer to Bafoussam about a year before we spoke. They could not influence the transfer process in any way; all they could do was to ask a friend in the national capital, Yaoundé, where such transfers are centrally organized, to go to the Department of Health and ask if the file had been processed. So, Nelson and his wife had to wait and hope indefinitely.

As a former police officer, Nelson had a pension that covered his basic costs in Bafoussam. But, after paying for rent and food, there was not much money left. He was suffering from diabetes and needed to buy medicine that he could not afford on his pension. That is why he regularly asked his second wife and his older children to support him by sending money for insulin or for equipment to monitor his blood glucose—both of which he used only when he could afford them.

His profession as a police officer was the reason why he left his village in the Northwest. After being posted to several stations throughout Cameroon and in neighboring Chad for some years, he retired at age fifty-five. Then, he oscillated between the households of his two wives. When talking about his past in the Northwest, Nelson often spoke of his house in Bamenda, which was much bigger than his small hut in Bafoussam. He particularly mentioned the conveniences he missed from his "former" life in the regional capital, where his house had four bedrooms and he did not have to go outside to relieve himself but used an indoor bathroom. When asked about his daily routines in Bamenda, before he was displaced, he said, "I stayed at the house or visited my friends and neighbors. On the weekends, I would travel to the village to work the farm with my wife." His first wife lived in their farmhouse and tended their small farm in the northwestern village where he was born. Nelson went back to help her, particularly with the harvest and with maintenance work around the house. I once asked him what his plans for the future had been before he came to Bafoussam, and he replied, "I don't know. I just kept going with the things I did. I went to the village, I went to Bamenda. That was all. I was a happy man." Nelson did not speak of any special plans he had had for his own or his family's future, and while taking into account that he might have simply forgotten them, or did not want to tell me, I could only suspect that his aspirations were for his life to stay the way it was.

His statements about his future plans differed when we talked about his time in, and on the way to, Bafoussam about a year and a half before we met. In 2017, he was kidnapped from his home in the village by separatists, who took him into the forest and abused him, pressing him for money and his service weapon. After two weeks of torture by his kidnappers, he was ransomed and allowed to go back to his home in the village. However, he told me:

I knew that they would come back. Once they knew I could give them money, they would come back for more. I told them that I had to return my gun when I retired and I don't have it anymore, but I lied. If they had found out, they would have killed me with it. So, we decided that I should leave and not come back so soon. I first went to Bamenda [to stay with his second wife], but I did not feel safe there and my wife was also scared.... Then I went to Dschang [in the francophone West region], where I stayed with a friend. I was there for two months, but I did not want to stay there. So I went to Bafoussam. My son and daughter are here, and I wanted to be closer to them. They visit me sometimes after school.

Nelson's words make clear that he had already altered his plans when he started on his escape from the village in the Northwest. As a logical consequence of the threat he had faced in his rural home, he decided to go to his second home in Bamenda, where there was no current threat, but where he still *felt* the danger of the violence he had previously encountered. Staying with his friend in Dschang was only a temporary option for Nelson, so he decided to continue to Bafoussam, where he could be near his two younger children. During his time in Bafoussam, he was in close contact with his wives and other villagers to learn about the situation in his village. Checking the news and exchanging messages with family and friends back home became an inherent part of his daily routine: "I read the news on my phone every day. I wait for news. What is happening there. What the Ambas do. My friends send me videos all the time and tell me everything they know. Yesterday they [the Amba Boys] burned my neighbor's house. It is crazy.... I hope that my wife is safe and they won't harm her. I hope."

Apart from the understandable concern for the safety of his wife, Nelson was also hoping to return, saying, "I really wish I can go back to be with my wife. But who knows when this thing [the violence] is over? I don't. I hope I can go back soon, but I don't think that the war will end soon.... I just want to be there. But now, I am here." After several months in the West region, the longing for a reunion with his second wife became so intense that they agreed to apply for his wife to transfer to the regional hospital in Bafoussam. They gathered all the required papers and handed them in at the Department of Health in Yaoundé. At the time of my interview, there was still no response from the authority in Yaoundé, and Nelson and his second wife were patiently waiting for a positive reply. When I asked if a refusal of the request seemed likely, he told me that he would not know and just hoped it would be approved. Finally, in summer 2021, about two and a half years after the application, the health department approved the request, as Nelson happily texted me via Telegram.

When I phoned him some weeks later, he seemed eager to find a new place for himself and his wife: "something neat and with a bathroom inside the house." When I asked him about their future, he replied that he hoped to go back to the Northwest one day, but for now his wife was with him, and that was enough. Nelson's case well elucidates the correlation of hope and aspirations. While the hope to return to the anglophone region imbued his displacement over time, it was evident that returning home became less important once he was to be reunited with his second wife in Bafoussam. More than that, his aspirations for their foreseeable future in the francophone West region shifted to the idea of finding a cozy and comfortable home for them to live in, if necessary, for good. Nelson's story illustrates how aspirations shift over time and are influenced by the importance of family relationships that have impacts on everyday life during displacement.

Harry and Florence

In contrast to Nelson, Harry lived with a large part of his family in a rented three-bedroom apartment in Bafoussam, close to a popular polytechnic. While Nelson lived in a sparsely inhabited area, where the roads were unusually empty for a bigger city like Bafoussam, Harry and his wife, Florence, lived in a bustling neighborhood and maintained close relationships to other people residing in the area. Due to the high volume of traffic, Florence had a small roadside stall, no more than a wooden table, where she neatly arrayed basic foods and other essential goods in small and large bags or plastic buckets, offering them for sale to passing residents.

I met Harry and Florence at the Catholic church that I regularly attended on Sundays. Florence approached me one day and told me that I had to meet her husband and talk to him, as she had learned from others that I was conducting research among the IDPs from the anglophone regions who had come to Bafoussam. She invited me to their place on one of the following days. On the assigned day, I arrived at the polytechnic, where Harry, a tall and quiet man in his early sixties, came to collect me. We walked toward his home, and he greeted some people on the streets. At his house, Florence was sitting outside in the sun, at the wooden table, watching the street and waiting for customers. They invited me into a spacious living room with several sofas and armchairs. In a corner, there was a desk with a TV placed on it. Three children were gathered around, watching cartoons. Harry shooed them outside to play and invited me to sit down. I asked how he and Florence had met each other and where they had lived before, and I learned that they had been married for more than twenty-five years. They had five adult children, of whom three lived with them in Bafoussam, while two remained behind in the village in the Northwest because they did not want to leave. "My oldest son was just elected mayor of our village," Harry told me proudly, showing me pictures of his eldest.

I wanted to know more about their life in the village, and Harry told me that he had worked as a police officer and retired seven years ago. He had been based in Yaoundé, Bafoussam, and Mbouda, a smaller town near Bafoussam, where he and his family lived for several years during his service. During this time, Florence, who was ten years younger than Harry, worked their small farm in their home village and took care of the children. As he had lived in francophone parts of Cameroon as a police officer, Harry spoke French well and had developed close relationships with his neighbors. After he retired, he said, "I did not want to sit around.

I wanted to work." So, he applied for a bank loan to invest in oil palm cultivation. "That was five years ago, before I came here [to Bafoussam]."

I learned that they had quite a big piece of land close to their home in their village, where he started planting palms and also practiced husbandry. At the time of our interview, Harry was still repaying the loan, and he mentioned that he used almost all his pension payments for this purpose. After each installment was deducted by the bank, there was only CFA 3,000 (approximately USD 4.82) left, which was, to put it in Harry's words, "literally nothing." While waiting for his first oil palm harvest, Harry sold cattle to pay the university fees for two of his children and some other minor expenses. At that time, prior to displacement, his aspirations for the future seemed to fill him with self-confidence, as he benefited from the cash flow from selling cattle and other crops and was aiming to finance the education of his younger children, as well as do something on his own behalf.

In the year he was expecting his first harvest, conflict flared up, and Harry and Florence had to leave their village. As a former police officer and a chairperson of the local high school, Harry was targeted by separatists. He had encouraged parents to continue sending their children to school, one of the things that the Amba Boys said parents should not do, in order to not support the government.

> One night, they came to my house. It was one o'clock in the night and we were sleeping. I woke up because there was a smell, something was burning. I got up and ran around the house, and then the kitchen was burning. They set it on fire, but it was not burning well. . . . They entered the house and beat me in the face. I had to kneel down in front of them, and they held a gun to my head. My wife and children were there and watched. I thought they would shoot me. They yelled at me, [saying] I should give them the money and stop talking to the parents [to tell them their children should continue attending school]. I knew them. They were boys from the village. . . . I gave them three hundred thousand [CFA] and then they left. I had more money—they didn't know that. . . . Then I knew I am not safe any longer, and the next morning I left the village.

Harry left his family behind to get to safety outside his village. At first, he stayed with a friend in Bamenda, but then decided to leave the Northwest altogether for Bafoussam, where a former colleague was from. The colleague rented out an apartment to Harry, and, after several weeks, Florence and their three younger children followed him. Florence started her small roadside stall soon after, and she kept herself busy with that and a reading group that discussed Bible texts every Monday. Harry often joined Florence while she was waiting for or serving customers, and from his chair he observed the scenery. He was also president of an IDP solidarity group and organized its meetings and administrative work. Together, Florence and Harry went to church every Sunday and "prayed that they could go home soon." But "soon" would not come, and when we met, they had spent almost one and a half years in Bafoussam. Unsurprisingly, Florence and Harry were hoping to go back home, just like Nelson. And, like Nelson, Harry checked the news from his village as often as he could, and he talked to his oldest son or to friends and neighbors. Usually, the news he received was devastating. One day, when I visited them, Harry was very quiet and absentminded. I wanted to know if he was all right, and he replied: "They [the Amba Boys] burned everything. They burned my whole farm. My neighbor just told me today. It's gone. They stole my cattle.... What will I do now?"

Although his house was reportedly untouched, Harry's investment was destroyed, and it meant that he had to repay the installments on his oil palm grove without any return. Following this incident, Harry's optimism and hope of return faded, and this influenced his everyday life in Bafoussam in different ways. The loss of his properties seemed to cause the loss of his energy, and while he had been telling me a lot about his village and his friends there, from that day onward he stopped speaking of them. He did not attend the biweekly meetings of the solidarity group, and Florence told me that he barely left the house. During one of our conversations, when I asked if he still hoped to go back to his home one day, Harry said: "I don't know if I will go back. It won't be same for me anymore. I lost everything, so why should I go?"

Things became even worse shortly after I had returned to Germany in March 2020. On a Sunday morning, I received a call from a friend in Bafoussam, who told me that Florence had unexpectedly died of a heart attack. I called Harry several days later and offered my condolences. He appeared composed and seemed grateful for my call. After two weeks, we spoke again, and I was surprised to learn that Harry had returned to his village. In a way, his return was not unusual, as, normally, after people die they are buried in their home villages. This was the case for Florence's burial, but Harry mentioned that he would only go back to Bafoussam occasionally, to see his children, and would rather stay in his house in the village.

In the end, it was Harry's personal loss that caused the shift in his future aspirations, even though the violence in the area had not ended.

Discussion and Concluding Thoughts

In this chapter, I have aimed to shift the focus toward the subtleties of how older IDPs in Cameroon built on their available resources and their engagement in familial relations to realign their notions of the future during protracted displacement. Rather than a mere shift in their future plans, and considering this to be an individual choice, the case studies I have presented show how displacement, as an unforeseeable disruption in the life course, can alter aspirations even at a later stage of life, and they also highlight the nonlinear character of these aspirations. At this point, older age is not an indicator of a predetermined future that only contains certain predictabilities, such as retirement, frailty, and, finally, death. Just as at earlier life stages, forced migration and displacement while aging come with uncertainties. While the wish and hope to return to their home villages or towns in the anglophone regions never fades completely, I have tried to demonstrate that older displaced persons are, against all odds, still in a position to actively make new plans for their future lives or to adapt the plans they had made before their displacement. The ethnographic examples of Nelson, Florence, and Harry illustrate clearly that there is a correlation between the intensity of hope and aspirations for the future, and these depend heavily on existing family relations. As previously suggested by other researchers (e.g., Brun 2015; Stock 2019), the two case studies reveal that, over time and with prolonged displacement, hope becomes subordinated to the challenges of the everyday, the shifting nature of close kin relations, and personal attachments to the new, though possibly temporary, home.

The results from my fieldwork demonstrate the importance of analyzing the spatiotemporal dimensions of protracted displacement with regard to the shaping of the future and the use of an aspirational lens over the life course. As Harry's case exemplifies, this includes looking at death—one's own or that of loved ones—to understand how this life incident can lead to shifting aspirations even while displaced. Moreover, learning about the life stories of displaced persons helps us better understand how, and on what basis, they decide to adapt their future aspirations. The findings also serve as a counterbalance to the picture of "the IDP" (and migrants more generally) as "being stuck" in time and place, waiting for the future, and instead show they are, with the resources they have, capable of acting and aspiring.

Acknowledgments

I would like to thank my research partners Nelson, Florence, and Harry for sharing their life stories and experiences with me so openly. I am also grateful to the editors of this volume and my research fellows of the Max Planck Research Group "Ageing in a Time of Mobility," and Victoria K. Sakti, in particular, for her inspiring and constructive feedback during the development of this chapter.

Notes

1. All names of the interlocutors in this chapter have been replaced by pseudonyms.
2. For more background and historical information on the Anglophone Crisis, see, e.g., Kofele-Kale (1980); Konings and Nyamnjoh (1997); Mbondgulo-Wondieh (2020).
3. The fighting between separatist groups and the military is concentrated in, but not limited to, rural parts of the Northwest and Southwest regions of Cameroon. Larger cities are less affected and are also places of refuge to some extent.

References

Appadurai, Arjun. 2013. *The Future as Cultural Fact: Essays on the Global Condition*. London: Verso.

Benjamin, Nancy Claire, Fatou Gueye, Dominique Haughton, Ahmadou Aly Mbaye, Romain Tchakouté, and Joel M. Tinga Yepdo. 2020. "The Informal Sector in Cameroon: Practices and Productivity." In *Formal and Informal Enterprises in Francophone Africa: Moving toward a Vibrant Private Sector*, edited by Ahmadou Aly Mbaye, Stephen S. Golub, and Fatou Gueye, 209–232. Ottawa: International Development Research Centre.

Brun, Cathrine. 2015. "Active Waiting and Changing Hopes: Toward a Time Perspective on Protracted Displacement." *Social Analysis* 59 (1): 19–37.

Bryant, Rebecca, and Daniel M. Knight. 2019. *The Anthropology of the Future*. Cambridge: Cambridge University Press.

Carling, Jørgen, and Francis Collins. 2018. "Aspiration, Desire and Drivers of Migration." *Journal of Ethnic and Migration Studies* 44 (6): 909–926.

Carling, Jørgen, and Kerilyn Schewel. 2018. "Revisiting Aspiration and Ability in International Migration." *Journal of Ethnic and Migration Studies* 44 (6): 945–963.

Cwerner, Saulo B. 2001. "The Times of Migration." *Journal of Ethnic and Migration Studies* 27 (1): 7–36.

Dalsgård, Anne Line, Martin D. Frederiksen, Susanne Højlund, and Lotte Meinert, eds. 2014. *Ethnographies of Youth and Temporality: Time Objectified*. Philadelphia: Temple University Press.

Gustafson, Per. 2001. "Retirement Migration and Transnational Lifestyles." *Ageing and Society* 21 (4): 371–394.

King, Russell, Eralba Cela, and Tineke Fokkema. 2021. "New Frontiers in International Retirement Migration." *Ageing and Society* 41 (6): 1205–1220.

King, Russell, Anthony M. Warnes, and Allan M. Williams. 1998. "International Retirement Migration in Europe." *International Journal of Population Geography* 4 (2): 91–111.

Kleist, Nauja. 2017. "Introduction. Studying Hope and Uncertainty in African Migration." In *Hope and Uncertainty in Contemporary African Migration*, edited by Nauja Kleist and Dorte Thorsen, 1–20. New York: Routledge.

Kleist, Nauja, and Stef Jansen. 2016. "Introduction: Hope over Time—Crisis, Immobility and Future-Making." *History and Anthropology* 27 (4): 373–392.

Kofele-Kale, Ndiva, ed. 1980. *An African Experiment in Nation Building: The Bilingual Cameroon Republic since Reunification*. Boulder, CO: Westview Press.

Konings, Piet, and Francis B. Nyamnjoh. 1997. "The Anglophone Problem in Cameroon." *Journal of Modern African Studies* 35 (2): 207–229.

Lamb, Sarah, Jessica Robbins-Ruszkowski, and Anna I. Corwin. 2017. "Introduction: Successful Aging as a Twenty-First-Century Obsession." In *Successful Aging as a Contemporary Obsession: Global Perspectives*, edited by Sarah Lamb, 1–24. New Brunswick, NJ: Rutgers University Press.

Lefebvre, Henri. 2002. *Critique of Everyday Life*. Vol. 2, *Foundations for a Sociology of the Everyday*. Translated by John Moore. London: Verso.

Mbondgulo-Wondieh, Zoneziwoh. 2020. "Women and the Anglophone Struggle in Cameroon." In *Gender, Protest and Political Change in Africa*, edited by Awino Okech, 131–147. London: Palgrave Macmillan.

Munn, Nancy D. 1992. "The Cultural Anthropology of Time: A Critical Essay." *Annual Review of Anthropology* 21: 93–123.

Oliver, Caroline. 2007. *Retirement Migration: Paradoxes of Ageing*. New York: Routledge.

Pine, Frances. 2014. "Migration as Hope: Space, Time, and Imagining the Future." *Current Anthropology* 55 (S9): S95–S104. https://doi.org/10.1086/676526.

Scheibelhofer, Elisabeth. 2018. "Shifting Migration Aspirations in Second Modernity." *Journal of Ethnic and Migration Studies* 44 (6): 999–1014.

Stock, Inka. 2019. *Time, Migration and Forced Immobility. Sub-Saharan African Migrants in Morocco*. Bristol: Bristol University Press.

UNHCR (United Nations High Commissioner for Refugees). 2021. *Cameroonian Refugees in Nigeria: Operational Update*. Geneva: UNHCR. https://reliefweb.int/sites/reliefweb.int/files/resources/UNHCR%20Nigeria%20Cameroonian%20Refugees%20Operational%20Update%20November%202021.pdf.

UNOCHA (United Nations Office for the Coordination of Humanitarian Affairs). 2021. *Cameroon: North-West and South-West*. Situation Report No. 37. New York: UNOCHA. https://reliefweb.int/sites/reliefweb.int/files/resources/ocha_cmr_nwsw_sitrep_novembre_2021.pdf.

Williams, Allan M., Russell King, Anthony M. Warnes, and Guy Patterson. 2000. "Tourism and International Retirement Migration: New Forms of an Old Relationship in Southern Europe." *Tourism Geographies: An International Journal of Tourism Space, Place and Environment* 2 (1): 28–49.

CHAPTER 9

"Setting Off from the Mountain Pass"

FACING DEATH AND PREPARING FOR THE JOURNEY AHEAD IN TIBETAN EXILE

Harmandeep Kaur Gill

Genla (teacher) Lobsang Choedak sat down on the bed, at the usual spot.[1] I sat down on the floor in front of him. I took off his sock and leg warmer, poured some medicinal oil on his leg, and started the massage. Genla closely followed my hands as they moved up and down and around his knee and leg. We could hear the chatter of the few elderly women gathered in the shared sitting area of the Tibetan Children's Village (TCV) old-age home. Here, inside Genla's room, there was silence. He was not a talker, with me or others.

I noticed the sparrows chirping outside and the sound of their wings flapping as they moved in and out through the open windows. The sky was crystal blue. Spring had slowly started lurking its way into the winter landscape of McLeod Ganj. Sunlight burst through the windows, warming up the old and bringing the promise of life. Life was all around, so overwhelming that one easily lost sight of decay, even at an old-age home. The elderly moved outdoors in the warmth of the sun. That was where one of the eldest residents, the ninety-three-year-old *Mola* (grandmother) Dawa, was usually found, either sitting outside on a chair or standing by the open windows, overlooking the Kangra Valley ahead. Genla, too, embraced all the life. He read Buddhist texts (*dpe cha*) outside in the sun.[2] He used the good weather to go for longer walks. Yet, every day he also prepared for death. All the life did not blind him to impermanence. Moreover, it served as a daily reminder.

While I massaged his leg, for once Genla chose to break the silence. "Mola passed away," he said to me.[3]

The news violently shook me out of the lightness of spring. It was the first time somebody had died while I had been there. I stopped the massage and looked up at him. "Who?" I asked immediately.

"Mola upstairs," Genla responded, pointing up. He tried to recall her name but to no avail. Half an hour later, when we had tea, it came to him: "Tsewang, Mola's name is Tsewang."

When the initial shock of the news had settled, I returned to the massage. "Did I know her, Genla? How did she look?" I asked, worrying whether it might be one of the *mola* I know.

"Ahhmm . . . tall body," he said.

"And black hair?" I added.

"Yes, yes," Genla nodded.

Mola Tsewang flashed before my eyes, walking down from Dal Lake in the company of one of the nuns, giving me a fleeting smile. I saw her strolling around on the rooftop. It was hard to comprehend that she was gone, when her figure kept lingering around in places, in moments in time, dissolved into the present.

"How do you feel, Genla? Did her death worry you?" I asked him.

Genla gave a short laugh, as he usually did when responding to something. "Now, all people from 1959 have passed away.[4] One by one, everybody is dying. I am also old, eighty-nine years old," he said.

That day, I did not attempt to console him by telling him that he was still fit and healthy. I am not sure that he needed it or even wanted it. On the contrary, he seemed to have accepted that death was the only inevitable end awaiting us all. Living at an old-age home, being surrounded by aging bodies, living with one himself, his daily preparations for death and the many deaths that were to follow in the spring made the impermanence of life strikingly present.[5]

This chapter explores life's end in a Tibetan exile context, through attention to the everyday life of Genla Lobsang Choedak, who is a monk and turned ninety-three years old in 2022. He resides in McLeod Ganj, a small hill station in northwest India, also known as Dharamsala. It has been the home-in-exile of the highest spiritual leader of the Tibetan people, the fourteenth Dalai Lama, Tenzin Gyatso, since 1960, one year after he escaped from Tibet, following the Chinese occupation of Tibet. Thousands of Tibetans followed him into exile. McLeod Ganj also houses the Central Tibetan Administration and other significant political, religious, and cultural institutions.[6] It is known as the capital of Tibetans in exile. Today, thirty-nine Tibetan settlements are spread across India, twelve in Nepal, and seven in Bhutan.

Like the rest of the elderly Tibetans living at the TCV old-age home, composed of monastics and lay people, Genla is a former employee of the TCV school.[7] And like many elderly Tibetans at the TCV old-age home and in the larger McLeod Ganj area, Genla was aging alone and faced death in the absence of family. His everyday life was devoted to Tibetan Buddhist practices in preparation for a peaceful death and a good rebirth, which is something all of my elderly companions aspired for and is the religious ideal among Tibetan Buddhists.

I came to know Genla in 2016, the year he moved into the TCV old-age home. At the time, I was doing preliminary fieldwork at the TCV old-age home in the preparation of a PhD proposal. When I began fieldwork for my PhD research on aging and dying among elderly Tibetans in January 2018, I resumed my engagements with Genla. He became one of five persons I followed throughout my fieldwork, and I have kept revisiting since. I gained access to Genla and my other elderly companions by massaging their legs and feet on a daily basis for thirteen and a half months.[8] Apart from the massages, we also spent time in each other's company by sharing meals, drinking tea, watching TV, or just sitting together in silence. I also assisted them during hospital visits, ran errands for them, and helped out with other practicalities, such as toilet visits. Over time, I was related to as an adoptive daughter, and even as a relative (*spun kyag*) from a past life.[9] Since the end of my fieldwork in December 2018, I have kept revisiting them and stayed in McLeod Ganj for longer periods.

This chapter tunes in to Genla Lobsang Choedak's aspirations of achieving a peaceful death and a good rebirth, which were shaped by his Buddhist faith, and explores how these were affected by having to age and die in the absence of family. I begin by outlining the central Buddhist notion of impermanence and how it steers aspirations for old age in the Tibetan Buddhist context, before providing a brief introduction to Tibetan exile. I open up my ethnographic explorations by describing how the impermanence of life manifested in Genla's life at the old-age home, giving rise to certain worries and fears, while also influencing his preparations for the coming of death and rebirth. In the end of this chapter, I put my ethnographic explorations in dialogue with some analytic perspectives on temporality. Here I take inspiration from Rane Willerslev, Dorthe R. Christensen and Lotte Meinert's (2013) notion of "taming" the objective ("impermanent") qualities of time with concrete religious or cultural technologies. I also draw on Michael G. Flaherty's (2011) notion of "time work," which tunes in to the customization of one's temporal experience in an attempt to deal with the objective workings of time. Together, this scholarship calls attention to how people deal with the forces beyond them, and attempt to clear a path in the midst of the uncertainty, with that which is given to them. Thus, I approach aspirations in the Tibetan Buddhist context and their associated practices as cultural resources that, for Genla, cleared a path and, in the process, also provided consolation in facing the decline of old age and the uncertain fate of death all alone.

The Impermanence of Life

In one of the two "Sūtra on Impermanence" (*Mi rtag pa nyid kyi mdo*) that are found in the Tibetan canon of the *Kangyur*, the Buddha speaks to his followers on one of the main characteristics of the samsaric existence: impermanence (Bernert 2019, line 1: 1–11).[10]

Samsaric existence implies that all life follows a cyclic existence, meaning that one's present life is part of a beginningless series of rebirths. Each life unfolds according to the karma (*las*) accumulated in the previous lives and in the present life. The Buddha comments that the four most cherished things in the world—good health, youth, prosperity, and life—are impermanent (Bernert 2019). Good health ends with sickness, youth ends with old age, prosperity ends with decline, while life ends in death (Bernert 2019). The impermanence of conditioned phenomena is regarded as the most fundamental teaching of the Buddha, and impermanence is described by the Buddha as the first principal characteristic of existence (Bernert 2019).[11] Hence, from a Tibetan Buddhist perspective, the uncertainty of life (deriving from its impermanent nature) is a radical type of uncertainty, meaning it is part of the human condition. As emphasized in Tibetan Buddhist literature and teachings (e.g., Changchan Gung Sonam Gyalpo 1963; Menriwa Lobsang Namgyal 1986; Gungtang Rinpoche 1975), in old age, this radical uncertainty manifests itself in all spheres of life: physical decline, illness, absence of family, and the future of death.

Thus, Tibetan Buddhists emphasize that old age is the time to meditate on death/rebirth and coming to terms with the impermanence of life. It is a life phase devoted to Tibetan Buddhist practices (*chos*), as a preparation for death and rebirth. Likewise, Genla spent his days in reading Buddhist texts, reciting mantra (*ma ni*), making offerings (*mchod*) at the home shrine, and doing prostrations (*phyag 'tshal*). Like my other elderly companions, Genla spent his days preparing for the journey ahead, aspiring for a peaceful death and a good rebirth.

As formulated by a ninety-one-year-old female companion of mine, at her age, one has reached the mountain pass. "La 'go thon gi 'dug," she has been repeating since I first met her in 2015. These words can be translated as "I am about to set off from the mountain pass/top." According to this metaphor, the journey of life is a continuous climb up the mountain, and reaching the mountain pass is when the journey comes to conclusion. What is important to remark is the particular verb ending of *gi 'dug* she used, which is an ending of the verb "to be" in the present tense. Furthermore, *gi 'dug* is also applied when one bears witness to something. Therefore, when she said these words, I understood that death for her was not somewhere in the distant future. The descent from the mountain pass was right in front of her; in other words, she stood face-to-face with death and felt its presence in her own body.

"I am going to die," she followed up next, as she tilted her head sideways with a smile, as if in an accepting gesture to herself. While the mention of death set me aback like an interruption, for her it was very spontaneous or natural. I found a similar pressing awareness of death in Genla. He was also at the lonesome timespace of the mountain pass, waiting to set off on the new journey, and through his daily religious practices, he attempted to come to terms with the impermanence of life.

However, as also highlighted by the Buddha's teachings, coming to terms with old age and death is far from an easy process and is fraught by common human sufferings, for example, afflictions, worries, and fears. Likewise, the impermanent nature of life, accompanied by the absence of family, gave rise to a lot of uncertainty for Genla.

Aging and Dying in Tibetan Exile

Genla Lobsang Choedak was born in Penpo, western Tibet. When he was about fifteen years old, he ordained as a monk at Ganden monastery, which in those days used to be a one-day walk from the Tibetan capital of Lhasa in central Tibet, he would tell me.[12]

When the 14th Dalai Lama escaped into exile in March 1959, Genla was thirty years old. Upon Genla's escape, the PLA was yet to reach Ganden monastery: "Lhasa was lost, but the Chinese had not entered Ganden. But later they came. A lot of monks started escaping. And I, with a party of four, left some time after.... We left Ganden and crossed the passes by walking in 1959.... We left Ganden on the fourteenth of the second month [April 1959] around afternoon."

The occupation of Tibet and the escape into exile were tragic events for him. Genla was forced to leave behind his entire family in Tibet. Like many others, Genla arrived in India in Tawang, which today falls in the state of Arunachal Pradesh in northeast India. From the first week in April 1959, the Indian authorities set up camps in the northeastern states to accommodate the Tibetan refugees. Many people died or fell ill after the difficult journey across the Himalayas and after exposure to the warm Indian climate. Soon the refugees were sent off to cooler areas in the Himalayan region in northwest India: Shimla, Chamba, and Kullu/Mandi/Kangra. There they took up work as road builders. Genla built roads in Chamba (which today falls under the state of Himachal Pradesh) for some time, before he traveled to Mussoorie, a small hill station in the state of Uttarakhand, established by the British Raj. He built roads for two years and then joined the Indian military.

Like the rest of the first generation of Tibetans in exile, Genla never planned to settle down in India, but intended to return to Tibet within a few years. But sixty-three years later, he finds himself at an old-age home in India, aging and facing death not only on a foreign soil but also in the absence of physical and moral support from family members, who he left behind in Tibet.

Today, many elderly Tibetans in exile, including the other elderly at the TCV old-age home, are facing a similar end to life. The precariousness of living as a stateless person in India and Nepal has pushed many younger Tibetans to migrate to "the west" in recent years (Wangmo and Teaster 2009; Choedup 2018; Gill 2022). Many are also leaving the Tibetan settlements for bigger Indian cities in search of better opportunities.[13]

As a result, older adults are aging and dying in the absence of children. Unlike them, Genla did not have children. Nor had his close family members migrated to the west. However, he shared with the other elderly Tibetans the circumstances of aging and dying alone, giving rise to similar types of worries.

According to Tibetan Buddhist faith, the family's presence is required at the moment of death and in the aftermath to carry out death rituals, which last for forty-nine days. These rituals are regarded as essential for ceasing the deceased's attachments to the living and in helping them to move on to a good rebirth (Childs 2004; Desjarlais 2016; Choedup 2018).

The absence of family raised many unsettling questions for Genla, for example: "In what state will death occur?," "Who will take care of the death rituals?," and "Have I done enough to gain a good rebirth?"

The Last Stop

Genla Lobsang Choedak's room, with a small kitchen and a bathroom, was located on the second floor of the TCV old-age home. It was squeezed between two other rooms. A small amount of sunlight entered through the kitchen window, but it was never enough to keep the lights off. Despite the darkness in Genla's room, it was a warm and welcoming space. Yellow, red, and dark maroon colors covered the room, just like the interior and exterior of a monastery.

As a monk, these colors have dominated his life. Like the top of doors and windows of monasteries, the entrance of the kitchen and the bathroom had small curtains above them, hung by Genla. The room was inviting. There was serenity in the way his few belongings were arranged. In his maroon robe and red jacket, Genla for me melted into the red monastic bubble surrounding him. The room felt like an extension of him, not only in terms of colors but also in its calm, inviting, and settled mood. Things were neatly tucked into their corners as if they were never to be used again, as if their owner would be leaving them any day.

His few pieces of clothing, such as his red- and maroon-colored jackets, were hung by the door on cloth hangers. His few robes and woolen shawls were neatly folded and placed on the top of a big iron trunk settled on a wooden table next to the TV. Below the table were his four pairs of shoes: two pairs of summer shoes and two pairs of winter boots. He also had two pairs of slippers to wear indoors. The shoes were all gifts from his younger brother's daughter. She was the only relative he had in India. But he saw her as rarely as once or twice a year because she kept moving between places, something Genla expressed that he was not very happy about. "She does not benefit me much," he said. Six pairs of shoes for an elderly monk seemed to be a lot to me, as if she were bringing a pair each visit, not only as a respectful and caring gesture but also to make up for her absence.

Other objects rested still, such as some perfectly folded blankets on the bed that he never slept in and the TV that rarely received a signal. At the center of the room was a beautiful, humble shrine. It was filled with photos of the Dalai Lama and decorated with one set of red and yellow plastic roses. At the front of the shrine stood a butter lamp offering and a row of water bowl offerings. On the wall next to the shrine were four more images. Two of them were scroll paintings (*thang ka*) of Buddhist deities: one of Chenrezig, the Bodhisattva of Compassion, and one of Sangye Menla, the Medicine Buddha. The other two were photos: one of the Dalai Lama and one of the Dalai Lama's teachers, the third Trijang Rinpoche, Lobsang Yeshe Tenzin Gyatso.

Unlike the homes of my other elderly companions, Genla's room was not overflowing with things gathered over a lifetime. No object stood in the way of another. Apart from the shrine, his two Indian vintage trunks pulled my attention. These

Figure 9.1. Prayer wheel spinning, symbolizing, among other things, the cyclic existence of death and rebirth. Photograph by Harmandeep Kaur Gill.

heavy trunks symbolized two significant periods in his life in India. The smaller one was placed on a table in front of the shrine and had the words "base" written on its side in a military green color. This trunk was a material trace of his time in the Indian military, when as part of the Special Frontier Force (SFF), he was stationed at Indian military sites across northern India. The SFF was a military unit consisting of Tibetan men. It was formed in 1962 after the Sino-Indian War (1960–1962) and was a joint Indian-Tibetan operation (McGranahan 2010, 139), formerly known as Establishment 22.

In 1984, after eighteen years of military service, he packed all his belongings in the small trunk and moved to the TCV school in McLeod Ganj. There, he took up work in the school kitchen and made Tibetan bread (*bag leb*). In the winter of 1995, he slipped on ice and broke his left hip. He was hospitalized for three months, and upon his return to TCV, he was allowed to retire. The TCV administration offered a small retirement residence on the outskirts of the school. During his time at TCV, he had bought a new and bigger trunk. He packed his few pieces of clothing, blankets, and utensils and moved to his new residence, which was also hidden from the sun. In 2016, the school administration offered him residence at the TCV old-age home, and, for the last time, he packed his belongings in those two heavy iron trunks and moved to the place that is the last stop on his journey.

When I asked Genla whether his room in the old-age home felt like his home, he responded, "This is where I am going to die." Genla's words made clear that the old-age home was not a place to settle in or to feel at home. Rather, it was a place from which to set off on his next journey. He had reached the mountain pass (figure 9.1).

The Pressing Presence of Death

The presence of death became rather stark after Mola Tsewang's death that spring, when several deaths followed one after another. To use Genla's words, people were literally dying "one by one." Butter lamp offerings burned continuously for months, and the sight of new, strange faces who had come to make offerings for the deceased became a part of life. Genla anticipated that soon he would be next.

When the next death occurred only two weeks later, no one had anticipated, certainly not Genla, that Mola Tsewang's death would be followed by that of her husband, who was only in his early seventies. Genla told me that he died after a long-term illness, which was even more surprising to me, because when I had met him two weeks earlier upon making offerings for Mola Tsewang, he had looked healthy and upright. Twenty days later, his death was followed by the death of the oldest resident of the old-age home, one ninety-five-year-old *pala* (father), who passed away after a long-term illness. But his death did not come as a surprise to Genla or to anyone else.

With each passing death, I sensed in Genla an increased anticipation about the unknown. Whenever I asked Genla what thoughts occupied his days, he only had one answer for me: "Death," he would say with a gentle, accepting smile.

The day after the ninety-five-year-old *pala* passed away, Genla said to me, "Now two more people are sick here. Pala Urgyen, who is eighty-nine years old, he is quite sick. And Mola Yangchen."

"What happened to her?" I asked.

"She has jaundice. Her face is all pale. She can't talk or open her eyes."

I decided to look in on Mola Yangchen on my next visit, which was only two days away. When I arrived at the old-age home two days later, visitors were moving in and out of Mola Yangchen and her husband's residence. By now, I knew what that sight signified. One of the elderly nuns was on her way to Mola Yangchen's room holding a ceremonial silk scarf (*kha btags*), which is offered along with the monetary donation for the butter lamps offerings. She whispered to me that Mola Yangchen had passed away the previous day.

While I lived as if time were a luxury, postponing my visit to Mola Yangchen, it struck me how Genla and others could never take time for granted. While the loss of another elder was something I still found hard to comprehend, for Genla and other elders at the old-age home, loss (and death) had become a part of life. They donated money for butter lamp offerings (*mchod me zhal 'debs*) and then returned to their everyday lives, albeit with a heightened awareness of death's looming presence and a concern about who would be the next to go, accompanied by the hope that they themselves would die a sudden death.

Worries over a Bedridden Death

Mola Yangchen was bedridden for three months before passing away from jaundice. Her husband, sons, and a young Indian helper took good care of her. On her passing, her husband said, "There was no *arraa . . . ooroo*. Without pain, she left quietly. That is very good. Otherwise, she would be in a lot of pain." Mola Yangchen's quiet passing without pain was a comfort for her husband. He himself hoped for a sudden and peaceful death, which is a sentiment shared by all of the elderly Tibetans I have come to know. The possibility of dying a bedridden death and in suffering, especially in the absence of family members, was feared. Mola Tsewang and her husband, who passed two weeks after her, had also died what the elderly called a sudden death.

Unlike them, Genla did not trust that his younger brother's daughter would come to his rescue in case of a severe illness. While the staff at the old-age home provided care, such as serving food and cleaning the body when an elderly person was bedridden, Genla did not have high hopes for how he would be supported. He said: "Sometimes my mind feels relaxed. That is how the mind is. Sometimes I have suffering in my mind. Sometimes the mind cannot be happy. Being old and wondering how it will go, it worries me sometimes. Here [at the old-age home] they won't do much for you. They will not provide support. That's my biggest worry. Many people have died here. Their corpse is taken care of. But that's about it."

Genla worried that he would "suffer in the absence of no helper" if the worst-case scenario became a reality. This had been the case with one of Genla's peers, Pala Urgyen, who resided on the third floor, exactly above Genla's room. The eighty-nine-year-old man had been bedridden for a long time. His only son resided in the United States and could not aid Pala Urgyen during his period of sickness. When I once visited Pala Urgyen, he did not notice me until I stood by his bedside. His things had been randomly stuffed into corners and in the shelves of the large wooden cabinet and left to decay. Most of the kitchen had been emptied by the TCV staff. Only a stove and some ingredients to make chai stood on the empty kitchen counter. It was as if I had walked into an abandoned home. Pala lay under several blankets, but I could not feel his presence. Moving closer to him, I saw that he lay there with eyes wide open—staring toward the ceiling—but he seemed to be somewhere far away. I asked whether I could make him more tea. But he could not hear me, nor was he able to respond. As I was about to move away from his bedside, he slowly moved his face toward me and nodded his head, perhaps saying yes to the tea or acknowledging my visit. Witnessing his condition, I could understand Genla's worries. The following week, Pala Urgyen was moved to the TCV hospital, where he passed away after a few months. His death was the type of death no one wanted to befall them. To die in sickness and pain not only is an undignified closure but also increases the chances of dying with a restless mind, resulting in a bad rebirth or, worse, wandering the afterlife as a ghost (Childs 2014; Desjarlais 2016).

As I sensed from Genla's words and the utterances of other elderly Tibetans, if the future might lead to a bedridden death, they were ready to die now and disappear while still able to look after themselves.

Meditating on Impermanence

For Genla Lobsang Choedak, his aging body was the clearest manifestation of death's looming presence. It was there in the weakening strength of his legs, arms, digestion, or eyesight. He said that old age had reduced him to half a person: "When one is young, one has the essence of a full person... in youth, one can do anything. One is fit, has physical strength. Mental strength. Now, in old age, the mind is not very lucid. And physically without strength, it is difficult."

For Genla, so much of who he used to be was gone and more was disappearing day by day. His words bring to mind the words of a high-standing monk official from the nineteenth century, Menriwa Lobsang Namgyal of the famous Tashi Lhunpo monastery in Shigatse in Tibet. In his poem titled "The Questions and Answers of the Weak and Old Man," Menriwa Lobsang Namgyal writes a dialogue between what supposedly is his younger and older self.[14] His younger self cannot accept, or recognize, what has become of him. In reply, the older self encourages him to come to terms with his own impermanence and the impending death. He says that the Lord of Death is just behind him and likens himself to a flower that has been touched by frost. He further asserts that he is also the frost itself, withering the flower away. Hence, he has already been touched by death, as Genla's words also conveyed. According to a Tibetan-Buddhist perspective, which informs Genla and Menriwa Lobsang Namgyal's understanding of the relation between life and death, death is present in life from the moment of birth, but as Menriwa Lobsang Namgyal writes, we only become aware of it once physical decline sets in. In old age, the process of dying speeds up. The Lord of Death takes hold of the body, to the point that death can no longer be ignored.

Because of the increasing manifestation of death in Genla's own body and through the many deaths at the old-age home, the time left could never be taken for granted. As advised by Gungtang Rinpoche (1762–1823) in his teaching *Advice from an Experienced Old Man* (1975), instead of dreading the coming of death, one should spend one's remaining time meditating on impermanence and dedicating one's "life—body, speech, and mind—to Dharma practice."

Preparing for Death and Rebirth

Genla's everyday life was dedicated, from early morning until evening, to Tibetan Buddhist practices. As a monastic, a rigorous daily practice was also essential to the fulfillment of his monastic vows. While my other elderly lay companions finished reading Buddhist texts during the morning hours and returned to the chanting of mantras during different parts of the day, for Genla, the reading of Buddhist texts and chanting of mantras extended from morning until evening. On a regular basis, Genla was immersed in his prayers when I showed up at his door. I tried to keep my visits short and leave as soon as possible after the massage and the cup of chai he offered me.

Regarding the daily Buddhist practice of monastics, an elderly nun had described it as a type of work. She said: "I have to keep reading until death. This is like my work. I have taken vows." The daily practices and preparations for death and rebirth can be understood as a type of work, especially in the case of monastics such as Genla and the old nun, and a continuous striving for transformations that does not cease until the moment of death.

However, working for a peaceful death and good rebirth in Genla's everyday life involved not only reading Buddhist texts, chanting mantras, attending prayer sessions at the TCV old-age home, or teachings at the Dalai Lama temple but also doing more practical preparations such as exercising daily in order to keep himself healthy and fit and making monetary offerings to ensure a good rebirth.

Exercise, in addition to Buddhist practices, was an important part of Genla's days. During my fieldwork in 2018, his morning water bowl and butter lamp offerings were followed by thirty prostrations, which for Genla is a form of both exercise and religious practice. In the evenings, he used to do another round of thirty prostrations. In January 2020, he had increased the amount to fifty-five, both morning and evening.[15] After a cup of tea, he headed out for his daily three-kilometer-long morning walk. On rare occasions, he would take the tiring steep climb to the TCV monastery, located at the highest point inside the TCV school area. But on a regular basis, he walked up to Dal Lake, following either the car road or the more peaceful path through the TCV school area, which are both more mellow steeps compared to the walk to the monastery. Reaching Dal Lake, he usually walked once around the lake on most days. His left hip had healed significantly since its fracturing twenty-five years ago, although his left leg was now slightly longer than the right. When he stood up, his knee could not be properly stretched. Apart from the moderate climb and the descent upon return, the condition of his left leg and old age also slowed him down. The entire walk took him between one and a half and two hours.

In addition to devoting himself to Buddhist practice and exercise to avoid the prospect of a bedridden and grim death and possibly a bad rebirth, Genla had also made all the necessary offerings to ensure a good rebirth: "I have offered twice to Gyalwa Rinpoche (the Dalai Lama). The first time I offered one hundred thousand. And the second time, I offered two hundred fifty thousand and water bowls."

Genla's second set of offerings was made in November 2017. That was nearly all of Genla's savings and also his final large offering. These days, he lives on the pension from the TCV school and from the Indian government for his military service. On top of the major two offerings to the Dalai Lama in old age, he had made other offerings to the Dalai Lama throughout his life in India.

It is a common practice among elderly Tibetans in exile to offer money or other precious possessions (e.g., jewelry) to the Dalai Lama and other holy lamas. Namgyal Choedup (2019, 87), in his work among elderly Tibetans in the Doeguling Settlement in south India, refers to this traditional practice as *bsngo rten*, meaning a dedication and aspiration offering for a good rebirth.

Furthermore, Genla had also put aside money for the TCV old-age home to take care of his corpse and attend to the connected rituals: "When one passes away, money is needed to take care of the corpse . . . for that I have put aside some money." Money is needed to buy wood for the cremation, make butter lamp offerings, and make offerings to monks who perform the rituals and prayers, and, as I witnessed, it was also a custom to offer chai or Tibetan butter tea to the fellow elderly and others who made donations for the butter lamp offerings. The staff at the old-age home cannot take care of these rituals unless the deceased has left behind money or someone (e.g., a family member) steps in to take care of the rituals.

The offerings that Genla had taken care of prior to his death are usually taken care of by family members, as they were in the case of Mola Yangchen and Mola Tsewang and her husband. By contrast, Genla felt that he could not trust someone else to make these bigger offerings on his behalf, so he undertook them himself.[16]

As Genla said to me, all of his thoughts were directed toward death. Waiting at the mountain top, Genla's gaze was, like others', fixed on the descent in front of him. While every day was an act of waiting and coming to terms with the uncertain and unescapable journey ahead, every day was for Genla also a precious opportunity to aspire for a peaceful death and a good rebirth. Every day could be his last, but was also another day to strive for better karma.

Surrendering to the Impermanence of Life

Death and rebirth triggered many questions and uncertainty for Genla Lobsang Choedak and my other elderly companions. Regardless of their numerous reflections and Tibetan Buddhist practices, both death and rebirth remained deeply uncertain and unsettling events, beyond their control. "When death strikes our loved ones, most of us stand defenceless and have to face the irreversibility of time," write Rane Willerslev, Dorthe R. Christensen, and Lotte Meinert (2013, 4) in the introduction to the book *Taming Time, Timing Death*. Following the anthropologist Alfred Gell, they refer to this time as the "objective time." They recognize, as my elderly companions did, that one cannot undo the flow of time, but still we need to cope with the objective, or abstract, qualities of time somehow. Many of the edited volume's contributors, including the authors themselves, explore how people cross-culturally apply concrete technologies, such as rituals or mummification, in their efforts to grasp the abstract qualities of time and in finding potential answers and solutions to the questions that death raises about time (Willerslev, Christensen, and Meinert 2013, 3). Among others, they draw on Michael G. Flaherty's notion of "time work" as one potential answer, something I also find useful.

In his book *The Textures of Time: Agency and Temporal Experience*, Flaherty devotes attention to the subjective side of temporality by examining "how people alter or customize various dimensions of their temporal experience and resist external sources of temporal constraint or structure" (2011, 3). He argues that what we experience as the textures of time are created by weaving together our desires and circumstances (2), which for Genla and other elderly Tibetans meant the desire or aspiration to meet a peaceful death and achieve a good rebirth, when the circumstance for him and many others was a lonesome old age. Furthermore, Flaherty argues that the modification of temporal experience is achieved through subtle and guarded practices: "time work," which he defines as "individual or interpersonal efforts to create or suppress particular kinds of temporal experience" (2003, 17).

Genla's daily religious practices and exercise routines could be referred to as a type of time work. Through these practices of time work and their repetitions, he created circumstances that evoked the desired form of temporal experience (Flaherty 2003). By doing so, he exercised some form of self-determination, in facing forces, that is, impermanence / the objective qualities of time that were beyond his control, as Flaherty argues. The agentive aspect of time work is central to Flaherty's argument. For the sake of analysis, he approaches time work through the categories of duration, frequency, and sequencing (Flaherty 2011, 12), which involve for him different ways of "doing time."[17]

I find that the duration of a particular practice (e.g., reading Buddhist texts, chanting a mantra slowly word by word, and clearing/making offerings at the home shrine attentively, doing prostrations), the frequency by which something is done (e.g., reciting mantras every single day, the total amount of mantras one recites daily, or going for walks on a daily basis), and, finally, the sequence of Buddhist practices (the order in which practices are carried out on a daily basis) also affected the temporal experience (of time left and time to come) of Genla. I argue that this was how he "did time" or attempted to use it wisely. But there were also exceptions.

There were days when he felt tired and was unable to keep up with his daily practices. However, there were also days when certain events, for example, someone's death in the presence/absence of family, enhanced the duration or frequency of his practices (reciting mantras, reading Buddhist texts, or exercising) because they brought a strong reminder of the lonesome death that possibly awaited him. Duration, frequency, and sequence were ways of doing time through which Genla and my other elderly companions modified their experience of time: they attempted to influence the precariousness of the timing of their death and aspired to improve their karmic destinies by using time wisely through daily Buddhist practices and, in Genla's case, also by exercising and making the necessary offerings for rebirth.

While such aspirational practices provided some consolation in facing the unknown future of death and rebirth all alone, I do not argue that these to Genla and others provided a sense of control over the objective, impermanent nature of time. They found themselves at the mountain top, standing face-to-face with the unknown journey ahead, and often in the absence of family. The time work involved in their Tibetan Buddhist practices did not seem to be fully about resisting "external sources of temporal constraint or structure," as Flaherty argues.

Instead, as Willerslev, Christensen, and Meinert recognize, through ritualized practices of taming time "we acknowledge, on the one hand, that we are limited creatures, overwhelmed by the impersonal workings of objective time, and on the other that we can, to some extent, redefine time, life and the cosmos" (2013, 3). This resonates with Genla Lobsang Choedak's expressions regarding the uncertain nature of death and rebirth and, at the same time, his attempts at clearing a path, informed by Tibetan Buddhist aspirations for old age, their associated religious practices, and his own adaptations of exercise routines.

In the Tibetan Buddhist context, using time wisely is based on an acceptance and even surrendering to the objective workings of time: of impermanence. Any day could be one's last. One could go to sleep today and not wake up tomorrow, as so wonderfully captured in a famous poem by the Buddhist philosopher Nāgārjuna.[18]

While making the best of one's remaining time by striving for Tibetan Buddhist aspirations is one solution provided by Buddhist teachers, the other is giving oneself over to the uncertainty of the samsaric existence. In fact, the crucial thing one needs to come to terms with in old age is the point made by Willerslev, Christensen, and Meinert: the acknowledgment that we are limited creatures and that death and rebirth (or the objective workings of time) cannot be brought within the realm of lay human control. One must surrender and come to terms with the objective workings of time—to impermanence, uncertainty, and the unsettling nature of death and rebirth.

Conclusion

Old age among Tibetan Buddhists is a life phase devoted to religious preparations for death and rebirth and coming to terms with the impermanence of life. Likewise, Genla Lobsang Choedak spent his days immersed in Tibetan Buddhist practices and exercise routines, aspiring for a peaceful death and a good rebirth in the absence of family. I have explored how impermanence manifested in Genla's daily life at the TCV old-age home through the many deaths that occurred there within a short period of time. I have described how each death brought a strong reminder of Genla's own ending, which he expected to meet in the absence of physical and moral support from family members. This gave rise to certain worries and fears for his future. By taking inspiration from Willerslev, Christensen, and Meinert's (2013) notion of "taming" the objective ("impermanent") qualities of time with religious technologies and Flaherty's (2011) notion of "time work"—as a customization of one's temporal experience—I have approached aspirations and their associated practices as cultural resources for dealing with death and rebirth, which remained beyond Genla's control. By immersing himself in aspirational practices, including religious rituals and exercise routines on a daily basis, Genla Lobsang Choedak cleared a path in facing the uncertainty of the future. These path-clearing aspirational practices also provided some consolation in facing the end of life all alone.

Acknowledgments

I would like to thank my wonderful teachers, professors Lone Grøn and Lotte Meinert, who gave me the opportunity to be a PhD student in their research project "Aging as a Human Condition: Radical Uncertainty and the Search for a Good

(Old) Life" at Aarhus University from 2017 to 2020. I am forever indebted to my precious teachers, Genla Lobsang Choedak and my other elderly companions for opening up their homes to me and sharing about their extraordinary lives. Moments spent with you while drinking tea, listening, or massaging your legs and feet will stand as one of the most precious periods of my life, despite its challenges. A heartfelt gratitude to Genla Tashi Tsering for finding the poem by Menriwa Lobsang Namgyal and the text by Changchan Gung Sonam Gyalpo among the towering collection of books at the Amnye Manchen Institute and generously offering to me their use in my writings. Finally, thanks to the editors Megha Amrith, Victoria K. Sakti, and Dora Sampaio for their generous feedback and enthusiasm with this book.

NOTES

1. *Gen* means "teacher," while *la* is a prefix added to names and titles as a respectful gesture. Tibetans usually refer to monks, among others, as "Genla." I refer to Genla Lobsang Choedak primarily as "Genla" throughout the chapter because that is how I refer to him in person. All names in this chapter, except Genla Lobsang Choedak's, are pseudonyms.

2. Tibetan words are transliterated according to the Wylie system of transliteration. Titles, names of individuals, and place-names are transliterated according to pronounceable transliteration used by Tibetans.

3. The English translation of Tibetan quotes has been done by the author.

4. The year 1959 was when the fourteenth Dalai Lama, Tenzin Gyatso, escaped into exile in India and was followed by thousands of Tibetans.

5. See also Whyte (this volume) for a discussion on anticipating death in later life in Uganda.

6. The Central Tibetan Administration was previously known as the Tibetan-government-in-exile.

7. In 2020, fifty elderly Tibetans had accommodation at the TCV old-age home.

8. Over time, the massages, among other things, opened for warm and intimate connections between the elderly Tibetans and me. That is why I refer to them as "companions" in my PhD dissertation and in this chapter. The words *informants* or *interlocutors* do not capture the intimacy we came to share and the impact of our ethical relationship on my writings and analysis.

9. My writings also draw on shorter fieldwork in Kathmandu in 2018, a preliminary research period of two months at the TCV old-age home in 2016, and years of living in the Tibetan exile community in McLeod Ganj since 2014. During my fieldwork in 2018, I conducted thirty structured and informal interviews with the elderly living in the McLeod Ganj area, including at the TCV old-age home and the Old People's Home run by the Central Tibetan Administration, and with health-care workers at the TCV old-age home and a local Tibetan nongovernmental organization that provides health-care services to the elderly. I also interviewed people from governmental institutions that provide welfare services to the elderly.

10. *Sūtra* refers to ancient Buddhist scriptures, and the *Kangyur* is "the translated words (of the Buddha)" (84000: Translating the Words of the Buddha).

11. The other two principal characteristics are suffering (*bdug bsngal*) and no-self (*bdag med*).

12. Ganden monastery, Sera monastery, and Drepung monastery are known as "the three seats" (*gdan sa gsum*) of the Gelug sect of Tibetan Buddhism. All three monasteries have been reestablished in exile, in south India, which houses some of the biggest Tibetan settlements.

13. Out-migration has become a common phenomenon across the Himalayan regions in India and Nepal; see Desjarlais (2016); Gagné (2018); Childs and Choedup (2019); Craig (2020).

14. The Tibetan title of the poem is "Nyams char rgan po'i dri lan."

15. In January 2022, he reduced his daily walks to a few times a week, partly due to the COVID-19 pandemic. To compensate for his lack of movement, Genla increased the daily amount of prostrations to 250.

16. He could not take it for granted that his younger brother's daughter would happen to be present in McLeod Ganj upon his death.
17. Flaherty also adds timing and allocation and "taking time."
18. Life flickers in the flurries of a thousand ills,
    More fragile than a bubble in a stream.
    In sleep, each breath departs and is again drawn in;
    How wondrous that we wake up living still! (Cited in Patrul Rinpoche 1998, 41)

REFERENCES

Bernert, Christian, trans. 2019. "The Sūtra on Impermanence." In version 1.22, *Toh 309, Degé Kangyur*, vol. 72 (*Mdo sde, sa*), fols. 155.a–155.b., edited by V. Paganuzzi. Fremont: 84000: Translating the Words of the Buddha. https://read.84000.co/translation/toh309.html.

Changchan Gung Sonam Gyalpo. 1963. *"A Moral Advice of an Old Woman" to Two Young Women, regarding Mortal Decay* [Rgan byis gsum gyi 'bel gtam snang ba rab gsal zhes bya ba bzhugso]. Edited and published by G. Tharchin. Kalimpong: Tibet Mirror Press.

Childs, Geoff. 2004. *Tibetan Diary: From Birth to Death and Beyond in a Himalayan Valley of Nepal*. Berkeley: University of California Press.

———. 2014. "Hunger, Hard Work, and Uncertainty: Tashi Dondrup Reminisces on Life and Death in a Tibetan Village." In *Buddhists: Understanding Buddhism through the Lives of Practitioners*, edited by Todd Lewis, 228–235. Chichester, West Sussex: John Wiley and Sons.

Childs, Geoff, and Namgyal Choedup. 2019. *From a Trickle to a Torrent: Education, Migration, and Social Change in a Himalayan Valley of Nepal*. Berkeley: University of California Press.

Choedup, Namgyal. 2018. "'Old People's Homes,' Filial Piety, and Transnational Families: Change and Continuity in Elderly Care in the Tibetan Settlements in India." In *Care across Distance: Ethnographic Explorations of Aging and Migration*, edited by Azra Hromadžić and Monika Palmberger, 75–94. New York: Berghahn Books.

Craig, Sienna. 2020. *The Ends of Kinship: Connecting Himalayan Lives between Nepal and New York*. Seattle: University of Washington Press.

Desjarlais, Robert. 2016. *Subject to Death: Life and Loss in a Buddhist World*. Chicago: University of Chicago Press.

Flaherty, Michael G. 2003. "Time Work: Customizing Temporal Experience." *Social Psychology Quarterly* 66 (1): 17–33.

———. 2011. *The Textures of Time: Agency and Temporal Experience*. Philadelphia: Temple University Press.

Gagné, Karine. 2018. *Caring for Glaciers: Land, Animals, and Humanity in the Himalayas*. Seattle: University of Washington Press.

Gill, Harmandeep Kaur. 2022. "Imagining Self and Others: Carers, TV, and Touch." In *Imagistic Care: Growing Old in a Precarious World*, edited by Cheryl Mattingly and Lone Grøn, 163–184. New York: Fordham University Press.

Gungtang Rinpoche. 1975. *Nyams-myong rgan-po'i 'bel-gtam*. Oral translation by Sharpa Rinpoche, notes taken by Alexander Berzin in 1975, Dharamsala, India. https://studybuddhism.com/en/advanced-studies/lam-rim/impermanence-death/paraphrase-of-advice-from-an-experienced-old-man.

McGranahan, Carole. 2010. *Arrested Histories: Tibet, the CIA, and Memories of a Forgotten War*. Durham, NC: Duke University Press.

Menriwa Lobsang Namgyal. 1986. "Nyams char rgan po'i dri lan." In *Dzo mo glang ma 2*, 62–63. Shigatse, Tibet.

Patrul Rinpoche. 1998. *Words of My Perfect Teacher: A Complete Translation of a Classic Introduction to Tibetan Buddhism*. Rev. ed. Translated by Padmakara Translation Group. New Delhi: Vistaar Publications.

Wangmo, Tenzin, and Pamela B. Teaster. 2009. "The Bridge from Then to Now: Tibetan Elders Living in Diaspora." *Journal of Applied Gerontology* 29 (4): 434–454.

Willerslev, Rane, Dorthe R. Christensen, and Lotte Meinert. 2013. Introduction to *Taming Time, Timing Death: Social Technologies and Ritual*, edited by Dorthe R. Christensen and Rane Willerslev, 1–16. Farnham, UK: Ashgate.

84000: Translating the Words of the Buddha. 2010. *Facts and Figures about Kangyur and Tengyur*. Accessed 10 July 2020, https://84000.co/facts-and-figures-about-kangyur-and-tengyur.

Afterword

Erdmute Alber

In Germany, on average, roughly 50 percent of the health costs for each citizen are paid during the last six months of a person's life. This statistic, other data, and widespread public speculations about the increase of health costs in later life or in the months before death have led to occasional political demands to reduce these costs.[1] Arguing that not every therapy for older people makes sense and should be covered by the public health system, some politicians postulated that hip replacement or knee surgery is unnecessary for people over eighty. In fact, their argument was that the brevity of their remaining life span did not justify the cost. Key is the argument of "generational justice."[2]

Of course, such claims could be contextualized in larger debates about the benefits, risks, and costs of the German welfare state and its specific logics in which the actually working population largely covers the costs for pensions and health costs of the whole population.[3] At the same time, the requests to change the system by paying less to the elder cohorts of the population reiterate a widespread image of older age as a phase of decay, in which the need for physical mobility decreases. On this assumption, old age is not at all imagined as a time of aspiration or hopes for the future.

So far, ethical and constitutional concerns and the very fact of an aging population, and therewith an increase of aged voters at political elections, have limited the space for such political voices in Germany that disadvantage older people. But my point is a different one than these political debates. Foregrounding an image of older age as a time of decay and the gradual ending of a life that had its best time in the past, these voices tend to ignore an ontological truth that is deeply interwoven in all the chapters of this book: always and at any moment, it is still one's *whole* life that lies in one's future, waiting to be lived. One never knows how long a life will last, but it is, at any moment, still something to be discovered, anticipated, desired, or feared—still waiting to be lived, in its full range of possibility, and in relation to what could be called the world. It is to be walked, if at all possible with functioning hips and knees, but also to be breathed and aspired. And it is this future orientation toward one's whole life that influences and shapes the present in any moment of a life span. This ontological truth about the openness of life ethically rejects ideas of cutting medical costs in a later phase of life: in fact, you never know what happens in the future, not even in the last moments of a life. Not even if the possibility of death is vividly present, as two of the chapters, namely, those of Harmandeep Kaur Gill and Susan Reynolds Whyte, show.

In this sense, *Aspiring in Later Life* makes us aware that every moment of a life has not only its particular present and past but also its very particular future and, therewith, future aspirations. Much has been written about the past, in anthropology and the humanities, about the work of collective as well as individual memory. It has been argued that the work of creating, remembering, and imagining specific but changing pasts goes in tandem with changing presents. Often, the task of transferring cultural and historical knowledge to the present and future, by memory and storytelling, has been mapped as the task of older generations, in anthropological approaches as well as in popular imaginations of older age.[4] The African proverb "When an old man dies, a library burns to the ground," which Malian writer Amadou Hampâté Bâ cited in a speech before the United Nations Educational, Scientific, and Cultural Organization (UNESCO), exactly represents this imagery of older age as carrier of the past, offering it to the present.[5]

In contrast to the enduring interest in memory and the past, reflections on the future, and the important role of planning and making, hoping, and aspiring, of fearing and coping with the insecurity of the unknown, only developed late, after the millennium turn, in anthropological theorizing. Among others, it was Arjun Appadurai's (2013) book *The Future as Cultural Fact* that helped to acknowledge the importance of *unequally distributed capacities to aspire* for an understanding of present actions as well as impediments of acting, and even more for global societies with increasing inequality. Aspirations are then conceptualized as modalities of living in a present that are always shaped by the horizons of an unknown, but imaginable, desirable, or frightening future. Indeed, again, future orientation is imagined to connect to a specific phase in the life course: even if discussed and framed as being part of the human condition, reflections on aspirations are usually implicitly or explicitly focusing on younger generations.[6] And, again, older age, overseen in these debates, remains linked to temporalities other than the future.

Exactly here, *Aspiring in Later Life* makes an important intervention. It sets a new and important accent by insisting that hopes and aspirations, and the related importance of future imagining for the present, are important in all phases of life and remain being tasks and maybe even human necessities until the end of life. If aspiring is breathing, as the authors claim, it could not end before death. Without ignoring the role of the past, of memory and of human desires to keep what has been achieved, the book opens a window onto the unexpected aspirations of middle-aged and older people, which makes a significant contribution to understanding their agencies.

The focus on aspirations in later life strengthens the argument that later life is not necessarily a phase of decay and immobility. In this volume, older generations are presented as active, innovative, and creative human beings, who could—like younger generations—be portrayed as *makers and breakers* (Howana and De Boeck 2005). A lively breath of aspiration blows through all chapters. This is a book saturated with anthropological wisdom, a wisdom produced by mainly younger scholars, or at least scholars younger than the research partners they portray. Along the way, they convey the fun of doing research with people in later life.

The volume provides narrations of unexpected experiences in older age: for instance, on the part of women who discover desire and fulfilled sexuality in later phases of their lives, when marriages have ended, children have left the household, and labor migration guides them to new working places that turn out to be places of love, sex, and enjoyment. Dumitrița Luncă found these experiences among Romanian transmigrants in Rome, and her descriptions of these living and loving women also gives the reader an insight into the beauty and joy of fieldwork with loving research partners.

In a similar direction, and with regard to domestic workers from the Philippines in Hong Kong and Singapore who liberate themselves in later life from some gendered norms and moralities of being primarily givers and breadwinners they had been attributed to, Megha Amrith argues that the "vantage point of midlife thus enables us to see how aspirations start to shift or take on renewed energies when migrant women reach their forties, fifties, and sixties." Her text, furthermore, compellingly demonstrates that women's aspirations are shaped in relation to multiple temporal horizons: through "letting go of past selves or undesirable past relationships, anticipating uncertain and insecure futures, and then reconfiguring projects of self and collective transformation in the present." Finally, she considers how migrant women themselves negotiate and challenge the aspirations that others (kin, states, public narratives) expect them to hold with their own aspirational horizons.

It is more than a coincidence that the third chapter in this section on desire and self-realization also focuses on women who underwent labor migration to a wealthier country in order to do domestic or care work. Seemingly, migratory experiences and the related possibilities to leave some norms behind in the country of origin without completely needing to take over all norms in the new country provides a space for some openness, especially when people's living conditions are establishing after some time in the new country. Lisa Johnson looks at Jamaican women working in Canada who are organizing their older age around desires and attachments to their homes (and often children) in Canada, on the one hand, and lifelong yearning for the country of origin, Jamaica, on the other. The compromising outcome is often to stay in Canada, while constantly traveling to Jamaica, a lifestyle they would possibly not even have imagined when young. Here, again, it is the aspirations that appeared at a later life stage that shape the very mobile ways of living old age of these Jamaican women.

Such lifeworlds—based on experience of migration, past care work for wealthier families abroad, and an increasing sense for self-care and fresh aspirations for older age—stand in contrast to those of women in Uganda whose experiences Susan

Reynolds Whyte narrates: women who never migrated and are currently confronted with the limitations of their remaining life spans, feeling the loss of energy and strength, finding they are less heard than before. In these conditions, they redirect their aspirations from their own life expectations to their hopes for their children. But even in this context of shrinking possibilities, the dignity of aspirations, now for others, not for themselves, is remarkable. It includes interactions, not only with kin and friends, but also with the researcher. It is a dignity that is based on acknowledging that living possibilities for older people themselves are, indeed, shrinking. However, hopes accompany a relatedness with the next generation. Here, Whyte adds another important dimension to discovering aspiration in later age: she outlines the importance of intergenerational entanglements of aspirational future-building. It might be children's aspirations that bring their parents into new places of living, near their children, where they are better cared for. Or the aspirations of older generations that influence the life paths of their children or grandchildren. The text makes us aware that an anthropology of aspirations should never be limited to individual aspirations shaping individual life courses, and thus involuntarily reproducing Western notions of the individual self. Instead, research on aspirations should at least be open to notions of multiple entanglements and *dividualities* Strathern (1988:3).

Intergenerational entanglements and especially the entanglements of aspirations and expectations are also key in Alfonso Otaegui's and Cati Coe's chapters, both again raising generational differences through experiences of migration. If elder generations constructed their selves through the notion of work and cannot stop working if they do not want to get bored, as one Peruvian interlocutor having migrated to Chile says in Otaegui's chapter, such notions are critically perceived by the younger generation. The latter might not want to dedicate their whole life to work but acknowledge that their parents' work is key for their position in the country they live in as second-generation migrants. But these older people who dedicated their whole lives as migrants in Chile to work also narrate feelings of unexpected vitality and feeling younger than their biological age.

In Coe's chapter, starting again from the experience of transnational migration of Ghanaian women in the United States and focusing on their intergenerational relations, aspirations in later age are strongly interrelated with flipping cultural scripts of self-reliance and interdependence. On the one hand, people invest in buildings and seek to generate resources through investments in order to live a decent life after retiring, and, on the other, they invest in care for kin and the related expectations of mutuality. In any case, projects of staying in the United States as well as return to Ghana, or life styles of constant mobility, are deeply interwoven with the life courses and actions of children and other kin and are based on changing and elusive ideas about a good life.

Other chapters add to a highly nuanced picture of the importance of aspiration in all phases of the life course. Not to forget Harmandeep Kaur Gill's chapter, which makes us aware that the dead and the anticipation of dying might be part of the horizons of aspiring and dealing with the future at any moment of life. Then,

Julia Pauli transgresses possible dichotomies of stagnation versus change. She portrays a setting of relatedness among different generations of women for whom *un poco más* ("a bit more") is an important aspiration: in the face of an insecure future that does not promise realistic chances of better living possibilities, *un poco más* of the same, just a prolongation of the current situation, becomes a desirable option for the future. Pauli's observation leads to an additional question about the present: wouldn't this aspiration of Mexican women to modestly live *un poco más* of the same, the desire that life might stay for a while with what the present offers, also provide an alternative to the seemingly omnipresent desire for growth and increase that others have called neoliberal "overheating" (Eriksen 2016)? Or, would that wish itself already be too much in the face of dramatic climate change and related threats? Do we not live in times in which the desire for a prolongation of what we have achieved is already too much? Of course, *un poco más*, expressed by Mexican women, would possibly not mean the same for the Romanian women had they claimed that they would just like to continue what they achieved.

Looking at a present that is desired as no more than *un poco más* also makes us aware that aspiring is not always and only linked to a notion of increase. Furthermore, it does not always need to be exclusively future-oriented. Rather, it often connects present, past, and future, an insight that is also expressed in Gill's and Nele Wolter's chapters. Gill portrays monks in a monastery in Tibet and their way of living toward and in peace with death and life so warmly that one might wish to sense the beauty of the landscape and the wind as the ethnographer did when following conversations with her research partners. Again, the book demonstrates the beauty of doing research with people in later-life phases.

In sum, *Aspiring in Later Life* finds a new way to ask the question: What can be learned from a careful perspective on later life? The book's answer is that it might not only be wisdom, accumulated through memory and past experience of a lived life, but aspirations saturated with life experiences and memory that connect the present with the past through a perspective on the future that might include birth and death. It argues that looking at aspiration in later life enables a nuanced perception of possibility. These aspirations might include gratefulness for things achieved, dreams for a better life, a sense of responsibility for others' lives, or a willingness to accept being cared for. *Un poco más* might be much more than it seems: it might be an insistence on continuing to live one's *whole* life into an open-ended future, as much as one has lived it in its past.

Acknowledgments

I am more than grateful to Koreen Reece and the editors of this book for careful reading and important comments on this text.

Notes

1. A differentiated and complex study about the medical costs for older people in Germany for could be found in Kruse et al. (2003).

2. See, for instance, the head of the youth organization of the Christian Democratic party, Philipp Mißfelder, arguing in *Der Tagesspiegel* that such public health insurance costs should be cut to ensure greater "generational justice." See Cordula Eubel, "Keine Hüftgelenke für die ganz Alten. Chef der Jungen Union fordert radikale Einschnitte bei Sozialversicherung / Rürup will Opfer von Neurentnern," *Der Tagesspiegel*, August 3, 2003, https://www.tagesspiegel.de/politik/keine-hueftgelenke-fuer-die-ganz-alten/436080.html.

3. In the so-called Bismarck social security system, present working generations are paying the pension and health costs for elder generations, assuming that next generations would cover for them. As the stability of the system depends, among others, on demographic balance, generational justice is regularly discussed in the media. The underlying logic is that every generation cares for older people, as previous generations cared for them.

4. To name but one in anthropology: a poetic but also critical description of the ambivalent role of elders as carriers of memory important for marriage arrangements can be found in Astuti (2000).

5. Amadou Hampâté Bâ, Goodreads.com, https://www.goodreads.com/quotes/1275451.

6. See, as only one example, Stambach and Hall's (2019) brilliant volume on students' hopes.

REFERENCES

Appadurai, Arjun. 2013. *The Future as Cultural Fact: Essays on the Global Condition.* London: Verso.

Astuti, Rita. 2000. "Kindreds, Cognatic and Unilineal Descent Groups: New Perspectives from Madagascar." In *Cultures of Relatedness: New Approaches to the Study of Kinship*, edited by Janet Carsten, 90–103. Cambridge: Cambridge University Press.

Eriksen, Thomas Hylland. 2016. *Overheating: An Anthropology of Accelerated Change.* London: Pluto Press.

Howana, Alcina, and Filip De Boeck, eds.. 2005. *Makers and Breakers: Children and Youth in Postcolonial Africa.* Oxford, UK: James Currey.

Kruse, Andreas, Eckhard Knappe, Frank Schulz-Nieswandt, Friedrich-Wilhelm Schwartz, and Joachim Wilbers. 2003. *Kostenentwicklung im Gesundheitswesen: Verursachen ältere Menschen höhere Gesundheitskosten?* Stuttgart: AOK Baden-Württemberg. https://www.uni-trier.de/fileadmin/fb4/prof/VWL/SAM/veroeffentl/Kruse-Knappe-Schulz-Nieswandt-Schwartz-Wilbers-Kostenentw-Ge.pdf.

Stambach, Amy, and Kathleen D. Hall, eds. 2019. *Anthropological Perspectives on Student Futures: Youth and the Politics of Possibility.* New York: Palgrave Macmillan.

Strathern, Marilyn. 1988. *The Gender of the Gift. Problems with Women and Problems with Society in Melanesia.* Berkeley: University of California Press.

Acknowledgments

There are many people and conversations that made this volume possible. We first began thinking about aspiring in later life at a panel we organized, "Later Life Negotiations," at the German Anthropological Association (DGSKA) meeting in Constance in autumn 2019. We thank the DGSKA for making this panel possible, as the fascinating presentations we heard and the discussions that ensued inspired us to find a way to continue these discussions in a deeper way. Aspirations in later life—and the different meanings infused in these aspirations—was a compelling thread connecting the papers in this panel. We then organized a workshop in 2020 involving more scholars working on different regions of the world. This was initially planned in-person but moved onto Zoom once we entered into the global COVID-19 pandemic. We would like to thank all of the contributors to this volume for their enthusiastic participation in our workshops and for remaining committed to this collective project despite the immense challenges of doing so in the midst of a global pandemic. We are grateful to Erdmute Alber for writing the afterword, bringing together the different strands of the volume into an overarching concluding reflection. We, as editors and scholars, have learned a great deal from the rich scholarship and from the myriad perspectives that the contributors have brought into our conversations around this theme of aspiring in later life. We also thank the guest participants at these workshops for engaging with us.

The work we did on this volume took place within the framework of the Max Planck Research Group "Ageing in a Time of Mobility," funded by the Max Planck Society and hosted by the Max Planck Institute for the Study of Religious and Ethnic Diversity in Göttingen, Germany. We are thankful for the financial support and to our colleagues at the institute for helping to make our work possible in an intellectually stimulating environment. Special thanks to Antje Menster for her support in organizing our 2020 workshop, which had to move from an in-presence to an online format, and also to Rami Higazi and Birgitt Sippel.

Our thanks also to Fatima Raja for her excellent editing support as we moved closer to completing a draft of our manuscript.

When we first had the idea to develop our conversations on aspiring in later life into a collected volume, we got in touch with Sarah Lamb, editor of the Rutgers University Press series Global Perspectives on Aging, which has published many volumes that have influenced our own understandings of aging in global contexts. We are incredibly grateful that she welcomed the volume into her series with enthusiasm and provided valuable insights that helped us to refine our initial ideas. Similarly, we thank Kimberly Guinta, editorial director at Rutgers University Press, for believing in our project; the two anonymous reviewers whose reports and feedback offered excellent and thought-provoking suggestions; the design and production teams working on our volume, with special thanks to Daryl Brower and Michelle Scott; Amron Lehte for her careful indexing work; and Jasper Chang and Carah Naseem for their truly wonderful editorial support as we developed our publication project with Rutgers University Press.

We must acknowledge that our conversations with older migrants, those experiencing displacement in later life, and also friends we have made along the journeys of our long-term research in different parts of the world have been fundamental to our thinking about aspirations in later life. Our field research has illuminated the creative ways through which older people imagine a good life for themselves and their families and the strategies they use to pursue that vision. Without wanting to romanticize their lives given the many social, economic, and political constraints within which they act, it was equally clear to us that later life is not at all about sedentariness or passivity but is a time to pursue aspirations, old and new. The older people we worked with showed us how, despite their adversities and challenges, they remain resilient and are able to live well. This is a lesson that we carry with us, and it is to them that we owe our most gratitude.

Notes on Contributors

ERDMUTE ALBER holds the chair of social anthropology at the University of Bayreuth, Germany. She has worked on kinship, childhood, intergenerational relations, aging, processes of class building, and the life course. She is the author and editor of several books on life course–related issues, including the book *Transfers of Belonging: Child Fostering in West Africa in the 20th Century*. Recently, she published on the entanglements of politics and kinship, for instance, by co-editing the volume *Politics and Kinship: A Reader* with Tatjana Thelen.

MEGHA AMRITH leads the "Ageing in a Time of Mobility" Research Group at the Max Planck Institute for the Study of Religious and Ethnic Diversity in Göttingen, Germany. Her research interests are on migrant labor, care, aging, inequalities, and belonging, with a current focus on aging migrant domestic workers in Asia. She is the author of *Caring for Strangers: Filipino Medical Workers in Asia* and co-editor of the volume *Gender, Work and Migration*.

CATI COE is professor of anthropology at Carleton University, Canada, and the author of several books on Ghanaian transnational families, including *The Scattered Family: Parenting, African Migrants, and Global Inequality* and *The New American Servitude: Political Belonging among African Immigrant Home Care Workers*. She is starting a new research project on how transnational migrants navigate social protection in later life.

HARMANDEEP KAUR GILL is a Carlsberg Junior Research Fellow at Linacre College and an associate member of the Faculty of Asian and Middle Eastern Studies, University of Oxford. Gill has worked with Tibetans in exile for over a decade, focusing on the lives of marginalized people. Her PhD thesis offered a phenomenological exploration of the experiences of old age and attitudes toward death and rebirth among lay and ordained Tibetans living in exile in India.

LISA JOHNSON is an associated postdoctoral researcher in the field of anthropology at the German Research Foundation–funded International Research Training

Group (IRTG) "Diversity: Mediating Differences in Transcultural Spaces" at the University of Trier, Germany. Her doctoral research was on the migratory practices, intergenerational narratives, and aspirations of return among Jamaican women in Montreal.

DUMITRIȚA LUNCĂ is a PhD fellow at the Institute of Social and Cultural Anthropology at the University of Hamburg, Germany. Her doctoral project, for which she has conducted extensive fieldwork among Romanian immigrants in Rome, Italy, aims to explore a side of migration focused on questions of love, sexuality, and intimacy by following the life stories of three distinct generations. Her current research interests are sexuality, mobility, and gender, with a regional focus on Europe.

ALFONSO OTAEGUI is assistant professor at the Pontifical Catholic University of Chile. He did research among Peruvian migrants working in Santiago, Chile, focusing on communicative practices related to aging and health care in new digital environments. He also carried out fieldwork among older adults adopting new technologies and is currently developing digital literacy initiatives and further applied anthropology projects.

JULIA PAULI, professor of social and cultural anthropology at the University of Hamburg, Germany, has done fieldwork in Mexico (since 1995) and Namibia (since 2003). She has published on migration, social class, gender, demography, kinship, and marriage. For *Africa Today*, she recently co-edited a special issue on migration and social class with Cati Coe.

VICTORIA K. SAKTI is a postdoctoral research fellow of the Max Planck Research Group "Ageing in a Time of Mobility" in Göttingen, Germany. She has conducted long-term research in Indonesia and Timor-Leste on aging, forced displacement, (im)mobilities, violence, memory, and social repair. Her publications deal with older refugee experiences, care practices within and across borders, aspirations related to a good life and death, local idioms of distress, and the temporal dimensions of displacement.

DORA SAMPAIO is assistant professor in the Department of Human Geography and Spatial Planning, Utrecht University. She is also a research associate with the Max Planck Research Group "Ageing in a Time of Mobility." Her research interests are on aging, migration, transnational families, care, and the life course. She co-edited a special issue of the journal *Area* on aging and migration. She is the author of *Migration, Diversity and Inequality in Later Life: Ageing at a Crossroads*, an ethnography of migrants aging in the Portuguese islands of the Azores.

SUSAN REYNOLDS WHYTE, professor in the Department of Anthropology, University of Copenhagen, carries out research in East Africa on social efforts to secure well-being in the face of poverty, disease, conflict, and rapid change. Her publications deal with the management of misfortune, gender and generation, changing health-care systems, disability, social lives of medicines, the response to HIV and other chronic conditions, and legacies of violence.

NELE WOLTER is a doctoral fellow with the "Ageing in a Time of Mobility" Research Group at the Max Planck Institute for the Study of Religious and Ethnic Diversity. She is also associated with the Department of Anthropology and African Studies at the University of Mainz. Her dissertation focuses on how anglophone internally displaced Cameroonians reconfigure their everyday lives in makeshift homes in the francophone part of the country.

Index

abuse, 139, 152
activism, 42, 46–48, 52
adelantarse, 11, 129
Adriana, 131, 132, 133–35, 140
AFP (Administradoras de Fondos de Pensiones), 98–99
aging: Alma on, 136; as concept, 145; cultural scripts of, 79–82, 90–91; impermanence and, 11, 159–62, 168, 171–72; "in place," 13, 14n8; late middle age as phase of, 7, 9–10, 95, 107–9; Peruvian migrants in Chile and, 97–100; Regina on, 137; in Tibetan Buddhism, 11, 161–64, 168, 170–72; between youth and old age, 22, 97–100. *See also* life course
Ágústsdóttir, Embla, 42
Ahearn, Laura M., 78
alcoholism, 113, 138
Alma, 131, 135–36, 141
Amba Boys, 147, 153, 155, 156
Ana, 98
Anastasia, 19, 22, 33
Andrei, 28, 33
Angel, 137
Anna, 117, 120, 125
Antonio, 135
Appadurai, Arjun, 3, 113, 114, 118, 178
aspirations: of caregivers, 122–24; constraints to, 50–51, 104; *vs.* gendered norms, 39–43; imaginings pasts and futures, 114–15, 130, 177–78; in later life, 3–5; life course and, 4–7, 13, 43–44, 81, 118, 146, 149, 156–57, 178, 180; migration and, 20, 140; as process, 1–3, 14n5, 149; scale and, 3, 5–8, 20; shifting of, 5–7. *See also* "good life"; hope, as term and concept; living in the present

Bâ, Amadou Hampâté, 178
badante, 19, 26, 30, 32, 35n2
Baldassar, Loretta, 20
becoming, 43, 53
belonging, 8, 49, 56, 67–68, 109
Berenice, 78–79, 81, 82–91
Berlant, Lauren, 82
Bismarck social security system, 182n3
Bloch, Alexia, 7, 22
Boccagni, Paolo, 43
Bonhomme, Macarena, 108, 109
breadwinner mentality, 39. *See also* financial independence
British Cameroon, 147. *See also* Cameroon
Brotherhood of the Lord of Miracles, 102
Brun, Cathrine, 148
Buddhism, 11, 159–74
Bunyole, Uganda, 113, 114, 116, 118, 125n1
Butler, Judith, 6

Cameroon, 146–57
Cameroonians, 11, 12, 145–57
Canada, 59–61. *See also* Jamaican migrants
caregivers, 122–24. *See also* home health workers
Caribbean Community of Retired Persons, 69
Caribbean immigration, 57, 59. *See also* Jamaican migrants
Carling, Jørgen, 20, 149
Carol, 61, 68
Catholicism, 106, 136, 142n8, 154
Ceaușescu, Nicolae, 23
Central Tibetan Administration, 160
Che, 46–48, 52
Chile, 96, 98. *See also* Peruvian migrants
Choedak, Genla Lobsang, 159–73

189

Christensen, Dorthe R., 161
Ciobanu, Ruxandra Oana, 29
civil war (Cameroon), 145–57, 157n3
Clara, 139–40, 141
Coe, Cati, 4
Cohen, Lawrence, 123
Collins, Francis, 149
colonialism, 5
communication. *See* messaging platforms; social media
compadrazgo system, 142n8
companionate marriage, 27–28. *See also* marriage
Cooper, Elizabeth, 90
Corina, 27–28, 33–34
Corwin, Anna I., 145
cosmetology, 86, 88, 90
COVID-19 pandemic, 1, 11–13, 57, 68–70, 87
cremation, 106–7
cultural scripts of aging, 79–82, 90–91
Culture and Well-Being (ed. Jiménez), 130
Cvajner, Martina, 22
Cwerner, Saulo B., 148

Dalai Lama, 160
dancing, 27, 28, 29, 34, 46, 116
Danely, Jason, 116
Dankyi, Ernestina, 89
Dawa, Mola Tsewang, 159–60, 166–67, 170
death: in Chile, 106–7; fear of, 166–67; Genla on, 159–60; presence of, 166; rebirth and, 168–70; Tibetan Buddhism on, 159–64; in Uganda, 116–17, 119–20. *See also* funerals
desire, 8–9. *See also* aspirations; sexuality
Dharamsala, India, 160
discrimination, 61
displacement, 145–57
divorce: in eastern Uganda, 114; in Mexico, 140, 141; migration and, 58, 83; religion and, 30; romance in later life after, 19, 25, 26, 27, 28, 30, 32; state socialism and, 23; vulnerabilities and, 69. *See also* marriage
domestic violence, 139
domestic workers, 9, 39–54, 101. *See also* home health workers
Dossa, Parin, 4
drug cartels, 135, 136

eastern Uganda, 112–25
education, 83, 85, 88, 89–90, 92n2, 115, 134
Elena, 105–7
emergence, 5
end-of-life health care costs, 177
erotic agency, 23
Esteban, 97–98, 99, 101

Estefanía, 97, 99, 101, 104–5
EU (European Union), 23–24
exile, 159–74
exploitation, 49

family reunification programs, 56
Federal Republic of Ambazonia, 147
Ferguson, James, 132
Fernandez, Nadine T., 21–22
Filipino migrants, 39, 40, 46–47
financial contributions by migrants, 39, 42, 46–47, 135, 137, 139. *See also* remittances
financial independence, 23, 44–46, 90, 134, 139. *See also* breadwinner mentality
financial insecurity, 150
Fischer, Edward F., 130
Florence, 154–57
Fokkema, Tineke, 29
food, 113, 116, 118–19, 124
forced migration, 145–57. *See also* migration
Francisco, 99
French Cameroon, 147. *See also* Cameroon
funerals, 116, 123. *See also* death
Future as Cultural Fact, The (Appadurai), 178
future mindset. *See* imagining pasts and futures

Gabriel, 29–30
Ganden monastery, Tibet, 163, 173n12
GED (General Educational Development), 85, 88, 92n2
gender differences: in migration, 24–25, 132; norms and cultural scripts on, 39–44, 51–52; in retirement, 79
gender equality, 23
generational justice, 177
Gerardo, 101
Germany, 24, 177, 182n3
Ghana, 79–80, 89, 92n4
Ghanaian migrants, 77–92
godparenthood, 142n8
González-López, Gloria, 22
"good life": anthropology on, 130; aspirations as process for, 1–6, 20; as concept, 52; labor migration and, 34; living in the present, 10–11, 134–36, 178. *See also* aspirations; well-being
Groes, Christian, 21

Hall, Stuart, 43, 57, 62, 63
Haraldsdóttir, Freyja, 42
Harry, 146, 154–57
Hasahya, 118, 120–121
Herminie, 68
Hirsch, Jennifer S., 22, 27–28

INDEX

holiday work, 98, 102, 109n7
home health workers, 82–83. *See also* caregivers; domestic workers
Hong Kong, domestic workers in, 9, 39–54
hope, as term and concept, 6, 20, 148, 153–54. *See also* aspirations
Horn, Vincent, 100–101
Horst, Heather A., 66
Hromadžić, Azra, 4
Hungary, 24

IDPs (internally displaced persons), 11, 12, 145–57
Ignacio, 98
imagining pasts and futures, 114–15, 130, 177–78. *See also* aspirations; living in the present; temporality
immobility. *See* mobility
impermanence, 11, 161–63, 168, 170–72
in-betweenness, 108–9
Indian migrants, 40, 48–50
Indonesian migrants, 40
inequality, 5, 50–52
inheritance, 61, 137–38
insurance, 79–80, 83, 86
intergenerational relationships, 9–10; in Ghanaian families, 81–91; in Peruvian families, 100–107; sandwich generation, as term, and, 95, 107; in Ugandan families, 112–25. *See also* kinship; transnational families
internally displaced persons (IDPs), 11, 12, 145–57
intimacy: defined, 35n5; migration and, 21, 24–27. *See also* romance and migration; sexuality
involuntary *vs.* voluntary return migration, 71n3
Isabel, 137–38

Jackson, Michael, 130, 131, 140
Jaja, 112–13, 117, 118–19, 123
Jamaica, 56–57, 68–70
Jamaican migrants, 9, 12, 56–71
Jansen, Stef, 6, 148–49
Janus (god), 102, 108, 109
Japan, 4
Javiera, 99, 103, 105
Josephine, 64
Judith, 114–15, 123–24

Kangyur, 161
Katz, Stephen, 64
Kavedžija, Iza, 4
King, Russell, 21, 22–23, 33–34, 108
kinship: kin-time, 10, 77; mobility and, 21–22; patrilineal, 114. *See also* intergenerational relationships; marriage; motherhood; transnational families
Kleist, Nauja, 6, 148–49

labor migration, 21, 24, 29–30, 46–47, 135, 137. *See also* migration
Laliberte-Rudman, Debbie, 64
Lamb, Sarah, 4, 145
Lambek, Michael, 130–31
land inheritance, 61. *See also* inheritance; remittance houses
language barriers, 32, 46
late middle age, 7, 9–10, 39, 41–44, 95–109. *See also* aging; life course; sandwich generation, as term
later life, as term, 7
Latvian women, 22–23
Lhasa, Tibet, 163
life course: aspirations and, 4–7, 13, 81, 118, 146, 149, 156–57, 178, 180; becoming and, 43–44, 53; cultural scripts of, 42, 91; intergenerational negotiations and, 87–88; kin-work and, 77; stages of, 78, 82. *See also* aging; late middle age
lifelong marriage, 27–28. *See also* marriage
Liliana, 106
liminality, 108–9
Lisa, 39
living in the present, 10–11, 134–36, 178. *See also* imagining pasts and futures; temporality
Lopez, Sarah Lynn, 132
Lulle, Aija, 22–23, 33–34, 43

Madhu, 48–50
Mai, Nicola, 21
Maia, 31–33
Manalansan, Martin F., IV, 42
Manuel, 137
Marcos, 107
Marian, 27–28, 33–34
Mariano, 97, 106
marriage: companionate, 27–28; as path to adult success, 89–90; polygamy, 151–52; state socialism and institution of, 23; virilocal, 114. *See also* divorce; kinship
Martín, 97, 106
matchmaking, 31
mayor, as term, 109n6
Mazzucato, Valentina, 89
McLeod Ganj, India, 160
medical care and medicine, 118, 123, 152, 177, 182n3
Medicare, 86
Meinert, Lotte, 161
messaging platforms, 31, 104, 133, 150. *See also* social media

methodological Santiaguism, 109n4
Mexican families and migrants, 129, 131–42
Miami, Florida, 68
migrants: Filipino, 39, 40, 46–47; Ghanaians, 77–92; Jamaicans, 9, 12, 56–71; Mexicans, 129, 131–42; Peruvians, 96–110; Romanians, 8–9, 19–35; Tibetans, 159–74
migration: aspirations and, 20, 140; due to civil war, 145–57; gender differences in, 24–25, 132; internal displacement due to political conflict, 11, 12, 145–57; intimacy and, 8–9, 21, 24–27; as mass phenomenon, 23–24; voluntary vs. involuntary return, 71n3; for work, 21, 24, 29–30, 46–47, 135, 137. See also mobility; return migration
migration studies, overview, 3, 21
Miller, Daniel, 66–67
Millicent, 78–79, 81, 82–91, 92n3
mobility, 57–70; in afterlife, 108; aging and physical, 117–18, 122; aspirations and, 2, 4, 5; within community or family, 112–13, 114–15, 119, 124; in late middle age, 95; temporality and, 148. See also migration
Montreal, Canada, 61
motherhood, 23, 89–90. See also intergenerational relationships; kinship
Museveni, Yoweri, 113

Näre, Lena, 20
Nelson, 151–54
Nepalese women, 78
norms, 41–44
nostalgic longing, 130, 131

Obrist, Brigit, 123
obuhwe, 120
Oportunidades program, 136–37

Pablo, 97, 102
Palmberger, Monika, 4
pandemic. See COVID-19 pandemic
Papadopoulos, Dimitris, 66
Parti Québécois, 61
past mindset. See imagining pasts and futures
patrilineal kinship, 114. See also kinship
pensions, 79, 83, 86, 98–99, 152
Peruvian migrants, 96–110
PLA (People's Liberation Army), 163
Plaza, Dwaine, 61
"Un poco más" (song), 129, 134, 135
poco más, un (concept), 3, 129, 134, 137, 141, 181
poetry, 32
Poeze, Miranda, 89
pollution, 136
polygamy, 151–52. See also marriage
poverty, 20, 62

Pratten, David, 90
present mindset. See living in the present
Pueblo Nuevo, Mexico, 129, 131–35, 137–38, 139–41

racial discrimination, 61
rebirth, 162, 168–70
Regina, 131, 136–41, 142n7
religion, 30, 106, 136, 142n8, 154
remittance houses, 131–33, 134, 135. See also land inheritance
remittances, 39, 42, 45, 47, 139. See also financial contributions by migrants
reproductive health and choices, 23
Republic of Cameroon, 147. See also Cameroon
research methodology, 35n3, 59, 133, 161
retirement: as concept, 145; of Ghanaians, 78–82, 86–88, 91; of Peruvian migrants in Chile, 98–99; of Rosalie, 56; studies on migrant domestic workers and, 43
return migration: by Ghanaians, 86–87; of Jamaicans, 56, 61–71, 71n1, 71n3; by Romanians, 28, 32–33. See also migration
Rhea, 44–46
right to free movement, 24
Río Lerma, 136
Robbins-Ruszkowski, Jessica, 145
Roberto, 98, 99, 101, 103
Roma ethnic group, 24
romance and migration, 8–9, 19–35. See also migration
Romanian migrants, 8–9, 19–35
Rome. See Romanian migrants
Rosa, 116, 118
Rosalie, 56, 61, 62, 64, 65–66
Rose, 118, 123

Samanta, Tannistha, 53
Sampaio, Dora, 33, 100
samsara, 161–62
Samwiri, 121–22
sandwich generation, as term, 95, 107. See also intergenerational relationships
Scheibelhofer, Elisabeth, 149
Sciortino, Giuseppe, 22
scripts, 77–78
self-expression, 44–46
self-realization, 7, 8–9, 12, 40, 41, 52, 179
self-reliance, 79–81, 91
senior citizen grants, 113, 115–16
Sera monastery, Tibet, 173n12
sexuality, 35n4, 45–46, 179. See also intimacy; romance and migration
Singapore, domestic workers in, 9, 39–54
Slater, Jen, 42

social justice, 46–48
social media, 28, 31, 48, 59, 133. *See also* messaging platforms
Sri Lankan migrants, 40
stability, 129
Stack, Carol, 77
state socialism, 23
Stefoni, Carolina, 108
Successful Aging as a Contemporary Obsession: Global Perspectives (Lamb), 4
"Sūtra on Impermanence," 161
Swidler, Ann, 78

Tamil migrants, 40, 48–50
technoscapes, 66
temporality, 7, 77, 148, 161, 170. *See also* imagining pasts and futures; living in the present
Tenzin Gyatso, 160
Teresa, 99, 101, 102
Tibetan Buddhism, 11, 159–74
Tibetan Children's Village (TCV), 159, 160
Tibetans in exile, 11, 159–74
Toronto, Canada, 61
transnational families: of Ghanaians, 77–79, 82–92; of Jamaicans, 9, 12, 56–71; of Mexicans, 131–42; of Peruvians, 100–109, 110nn9–11. *See also* intergenerational relationships; kinship
Tsianos, Vasilis S., 66

Uganda, 112–25
ultimogeniture, 137–38
uncertainty, 6, 24, 148–49, 161–62, 170, 172
United States, 83, 86. *See also* Ghanaian migrants

Vera, 30–31, 33
Victoria, 28, 33
viejo, as term, 109n6
virilocal marriage, 114. *See also* marriage
virtual communication networking, 31, 66
Vlase, Ionela, 24
voluntary *vs.* involuntary return migration, 71n3. *See also* migration; return migration

Walsh, Katie, 20, 21
well-being, 129–41. *See also* "good life"
Willerslev, Rane, 161
Williams, Raymond, 5
witchcraft, 86, 89, 91–92n3
workaholism, 98, 100, 103, 108

yearning, 9, 65
Yokosofati, 118, 121, 122
Yolanda, 136, 137, 139

Zambian migrants, 132